Landmark Visitors Guide

Cor

Cathy H

Cathy Harlow is a travel writer, photographer and naturalist tour guide, fluent in five European languages. After completing the Landmark Visitors Guide: Iceland, she spent 14 weeks exploring Corsica by road and on foot, gathering material for this book and vividly capturing the island's landscapes on camera. Cathy lives in Cumbria but devotes the winter months to working among killer whales in northern Norway and the summer to guiding French groups around Iceland.

Many people helped in great and small ways during both the research and writing of this book. My thanks go to Penny Bains, who supplied the paintings of birds and a mouflon, Caroline and John Little, Marie-Lou Torresi, Joy and Peter Treeby, Libby Hoseason, Anne-Christine Jaunin, Dominique Ogilvy, Nicky Beecham and Phillippe Berthelin. Thanks also to the staff of the many island tourist offices who were generous with their time and information and the many strangers who gave me lifts all over the island when the buses didn't turn up!

Published by
Landmark Publishing
Ashbourne Hall, Cokayne Ave, Ashbourne,
Derbyshire DE6 1EJ England

Corsica

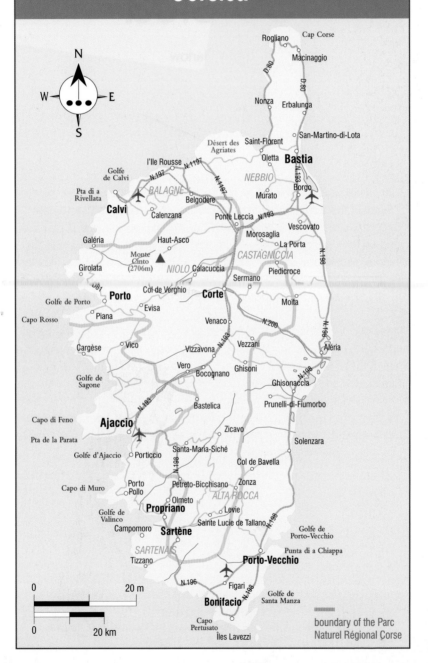

Landmark Visitors Guide

Corsica

Cathy Harlow

*a hiking trail runs the length
of the Sartenais coast, with its
beautiful deserted beaches*

Contents

Welcome to
Corsica

The Greeks called it *Kalliste*, 'the most beautiful', while today Corsicans refer to their home as *L'Île de Beauté*, a cliché that somehow falls short of doing it the justice it deserves. The Mediterranean's greenest isle is undeniably gorgeous, cloaked in fragrant *maquis* and majestic forests of pine and holm oak and fringed by a coastline of dazzling, sun-soaked beaches. Rising from the sea and soaring to over 2,700m (8,850ft), a chain of pinnacled peaks runs the length of the island. Embracing its most eye-catching landscapes, the vast Parc Naturel Régional Corse protects this fragile natural heritage, and offers boundless possibilities for walkers.

Top Tips

Golfe de Porto

This is a region of superlatives and unforgettable sunsets, where the pinnacles of Les Calanche and dizzying heights of the Gorges de Spelunca vie with Scandola Reserve's bizarre red volcanic formations for the title of the island's most spectacular landscape.

Bonifacio

Corsica's most dramatic town, with its impossibly tall houses and labyrinth of sunless passageways, stands defiantly on precipitous chalk cliffs, guarding the southern tip of the island.

The Mountain Villages

Perched on rocky ridges, stacked up on the mountainsides or nestled deep in the valleys, Corsica's mountain villages are timeless and beguiling.

Lavezzi Islands

Sandy coves, turquoise seas and a rich and varied marine life are set among chaotic granite boulders on a tiny offshore archipelago in the Straits of Bonifacio.

Romanesque Churches

In their villages, hidden in the depths of the forest or standing incongruously alone in a field, dozens of little medieval churches, embellished with fine stonework, are testimony to Corsica's rich architectural heritage.

The Beaches

It's not surprising that Corsica regularly features in surveys of the world's best beaches. From secluded coves framed by sculpted granite and lapped by gentle turquoise sea, to great arcs of surf-pounded soft sand, each has its own character. Some are popular with families, while others are so isolated they can only be reached on foot or by boat.

The Forests

From the heady scent of the coastal *maquis* to the luxuriant holm oak and chestnut groves enveloping the hills and stands of majestic mountain pines, Corsica is the Mediterranean's most forested island.

Bathing in River Pools

Fed by melting mountain snow, Corsica's youthful rivers leap from boulder to boulder, forming chains of natural, gin-clear pools that are perfect for a refreshing dip in the heat of the day.

The Mountain Lakes of Melo and Capitello

A duo of cobalt-blue lakes, set among soaring peaks in a glacier-scoured basin at the head of the beautiful Restonica Valley.

The Peaks of Bavella

This iconic ridge of serrated peaks is one of the most enduring images of Corsica, especially at sunset.

Corsica's Emblem

Most of the island's inhabitants live in the twin regional capitals of Ajaccio and Bastia, but visitors flock to the little resort towns of Porto Vecchio, Bonifacio, Porto and Calvi, that developed around the towers and citadels thrust up by the Genoese to protect the coast from invaders. Inland, the university town of Corte lies at the island's heart and is a focal point for Corsican culture. Much of the architectural heritage is to be discovered in the sober granite and schist villages lying stacked up on the flanks of rugged ridges. Here too visitors will find mysterious, megalithic menhirs peppering the landscape, and Romanesque churches, some dating back one thousand years, defying the test of time and enduring in their simplicity.

Corsica is keen to avoid mass tourism and most of its coastal development is low-rise and low-key, yet not elitist. The island succeeds in being both chic and unpretentious, with a rustic edge to it, most notably in the cuisine, where the emphasis is on locally produced *charcuterie*, pungent ewe's cheeses, honey, chestnuts, olive oil and wine. Above all, it is Corsican, yet as part of France it is naturally very French as well. Don't expect signs in English, nor any chain restaurants and hotels – there aren't any. A little knowledge of French will help, but Corsicans are by nature polite and patient and English-speaking visitors are welcomed.

Organising your trip

Self-drive or public transport?

Most visitors planning to explore Corsica opt for the flexibility of renting a car. Many would say it is impossible to get by without one. There are, however, downsides to driving on the island, especially in July and August, when the roads can be very choked and parking becomes a nightmare. Whatever the season, driving in Corsica requires concentration, extra care and attention because the roads are narrow, winding and often have steep drops to the side.

If you plan to spend most of your holiday on the beach and stay in a hotel rather than self-catering accommodation, you may be able to get by without a car. In the Porto Vecchio area there are bus services between the town and the main beaches in July and August and the Balagne tramway plies between Calvi and Île Rousse stopping at beaches along the way. The main resorts of Bonifacio, Porto Vecchio, Propriano, Ajaccio, Calvi and St Florent offer a range of sightseeing trips by boat. Ajaccio, the Gravona Valley, Vizzavona, Corte, Bastia, Île Rousse and Calvi are linked by train.

Public bus services are infrequent or non-existent from September to June and even in high season they may only run once a day, but with careful planning you could construct a tour of the island using only buses and trains.

A car is essential if you plan to do

day hikes or short walks and get out and about exploring the villages and mountains.

Package Holiday or Independent Travel?

Booking a package tour to Corsica with flights, accommodation and transportation or car hire included takes a lot of the worry and hassle out of your holiday and if things go wrong there should be a representative of the holiday company at hand to sort things out. Reputable car hire and transportation firms are used and the accommodation has been inspected and probably a few adjustments have been made to fit in with the needs of UK or North American visitors. The downside is that your holiday may cost you a little more.

However, it is worth remembering that tour operators are able to negotiate good rates on accommodation and in high season their prices may work out cheaper than booking direct.

There can also be savings by booking independently and it can be a lot of fun to search out the best flight deals and find the right accommodation. There are a number of internet sites dealing with self-catering accommodation and you may find that savings out of season can be considerable by booking direct. It can also be a lot of work and if the establishments you are dealing with do not have email, you may need to have a French speaker to help you out with booking over the phone.

If you're booking self-catering accommodation independently, it is important to check that the start and end day of the rental correspond to the flight arrival and departure dates. This can be a problem if you are arriving on the direct charter flights from the UK to Corsica on Sundays.

How long do you need to see the island?

If you're flying direct to Corsica from the UK on one of the charter flights, you will probably have to choose between a stay of one or more full weeks. If you fly via France or opt for a flight to Nice, Marseille or Pisa and then the ferry to Corsica, you will have more flexibility, but you will spend longer getting there. For a one-week stay, it is best to base yourself in one area of the island. In two weeks, you could combine two regions, or do a circular tour. Corsica is on the face of it a small island, but its roads are very slow.

When to visit

For beach holidays

The best months for a beach holiday are late May, June and September. April and early May have less reliable sunshine and the sea is a little chilly. July and August are peak season and the island's roads, beaches, hotels, campgrounds, restaurants and beauty spots are stretched to the limit, with the deluge of visitors pouring in from France and Italy. Prices are higher at this time, making it poor value for money. The weather and sea temperature can still be ideal right through October but some rain is to be expected from mid September onwards.

Suggested Itineraries

When coastal Corsica is so undeniably beautiful, it is hard to tear yourself away and head inland. But this would be a pity as there is as much to see and do in the interior, especially if you enjoy walking. The following itineraries will give an idea of what can be seen within a given time frame.

A week in the north

Day 1	arrive Calvi
Day 2	Calvi, Île Rousse and Balagne villages
Day 3	St Florent, Agriates and the Nebbio
Days 4 & 5:	Cap Corse and Bastia
Day 6:	Corte and the central mountains
Day 7:	Corte and the central mountaino
Day 8:	depart Calvi

A week in the south

Day 1	arrive Figari; Bonifacio
Day 2	Bonifacio and Lavezzi Islands
Day 3	Porto Vecchio
Day 4	Aiguilles de Bavella
Day 5	Alta Rocca villages and prehistoric sites
Day 6	Sartène and Filitosa
Day 7	Sartenais coast and megalithic sites
Day 8	depart Figari

A week in the centre and west

Day 1	arrive Ajaccio
Day 2	Vizzavona and Corte
Day 3	central mountains
Day 4	Niolo Valley
Day 5	Evisa and the Spelunca gorge
Day 6	Porto and Scandola boat trip
Day 7	Porto, Piana and Les Calanche
Day 8	depart Ajaccio

Two-week tour of Corsica

Day 1	arrive Bastia
Day 2	Cap Corse; overnight Macinaggio, Luri or Centuri
Day 3	Cap Corse and Nebbio; overnight St Florent area
Day 4	Balagne villages and overnight Calvi area
Day 5	coast road to Porto; 3 nights Porto area
Day 6	boat trip to Scandola reserve; Les Calanche and Capo Rosso
Day 7	Ota, Evisa and Spelunca Gorge
Day 8	forest of Aïtone, the Niolo and Scala di Santa Regina; 2 nights at Corte
Day 9	Restonica Valley
Day 10	Vizzavona, Ajaccio, Filitosa and Propriano; overnight Propriano/ Sartène
Day 11	Sartène, megaliths of the Sartenais to Bonifacio; 2 nights Bonifacio
Day 12	Bonifacio and boat trip to Lavezzi Islands
Day 13	villages of the Alta Rocca, Aiguilles de Bavella; overnight Zonza

Corsica is a hiker's paradise

crushing defeat at Ponte Nuovo, Paoli fled to London.

Biding his time, Paoli returned to stage a second bid for Corsica's freedom, but this time enlisting the help of the British fleet in 1794, who laid siege to Bastia, St Florent and Calvi. Meanwhile, those loyal to France, among them the Bonaparte family, fearing civil war, fled the island. But the Anglo-Corsican accord was neither peaceful nor successful as the British-nominated viceroy, Gilbert Elliot, replaced Paoli, aggravating the Corsican supporters, who allied with the French. With Paoli's departure into exile, in 1796 the French invaded under the young Corsican-born officer Napoleon Bonaparte. In 1811, by Imperial Decree, Corsica became a single *département* of France with its capital at Ajaccio.

The Corsican Exodus

French citizenship may have brought the benefits of political stability, but Corsica's development in the Napoleonic era was slow. The town of Yauco in Puerto Rico in the Caribbean bears a plaque to commemorate the Corsican immigrants who settled there

Protecting the Environment

Over one and a half million visitors pour into Corsica each year, mostly from France and Italy and the vast majority in July and August. While some never leave the beach, many are drawn to explore further, meandering inland on the twisting mountain roads or working up a sweat on the 1,600km (1,000 miles) of footpaths criss-crossing the island.

Created in 1972, the *Parc Naturel Régional Corse*, often shortened to PNRC, has the job of protecting almost 40% of Corsica's surface area that falls within its boundaries. Building and maintaining the huts and trails, waymarking with splashes of bright paint and cairns and erecting signs is just part of it. The park also renovates traditional architecture such as olive and chestnut mills, bread ovens and mountain *bergeries*, encouraging shepherds to continue cheese-making activities, and preserving a way of life that is threatened by depopulation. The greatest challenge is in raising public awareness of the fragility of the flora and fauna and the need for respect and care. For this reason, camping in Corsica, both in and outside protected areas, is only allowed at designated campgrounds.

Along the coast, several smaller reserves, among them the unspoiled tip of Cap Corse, the Agriates Coast and Sartenais Coast, are managed by the *Conservatoire du Littoral*, who since 1975 have been buying up land to prevent development.

The island's public enemy number one is fire and on a yearly basis, almost 10,000 hectares (25,000 acres) of forest and scrub fall victim to what shockingly are often deliberately started fires. Visitors can do their bit by not lighting fires, anytime, anywhere, and not smoking in cars or in the countryside. In high winds, the risk of fire is elevated and some areas may be closed to foot and vehicle traffic. Visitors should watch for and respect any notices.

in the nineteenth century 'enriching our culture with their traditions and helping us to progress through their hard work'. Four percent of Puerto Ricans are of Corsican descent. Over 6,000 Corsicans emigrated to Venezuela.

For centuries Corsicans had uprooted and left their homeland, first as mercenaries in the armies of France and Genoa and later to escape desperate poverty. The greatest wave of emigrants departed in the wake of the decimation of the vineyards from phylloxera in the 1870s, which coincided with a population explosion as the island's inhabitants topped 273,000.

Just as 10,000 Corsicans had filled the ranks of Napoleon's armies so too they signed up to fight for France in the First World War. The village war memorials are a poignant reminder of how huge the loss was – 20,000 did not return. Occupied by Italian and German troops in World War II, the island secretly trained up a resistance force of 12,000, which took the name of the *Maquis*, the island's thorny impenetrable scrub. When the last of the occupying forces retreated in 1943, Corsica became the first French *département* to be liberated, but Corsica's repeated sacrifices to France are seldom acknowledged.

By 1960, the population had dropped to 160,000 as the islanders continued to leave for France and the colonies. Today's population of 260,000 includes many immigrants and less than two thirds of the inhabitants were born on the island. By contrast, around 70,000 people living in mainland France were born in Corsica!

Corsica and its people today

Tourism is the biggest private sector employer on the island accounting for ten per cent. Over a third of jobs in Corsica are in the public sector and just a small percentage is represented by agriculture and industry, most of which are small scale. With an increasing population of retirees, a continuing shift from rural to urban living and a principal industry that provides only seasonal employment, many Corsicans are pragmatic about the benefits of the island's ties to France, especially given the one billion euro annual subsidy. But not all. Since the 1970s, when a protest against the *'pieds noirs'* wine producers on the plains of Aléria turned to violence, a small but dedicated faction of radical nationalists has surfaced under different banners.

Under the FLNC (Fronte di Liberazione Nazionale di Corsica), a sustained campaign of assassinations and bombing of public buildings took place in Corsica and on mainland France, allegedly financed by racketeering and extortion. Fragmentation of the nationalist movement and its ideology into many factions made negotiations with the government increasingly difficult. Things came to a head with the murder in 1998 of Claude Erignac, the *Préfet* and most senior government official on the island, an event that deeply shocked most Corsicans. However, support for the anti-violence movement waned when Erignac's successor, Bernard Bonnet, was found to be behind an arson attack on a *Paillote*, a beach restaurant owned by a radical militant on the coast south of Ajaccio,

The *Maquis*

Napoleon claimed he could smell the pungent Corsican *maquis* from prison on Elba. True or not, islanders living abroad cite the evergreen, thorny, pungent scrub as the most nostalgic and evocative scent of their homeland.

The heady mixture of aromas comes from several species, some, like French lavender *Lavandula stoechas*, rosemary *Rosmarinus officinalis* and juniper *Juniperus phoenicea*, easily recognizable. Others are less so – the curry-aroma of *Helichrysum stoechas* may have you puzzled until you track down its yellow flower heads. Myrtle *Myrtus communis* has beautiful, large white flowers and its pungent blue-black berries are picked to flavour local dishes and liqueurs. Another prolific berry-producer is the strawberry tree *Arbutus unedo*, whose red fruits are edible, though tasteless. The spring foliage of the mastic tree or lentisc *Pistacia lentiscus* and flower-laden branches of tree heath *Erica arborea* add to the olfactory cocktail but the *maquis* will also surprise you with its dazzling shades. From April to June, but especially in May, rockroses are in bloom and the papery, saucer-shaped pink flowers of *Cistus incanus ssp. corsicus* contrast vividly with the white of *Cistus salvifolius*.

Once you've walked any of the coastal paths you'll start to recognise the culprits that snag at your clothing and draw blood, in particular the broom *Genista corsica*, whose yellow flowers are borne on thorny stems. Forming an impenetrable dense undergrowth from the coast to the foothills of the mountains, *a macchja*, as it is known in Corsican, was the perfect retreat when Saracens attacked, a safe hideout during a *vendetta* and a place to hunt wild boar and partridges.

and many ordinary islanders took to the streets in protest. As demands for greater autonomy grew, plans were drawn up to address the issues that had given rise to the radical movements in the first place, among them lack of investment in the island's infrastructure, the status of the Corsican language, the university at Corte and preferential tax laws. In 2001, an historic agreement was signed, giving the island its own Regional Assembly. Since then extremism continues to rear its ugly head from time to time, as public buildings and French-owned businesses are singled out, but tourists have never been targets of political violence in Corsica.

Corsicans are justly proud of their island and its *'Corsitude'* – the quality of things Corsican. While tourism is enormously important, it is embraced with a degree of caution to avoid the pitfalls of over-development that other Mediterranean islands have suffered. Many local tourism businesses like hotels, restaurants and shops are locally owned and run and small-scale local producers of traditional crafts and foods are encouraged.

As many as seventy per cent of Corsicans may be conversant to a degree with the island's language *Corsu*, which shares common ancestry with a dialect of Tuscany, but far fewer are fluent.

For years, the language was suppressed, particularly in schools, though today Corsican is taught from primary level to university, but it is not compulsory. It is still spoken by older people, notably in rural areas, but with the resurgence in island pride, more young people are taking an interest in learning.

Traditional values continue to be important and while few islanders live year-round in the mountain villages, they maintain a strong sense of attachment to their ancestral homes. Family ties are strong but so too are allegiances on a 'clan' level, where a well-placed relative can influence many aspects of daily life, from getting jobs and promotion to building regulations and business development, though Corsica is not unique among Mediterranean regions in this respect.

Attitudes to women have changed greatly over the last thirty years, but they remain conservative. Women gain most status and respect as mothers, especially of a son. Interestingly, there are a large number of women mayors in Corsica. Most preside over inland mountain villages but, curiously, are not always expected to reside there.

Topography of the island

With a surface area of 8,712 square kilometres (3,365 square miles), Corsica is slightly larger than the county of North Yorkshire but one-third the size of Switzerland and the state of Vermont. It measures 183km (114 miles) from north to south (including Cap Corse) and is 85km (53 miles) wide at its broadest. The island is situated 160km (100 miles) from Provence, but just 82km (51 miles) from the Tuscan coast. A shallow 12km (7.5-mile) channel divides Corsica from Sardinia but sea depths of 400m (1,312 ft) exist between Corsica and the Tuscan Islands.

Wherever you are in Corsica, the **mountains** are the most striking feature of the landscape, and for an island this small they are both huge and impressive. The island possesses an astonishing 50 or more summits over 2,000m (6,560ft) in height and one-fifth of the terrain lies above 1,000m (3,280ft). The highest peaks of 2,706m (8,876ft) Monte Cinto, 2,622m (8,600ft) Monte Ritondo and 2,525m (8,282ft) Paglia Orba straddle the dividing range and watershed that cuts the island in two, presenting a formidable barrier to communications. Only four road passes traverse the range: Col de Verghio, Col de Vizzavona, Col de Verde and Col de Bavella. Brooding, **forested valleys** plunge from the western side of the range and one rocky ridge after another disappears abruptly into a deep, blue sea. This is Corsica's granite scenery at its most alluring and infinitely photogenic. In the south, the landscape is gentler and the granite is shaped by wind and water into monstrous, elemental sculptures, some pierced right through to form the characteristic *tafoni*.

It was intrusive plutonic magma, erupted within the earth's crust, that formed the island's granite heart of **crystalline rocks** between 340 and 240 million years ago. Where eruptions penetrated the surface, **volcanic lava**, **pyroclastite** and **ignimbrites** are evident, as in the Fango Valley, Scandola peninsula and on Monte Cinto. Granite

Corsica is bounded by St Florent in the north, Corte in the centre and Solenzara in the south-east, where a central depression gives way to the **metamorphic schists**, punctuated by gabbro and serpentine intrusions, that occupy the regions of Castagniccia and Cap Corse. These are geologically younger, having formed in an ancient seabed and adjacent continental margins between 170 and 60 million years ago. Subjected to the same metamorphic forces of heat and folding as the Alps around 30 million years ago, compression compacted the rock to produce the dark-green, slate-like **polished schist**, typical of the villages in this eastern region of Corsica. Here the topography is less abrupt and the mountains lower in altitude, culminating in 1,767m (5,795ft) Monte San Pedrone.

Sometime after 30 million years ago, Corsica and Sardinia broke away from the south of France, embarking on an anti-clockwise rotation of about 30 degrees that brought them to their present position around 18 million years ago. The island's east coast, with its **flat plain** and long sandy shore broken by a string of **coastal lagoons**, is formed of more recent Tertiary and Quaternary sediments, as are the chalk deposits, crowning the southern tip of Corsica. Relentless pounding by sea and wind have shaped Bonifacio's chalk into a belt of **high cliffs**, peppered with grottoes.

The effects of the Ice Age **glaciation** are clearly visible in the U-shaped valleys, sharp ridges and deeply scoured glacial basins or cirques, now occupied by mountain lakes like those of Capitello and Melo in the upper Restonica Valley. Here too, the granite has been polished and striated by debris transported by the moving glaciers. There are no longer any permanent ice fields in Corsica's mountains but pockets of snow can be found in shaded gullies and on north-facing slopes well into summer.

Corsica has many tumultuous, fast flowing **rivers**, fed by melting snow and high rainfall. Among them are, to the east, the Tavignano and Golo, while the Liamone and Taravo drain off west of the divide. Several have been dammed for hydroelectric production, drinking water and irrigation. There are numerous spectacular **river gorges** in Corsica: the Spelunca, near Porto, the Scala di Santa Regina in the Niolo, the Tavignano and Restonica near Corte and the famous *défilés* of Lancone, Inzecca and Strette to the east.

With 1,000km (625 miles) of largely unspoiled coastline, Corsica also has more than its fair share of beautiful **beaches**. For families with young children, the most suitable are around Porto Vecchio in the south, where powdery white sand fringes shallow and mostly sheltered bays. The beaches around Bonifacio are popular with windsurfers, while those along the west coast shelve more steeply and are often exposed, but there are exceptions. The north has a mixed bag of surf-lashed sands backed by dunes and idyllic, sheltered coves, while the east coast is one great long stretch of sand, with plenty of space to spread out.

Flora & Fauna

Corsican Flora

Over two and a half thousand plant species are found in Corsica, of which 12% are endemic to the region (which includes Corsica, Sardinia and the Tuscan islands) while 131 species are only found on Corsica. This relatively high level of endemism is explained by the island's isolation, while the high number of species is bolstered by the variety of habitat and climate from coastal to alpine.

The Forests

With 70% forest cover, Corsica has more trees than any other Mediterranean island. High rainfall, resulting from the mountainous topography, keeps the island noticeably greener and lusher than neighbouring Sardinia.

About 43% of Corsica is covered by *maquis*, a fragrant but fire-prone scrub, while 27% of the island supports a mix of evergreen and deciduous tree species. Of these true forests one quarter are holm oak, while maritime pine and sweet chestnut account for one fifth each, endemic Corsican or Laricio pine about one sixth and the rest shared by beech, cork oak, silver birch and endemic fragrant alder. The tree line lies at around 1,900m (6,200ft), where only the alder and birch form continuous cover. Laricio pines, beech and silver birch are middle to high altitude species, while sweet chestnut, maritime pine, holm oak and cork oak thrive in the hills and valleys lower down.

Traditionally, Corsica's exploitation of its forests has been sustainable. Chestnuts and olives were planted for food and oil and cork oaks were stripped of their bark for corks for the wine industry, but the bark regenerated within a decade. A variety of species were used for fuel and charcoal, but it was the Laricio pines, whose tall, straight trunks were needed for ships' masts, which were exploited commercially, hauled by mules down to the coast from the Tavignano and other mountain forests.

Wild Flowers

From the coast to the alpine zone, Corsica's flowering plants are as vivid as they are varied. Among the endemics are some real rarities like *Romulea corsica*, a **sand crocus** known only from Cap Corse and the extreme south and the **star of bethlehem** *Ornithogalum excapum* found only on Bonifacio's alkaline soil, though locally abundant. **Corsican stork's bill** *Erodium corsicum*, a member of the geranium family, has hairy leaves and pink flowers and blooms along the west coast from Calvi to Ajaccio. Several endemic species of *limonium* flourish above the tidal zone and can be seen at Tour de la Parata, near Ajaccio.

One of the most beautiful endemics is the white-flowering **Illyrian sea lily** *Pancratium illyricum*, which is widespread on the island up to a height of 1,000m (3,280ft). If you visit the Lavezzi Islands, look for one of Corsica's flashiest and most interesting plants, the **dragon arum** *Dracunculus muscivorus*, in among the rocks. This is one of only thirteen localities on Corsica where this fetid-smelling plant, with a huge burgundy-hued flower, grows. Allegedly it was eradicated from the nearby exclusive resort island of Cavallo because its smell troubled the clients!

Late April, May and June are the best months for flowers but at higher altitudes there are species in bloom well into summer. As early as February, delicate **crocuses** carpet the verges, while woodlands are ablaze with **cyclamen**. Tall, white-flowering stems of **asphodels** are at home in bare, open ground and occur in great densities in early spring, along with splendid stands of **Corsican hellebore** *Helleborus lividus ssp. Corsicus*. **Orchids**, of which there are 40 species, are a little more discreet – look for the beautiful burgundy-coloured *Serapias* and *Ophrys morisii*, which is only found on alkaline soils around Bonifacio and St Florent.

In the sub-alpine and alpine zones, the delicate papery flowers of the endemic *Helichrysum frigidum* can be seen wedged in rock crevices, but the one to hunt down on the high massifs of Ritondo, Rinoso and Incùdine is the rare **daisy** *Margarita minuta*.

Many species of flower are protected by law in Corsica but you should make it a rule not to pick or disturb any flowers or plants. Instead, leave them for others to enjoy.

The Fauna

Because of their isolation, islands are typically poor in diversity of land mammals, but may host a variety of birds, reptiles and amphibians, which are more easily able to colonise. Corsica is no exception in this respect but interestingly fossil remains suggest that before the last glaciation, a rich and varied mammalian fauna, including species of elephant, monkey and hippopotamus resided on the island. The last of these mammals, *Prolagus sardus*, a type of 'rabbit/rat', became extinct as recently as the Iron Age and was possibly a source of food for the island's early inhabitants. Scientists generally agree that the larger land mammals present on Corsica today – mouflon, red deer and wild boar – can neither have colonised from mainland Europe using a land bridge, nor swum across, which leaves only one other possibility: that they were introduced by man.

Land Mammals

Although you are very unlikely to see most of them, a surprising number of mammals survive in the wild in Corsica: hedgehog, pygmy white-toothed shrew, lesser white-toothed shrew, mouflon, red deer, wild boar, red fox, weasel, woodmouse, edible dormouse, house mouse, brown rat, black rat, rabbit and brown hare. There are no squirrels but at least 25 species of bat, most of which are protected.

Of the larger mammals, **wild boar** *sus scrofa* (*sanglier* in French) are abundant and widespread numbering around 25,000–30,000, of which as many as 10,000 are hunted each year. Understandably, they are wary of man, secretive and mostly active at night. You may hear them crashing through the *maquis* but you are unlikely to see them. Their presence is easily noted where they dig up the ground foraging for roots and fruits – they are not popular with gardeners! **Mouflon** (see feature box in the Central Mountains chapter) are most easily spotted in the upper Asco valley early in the morning but they are also shy. The **Corsican red deer** *Cervus elaphus corsicanus*, smaller in size than neighbouring populations, was originally introduced by the Romans.

Once common, by the 1930s they had dissappeared from most of the island and after the last confirmed sighting on the east coast in 1970, it was assumed that the race had died out. In an enclosure just outside Quenza in the Alta Rocca, a new breeding stock has been introduced from Sardinia, which it is hoped will be successfully reintroduced into the wild. The **edible dormouse** *Glis glis* (*loir* in French) is nocturnal and seldom seen, but easily recognised by its bushy tail. An adept climber, it is still hunted for food in the Taravo region.

Marine Mammals

Corsica's last **Mediterranean monk seals** *Monachus monachus* were shot in 1970. The species had been in decline for years, the last surviving animals taking refuge in caves along the west coast. Today it survives only off West Africa and in the eastern Mediterranean. A variety of whale and dolphin species are regularly observed in the island's offshore waters. In the Gulf of Genoa, currents cause upwelling of nutrient-rich sea from below, attracting plankton-feeding **fin whales** *Balaenoptera physalus*, the second-largest whale species, which can weigh 75 tons and reach 23m (75ft) in length. Closer to the coast, **bottlenose dolphins** *Tursiops truncatus* are regularly observed and may approach boats to bow ride.

Reptiles and Amphibians

You'll be relieved to hear that there are no venomous snakes in Corsica. Of the two species found on the island the **grass snake** *Natrix natrix* is shy and harmless, while the **whipsnake** *Coluber viridiflavus*, black with yellow-green markings, is best avoided because it can be aggressive and deliver a painful bite.

If you are very lucky, you may see a **Hermann's tortoise** *Testudo hermanni* in the cork oak groves of southern Corsica and areas of lowland pasture. Once widespread, they are now restricted to pockets of Italy, France, Spain and the Balkans. In Corsica they are threatened by fires but their main predator elsewhere, the badger, is absent. You can see them in captivity at the Cupulatta tortoise centre near Ajaccio and at Moltifao tortoise village in the lower Asco valley. To see the **European pond turtle** *Emys orbicularis*, **green**

Top Birdwatching Spots

- Biguglia Lagoon (south of Bastia)
- Urbino Lagoon (access on bumpy dirt road passing south of the lagoon, signed to Restaurant Albarettu)
- Northern tip of Cap Corse (migrants March to May and Audouin's gull)
- Scandola & Girolata (osprey)
- Asco & Restonica Valleys (forests and alpine zone, lammergeier, Corsican nut hatch, citril finch, wallcreeper)
- Forest of Bonifatu near Calvi (lammergeier)
- Forest of Aïtone (Corsican nuthatch)
- Capitello (by the Prunelli estuary, south of Ajaccio)

frog *Rana bergeri* and **Sardinian tree frog** *Hyla arborea sarda*, you'll need to head for natural wetlands and river estuaries – the Fango estuary south of Calvi is good for pond turtles.

You'll need to wait for a rainy day to see the splendid **fire salamander** *Salamandra salamandra corsica*. These slow-moving, nocturnal salamanders live in damp woodland near streams but are almost entirely terrestrial. It is only the female who must enter the water to give birth to her larvae. Look for them after rainfall, lumbering through the leaf litter of holm oak, beech and chestnut forests, usually at an altitude of 500–1,300m (1,600–4,200ft). Another member of the salamander family is the endemic *Euproctus montanus*, which can only survive in pure, clean mountain streams. It is never found far from water as it has no lungs and must breathe through its skin.

Fast-moving and jittery, **Tyrrhenian wall lizards** *Podarcis tiliguerta* are widespread up to about 1,700m (5,500ft) where they prefer open rocky ground, including walls. Their shading and markings are very varied but females are usually striped, while males are spotted. They are often confused with the introduced **Sicilian lizard** *Podarcis sicula*, which is noticeably greener on the front half of its body. The endemic **Bedriaga's wall lizard** *Archaeolacerta bedriagae* mostly favours high-altitude habitats, where it lives among granite boulders shaded by Laricio pines, but it can also be seen on the rocks at Campomoro, down at sea level! Corsica's rarest lizard is *Algyroïdes fizingeri*, most common around Bonifacio and unmistakeable because of its small size,

bluish throat and orange belly.

At night you may spot the **gecko** *Tarentola mauritanica* scuttling up smooth vertical surfaces, which it clings to by pads on its fingers and toes. Their preferred hunting spots are well-lit walls, which attract insects and moths, and as they are territorial they return to the same place night after night.

Birds

With an abundance of forest, a huge variation in altitude, and all sorts of habitat from coastal lagoons to soaring peaks, Corsica would be teeming with birdlife were it not for the island's obsession with hunting. But, armed with binoculars, a field guide to the birds of Europe and plenty of patience, a visit between March and May should yield good sightings of both migrant and resident species. Autumn and winter can also be rewarding but in summer many birds keep a low profile to avoid the heat.

The Coast

Around the coast, **Cory's shearwaters** *Calonectris diomedea* nest on the Lavezzi and Cervicale Islands and **yellow-legged gulls** *Larus cachinnans* and **shags** *Phalacrocorax aritotelis* are observed on offshore islet and rocks, where they breed readily. The rare **Audouin's gull** *Larus audouinii* is more specific in its nesting requirements and is only found on three island locations. Rocky pillars on the Scandola Peninsula provide ideal nesting spots for fish-eating **osprey** *Pandion haliaetus*, which can also be seen in flight over the Golfe de Porto, with another cliff-dweller the **peregrine falcon** *Falco peregrinus*. The **blue rock thrush** *Monticola solitarius* is at home on coastal

Charcuterie

Made from free-ranging pigs, who browse on acorns and chestnuts, the secrets of Corsica's famous (and expensive) *charcuterie* are passed down from generation to generation. Pigs are usually slaughtered between November and January once they reach the age of two. *Coppa* and *lonzu*, the highest quality of *charcuterie*, are ready for consumption within six months, but ham *prisuttu* traditionally takes two or three years. *Figatelli* sausages must be eaten fresh.

The demand for genuine Corsican *charcuterie* greatly exceeds the supply and unless you buy directly from the producer, you cannot be sure that it is the real thing – made that is from Corsican, rather than imported pork. But there again, if it tastes good, buy it anyway! You are more likely to find the real stuff earlier in the season – by August, most of it has found its way into mainland France's larders.

cliffs and on mountain rock faces, while other high mountain species such as the **alpine accentor** *Prunella collaris* and **wallcreeper** *Tichodroma muraria* often descend to coastal cliffs in winter.

Wetlands

Coastal wetlands, lagoons and river estuaries are the preferred habitat for many aquatic birds, among them **little egret** *Egretta garzetta*, **little grebe** *Tachybaptus ruficollis*, **water rail** *Rallus aquaticus*, **coot** *Fulica atra* and **moorhen** *Gallinula chloropus*. Rarities such as **purple heron** *ardea purpurea*, **great crested grebe** *Podiceps cristatus*, **little bittern** *Ixobrychus minutus* and **moustached warbler** *Acrocephalus melanopogon* are limited to one or two locations. **Reed warbler** *Acrocephalus scirpaceus*, **great reed warbler** *Acrocephalus arundinaceus*, **Cetti's warbler** *Cettia cetti* and **fan-tailed warbler** *Cisticola juncidis* are more readily seen. At Biguglia lagoon, you may be very lucky and see the **white-headed duck** *Oxyura leucocophola*, which is being reintroduced here after serious decline throughout Europe in the 1990s. Birds

of prey common to wetlands are **marsh harrier** *Circus aeruginosus* and **hobby** *Falco subbuteo*.

Rivers and streams

Corsica's freshwater streams and rivers run from the alpine zone to the coast attracting a variety of birds. Look for **grey wagtail** *Motacilla cinerea* and **dipper** *Cinclus cinclus*, which both feed and nest along riverbanks. Near estuaries, where flow is reduced by meandering, colonies of **European bee-eaters** *Merops apiaster* and pairs of **kingfishers** *Alcedo athis* dig out nest tunnels in sandbanks.

Pasture and cultivated terrain

Corsica has escaped the problems associated with monoculture and its vineyards, orchards, pasture and wasteland support plentiful birdlife. There are good pickings for **buzzard** *Buteo buteo*, **red kite** *Milvus milvus* and **barn owl** *Tyto alba*, but some of Corsica's most colourful birds are also found here, including **hoopoe** *Upupa epops*, **golden oriole** *Oriolus oriolus* and **woodchat shrike** *Lanius senator*.

Rock faces and sparsely vegetated rocky terrain

This is the realm of the **golden eagle** *Aquila crysaetos*, which number about thirty pairs in Corsica, and the even rarer **lammergeier** *gypaetus barbatus*, down to just nine or ten breeding couples. The dunnock-like **alpine accentor** *Prunella collaris*, recognised by a yellow patch on the beak, nests under rocks and is often very tame at picnic sites. Acrobatic and often gregarious, **Alpine choughs** *Pyrrhocorax graculus* have prominent yellow beaks and like to nest in *tafoni* or caves. **Wallcreepers** *Tichodroma muraria* flit around on rock faces, flashing their bright red wing patches as they hunt out insects and spiders. **Rock thrushes** *Monticola saxatilis* are shy but the brilliant red breast and underside of the male flitting from rock to rock in search of insects often gives away its presence. The **water pipit** *Anthus spinoletta*, in spite of its name, is an alpine bird in summer.

The *Maquis*

Thorny and dense but laden with blossom in spring and fruit in autumn, the *maquis* is home to many different bird species. You may hear them, but not always see them and because they are hunted some like the **quail** *Coturnix coturnix* and **red-legged partridge** *Alectoris rufa* are secretive and jittery. Typical of the low-growing *maquis* shrubs of cistus, juniper and tree heath are **cuckoo** *Cuculus canorus*, the nocturnal **nightjar** *Caprimulgus europaeus*, **woodlark** *Lullula arborea*, **stonechat** *Saxicola torquata*, **blackbird** *Turdus merula*, **spotted flycatcher** *Muscicapa striata*, **cirl bunting** *Emberiza cirlus*,

Brocciu

Pronounced 'brewch', this is Corsica's best-known and most versatile cheese, which most resembles Italian ricotta – though locals will disagree! Made from ewe's milk whey, with added whole milk, it is produced from winter until June and during this time is eaten fresh, often as a dessert. Salt is added to conserve it for use in savoury dishes, such as *ravioli*, *omelettes*, *tartes* and *beignets*. To be sure of getting the genuine article, look for the AOC label – like wine, this famous cheese has its own *appellation d'origine contrôlée*. Best of all visit one of the mountain *bergeries*, where it is still made according to local traditional methods.

goldfinch *Carduelis carduelis* and **greenfinch** *Carduelis chloris*. Here you can also find four species of warbler, sharing the same habitat but at different heights and utilising different sources of food – the **Sardinian warbler** *Sylvia melanocephala* with its black head and red eye, greyish **Marmora's warbler** *Sylvia sarda*, **Dartford warbler** *Sylvia undata*, with a burgundy throat and breast on the male, and **subalpine warbler** *Sylvia cantillans*. Where the canopy is higher and more substantial trees are present you will also find **great spotted woodpecker** *Dendrocopus major*, the diminutive **firecrest** *Regulus ignicapillus*, **chaffinch** *Fringilla coelebs*, **jay** *Garrulus glandarius* and four tit species. Many passage migrants make use of the *maquis*'s autumn fruit larder.

Corsican marmelade & jam, fish and cheese.
Most of Corsica's cheese is made from ewe's milk.

A Castagna
–the not so humble Chestnut

The chestnut was for centuries the staple food of Corsica's mountain people. It spread into Europe from Asia Minor and may have been introduced into Corsica by the Romans. This versatile and nutritious fruit comes from *Castanea sativa*, which grows readily between the altitude of 600 and 800m (2,000 and 2,600ft), preferring a slightly acidic soil. The trees can grow to 35m (115ft) in height, with a vast horizontal spread, but they benefit from regular pruning. They begin to fruit at 20 years of age and can live for up to 500 years. As the fruit begins to fall in late September, it separates from the spiny husk and is easily collected from the ground. The fruits must be sorted by hand to remove any bad ones that may taint the rest. The tough and inedible skins are today removed by machine and the chestnuts are placed on trays and dried above a low heat before the milling process, which produces the fine chestnut flour.

Chestnuts grow in many parts of inland Corsica, and particularly in the Castagniccia region, whose name is derived from the Corsica word *castagna*. There were once hundreds of thousands of chestnut trees, but because so many mountain villages are no longer inhabited year round many of the chestnut forests are neglected and the trees unproductive. Over 90% of the chestnuts harvested today are for pig fodder and only a few hundred tons are made into flour, by around thirty working mills.

Known locally as the 'bread tree', the staple flour was used to make bread and pastries, desserts such as the famous *fiadona*, as well as enhancing the taste of soups, stews and *eau de vie*. Chestnuts are used to flavour the award-winning local Pietra and Serena beers.

Laricio pine forest

Twenty-nine species of bird nest regularly in this uniquely Corsican habitat. Many are also found in the maquis, while others are more specific to this habitat and include **sparrowhawk** *Accipiter nisus*, **goshawk** *Accipiter gentilis*, **long-eared owl** *Asio otus*, **scops owl** *Otus scops*, **wryneck** *Jynx torquilla*, **chiffchaff** *Phylloscopus collybita* and **treecreeper** *Certhia familiaris*. With patience you should also spot the island's two endemic birds, the **Corsican nuthatch** *Sitella whiteheadi*, and Corsican finch *Carduelis corsicanus* and the **crossbill** *Loxia curivrostra*, all of which are dependent on this habitat.

Corsica's Climate

In the nineteenth century, the British flocked to Ajaccio to escape the harsh winters of the UK. While Corsica today is not normally considered a year-round destination, winter frosts are rare, at least on the coast. In July and August, coastal temperatures, especially in the north, can soar to 35°C (95°F) but usually hover around a pleasant 27°C (81°F).

Typical of Mediterranean islands, winters are wet and summers hot and dry, but with one notable exception: because of its high mountain terrain Corsica sees a fair amount of rainfall in spring and autumn and its average of 30 to 35 inches is higher than in the

Corsican Music

The origins of Corsican music are obscure. Some suggest links with Italian madrigals or North African music but more research is needed before any conclusions can be drawn.

Before its resurgence during the national political awakening in the 1970s, this deeply emotive traditional form of singing was practically unknown outside the island, yet today, along with wine, cheese and *charcuterie*, it is probably Corsica's most famous icon and, more than any other form of art, expresses the cultural spirit of its people.

Polyphonic (many voices) singing characterises the **Capella** style, in which three parts are sung. The *secunda* is the lead voice, then there is the *bassu* and the *terza*, which provides the high melodic notes. Yet there is often the distinct impression of a fourth part, the 'voice of the angels', mysteriously and evocatively weaving in and out of the songs, which can be both religious and secular. This music is traditionally sung by male voices in groups of between three and nine. Live performances are particularly intense as the singers often group closely together, hands cupped around ears and deep in concentration.

Women also sing but traditionally performed solo, as in the **voceru**, a lament sung at a deathbed, which was spontaneously composed in praise of the deceased and, in the case of a murder, to incite vengeance. Nowadays women are increasingly performing in mixed and female-only groups.

The best place to hear Corsican polyphonic singing is at the many music festivals and concerts, which take place over the summer months. But you can also hear it spontaneously break out in bars or behind the shutters of local houses and purely for the sheer pleasure of singing. As well as for entertainment, polyphony is sung by some lay brotherhoods, the **cunfraternita**, which were established in the Middle Ages and continue today to arrange the processions for religious festivals and church music.

Around eighty groups perform and of those who also record the best-known are **A Filetta**, **Canta u Populu Corsu** and Jean-Paul Poletti's **Choeurs de Sartène**, who maintain the purest form, while the popular **I Muvrini** and **I Surghjenti** produce a more contemporary sound, at times using modern instruments. **Soledonna** is an all-women polyphonic singing trio who have received critical acclaim.

Another musical tradition, which visitors may come across at the **Santa di u Niolu** festival, is the singing dialogue known as **chjam' e rispondi** (call and reply), where two singers try to outwit one another with their improvised rhyming verses, which follow strict conventions though the subject matter can be mundane. The winner in this verbal duel leaves his opponent without a suitable reply and elicits the most laughter and applause from the audience.

Among the many instruments featuring in traditional Corsican music are the *cetera*, a lute-like sixteen-stringed instrument, the *caramusa*, a kind of bagpipe, the *pifane*, a goat's horn flute with three to five holes, the *pirula*, a primitive reed recorder and the *riberbula*, similar to a Jew's harp.

wetter parts of Great Britain. This is a result of the abrupt topography – barely 22km (14 miles) divide the coast from the highest summit, Monte Cinto. This also means that in summer, convection brings in warm moist air from the sea, forming clouds and occasionally thunderstorms in the mountains. Conditions are almost always clear by nightfall but downpours can be hazardous for walkers as innocuous streams turn to raging torrents, and they can also block roads, creating chaos for motorists. Winter snow falls above 1,000m (3,280ft) between November and April but in recent years this has rarely been sufficient to open Corsica's ailing ski stations.

May, June, September and October usually offer ideal conditions for travelling around the island and for walking, though May is a little too early for the GR 20 mountain route.

Whenever you visit, you will probably notice one or another of Corsica's winds, each of which has its own name, character and vices. The *Libecciu* is a strong south-westerly wind, bringing rain to the west of the island, while the *Punente* from the west buffets the straits of Bonifacio. From the Sahara, the moisture-laden *Sciroccu* can bring mist and rain, though the *Livante* affects mostly the east coast. The *Gregale*, from the north-east, brings humid conditions to the north but drier weather in the south.

Corsican Food & Drink

Don't look for the refinements of French cuisine in traditional Corsican cooking. The island's food traditions are, by necessity, unrefined and based on a limited range of ingredients: *porc* (pork), *agneau* (lamb), *cabri* (goat), *châtaigne* (chestnut), *fromage* (cheese) and *huile d'olive* (olive oil) supplied from the land.

Meat

Domesticated pigs run free in many parts of the island, eating a natural diet of acorns and chestnuts, which give the meat a special taste. *Côte de porc* (pork chops) feature on many menus but try and get to taste *figatelli* (liver sausages), which are often served with chestnut flour *polenta*. A popular country dish is *tianu* (pork stew) or *ragout de porc*. Many menus also offer *sanglier* (wild boar), but it will only be fresh during the autumn and winter hunting season. Goat and lamb, also free-range, are usually roasted as *cabri rôti* or *agneau au four* or *stuffatu* (stewed).

Where Corsica really comes into its own is with its home-made *charcuterie*. Smoked ham *prisuttu* is eaten raw or grilled. Spicy *salsiccia*, *coppa* (shoulder) and *lonzu* (pork fillet) are often served as an entrée.

Fish

Corsicans traditionally looked more to the land than the sea for their survival, with a few exceptions. The inhabitants of Cap Corse fished for *langouste* (lobster), while on the east coast *huîtres* (oysters) and *moules* (mussels) are a speciality and farmed in the coastal

> *'Per un pate ne brama'*: a Corsican proverb meaning 'conserve, so you will never be wanting'.

Étangs de Diana et d'Urbino. *Oursins* (sea urchins) are eaten raw, but only for a few days in spring, when people are allowed to collect them. On local menus, look for *aziminu*, Corsica's answer to *bouillabaisse* (fish soup). *Grondin* (guernard), *rouget* (mullet), *loup* (sea bass) and *daurade* (gilthead sea bream) are popularly served grilled with fennel. *Truite* (trout) features on mountain menus but it is likely to be farmed.

Soups and Starters

Corsica's traditional *soupe Corse* is thick, almost stew-like and a meal in itself. It is vegetable-based, with haricot beans and unfortunately for vegetarians pork fat or pieces of meat are added. Delicious *beignets* (battered vegetables or cheese) are often served as a starter as is *charcuterie*.

Snacks

Crêpes, both savoury and sweet, are a perfect snack when you can't face a full meal. In local bakeries, look for delicious savoury tarts, or pasties like *feuilletés de blettes* (a pasty filled with swiss chard and herbs).

Pasta and Pizza

Pizzas are found just about everywhere in Corsica and are usually very good. Pasta is an ingredient of traditional Corsican cuisine and sometimes accompanies main courses, unlike in Italy where it is always a starter. Pasta with lobster is sometimes featured on fish menus but the most typical and delicious pasta dishes are *ravioli* or *cannelloni*, stuffed with fresh *brocciu* cheese and mint.

Cheese

With the exception of *brocciu* (soft ewe's cheese), most Corsica *fromages* are strong on the palate and not to everyone's liking. Both sheep's and goat's milk is used and each cheese-producing region, the Niolu, Venacais, Calenzana and Fium'Orbo has its own style, hard and crumbly or soft and creamy. There's even a cheese which comes with its own worms, the famous *casgiu merzu*, but you'll have to hunt it down as it's not advertised on restaurant menus. Cheese is often served with its perfect complement, home-made fig jam.

Desserts

Fiadone is a kind of thick egg-custard with *brocciu*, sometimes soaked in liqueur. Chestnut flour *gâteaux* and fruit tarts are also popular but in general Corsica is not big on desserts. In bakeries, look out for *canistrelli*, traditional dry biscuits made with chestnut flour and aniseed.

Vegetarians and Vegans

Végétarien (vegetarian) and *végétalien* (vegan) are concepts that are better understood today than even ten years ago but if you are a vegan, then self-catering is really the only safe option as most dishes contain eggs or cheese. Vegetarians are quite well catered for in Corsican restaurants with dishes containing *brocciu* cheese such as *omelette au brocciu*, *ravioli* and *cannelloni au brocciu*, *beignets de courgettes*, *aubergines à la Bonifacienne* (aubergines stuffed with tomatoes and cheese) and *tartes*

Corsican Honey

There are so many flowering plants on the island that bees are spoiled for choice in Corsica. There's a long tradition of bee-keeping and honey production but not always with sweet intentions – bees were sometimes used as weapons to defend villages under attack. Today's honey is divided by season. *Miel de printemps* is made in spring and is light and delicate, the bees feeding on citrus and asphodel blossom. *Miel de maquis*, made in summer, is full of the heady scent of helichrysum, thyme and broom while the autumn version is also strongly flavoured and even slightly bitter. Corsican honey has its own seal of quality, the AOC Mele di Corsica.

aux herbes and the like, with pizzas as a standby. Vegetables are not often served with main meals, though a salad will often accompany a dish.

Wine

Corsica produces some really rather good wines but they are little known outside the island because production at most vineyards is small. In the interests of preserving quality, the total acreage of vineyards was drastically cut and today it is one third of what was under cultivation in the 1960s.

The Greeks and Romans probably established the island's first vineyards and today 30 traditional grape varieties are still grown, principally *Vermentinu* (white) and *Nielluccio* and *Sciacca-rellu* (red) alongside imported varieties. Granite, schist and chalk soils each give their own character, while the sun-drenched slopes on which many vineyards are sited work their magic.

The system of AOC (*Appellation d'Origine Contrôlée*) is complex and depends on the proportion of native grape varieties used. The 'Corse' *appellation* is for wines with a high level of imported grape varieties, mainly on the east coast; the 'Corse-Village' *appellation* is for mostly Corsican grape varieties and applies to Calvi, Cap Corse, Figari, Porto Vecchio and Sartène; the 'Cru' *appellation* is given to Ajaccio and Patrimonio.

Reds are full-bodied and those for keeping are generally from the Sciaccarellu grape, while the Niellucciu is similar to the Chianti grape Sangiovese. Vermentinu is the principal variety on Cap Corse, producing fine **whites,** varying from pale to golden yellow.

Many vineyards have a sales outlet but it is usually advisable to ring ahead of your visit. A leaflet listing all the island's vineyards is available at Tourist Offices, or on the AOC website. And of course, don't forget to taste before you buy!

AOC Corse Figari: Tarabucetta, Clos Canarelli ☎ 04 95 71 07 55

AOC Corse Porto-Vecchio: Lecci, Domaine de Torraccia ☎ 04 95 71 43 50

AOC Corse: Ponte Leccia, Domaine Vico ☎ 04 95 36 51 45

AOC Corse Sartène: Tizzano, Domaine de Tizzano ☎ 04 95 77 01 05; Domaine Fiumiccioli ☎ 04 95 76 14 08

AOC Ajaccio: Mezzavia, Domaine Compte Peraldi ☎ 04 95 22 37 30

Corsican Villages

Straddling the ridges, perched on rocky outcrops, sprawled over the mountainsides or huddled in the depths of the valleys, each region of the island has hundreds of hamlets and villages. Some are just a cluster of crumbling stone buildings; others could almost be towns. With their tall stern granite or schist houses clumped together, they look almost fortress-like, which they needed to be to resist the Saracens, Genoese, French, English or whoever else felt inclined to attack their poorly defended mountain strongholds.

Wandering through what is often a single street, flanked by dark, sunless passages and blind alleys, one is struck by the silence. The villages are all but deserted for most of the year, shutters drawn tight. The village school has long ago closed and a mobile shop passes once a week for the handful of retired people who can't or won't leave. But come July and August, they are choked with cars. Bars and restaurants open from nowhere and children's voices fill the streets. Whatever state of decay the houses are in (and some look set to topple) they are almost always privately owned by the descendants of those who once lived there. They live in Ajaccio, Bastia, Marseilles, Paris or even the Caribbean and they are many. Inheritance laws mean that properties are divided between all the children . . . and their children . . . and so on until a single property has twenty or more owners spread all over the world and no one can agree on whether to sell, to renovate or anything else. And being Corsicans they have a special attachment to their village and family home and they return each summer. It's not hard to see why. Stop at one of the war memorials and you'll discover that there may be as few as two or three surnames in one village. The ties are strong.

AOC Corse Calvi: Muro, Clos Reginu ☎ 04 95 61 72 11; Feliceto, Domaine Renucci ☎ 04 95 61 71 08

AOC Patrimonio: Patrimonio, Orenga de Gaffory & San Quilico ☎ 04 95 37 45 00; Domaine Giacometti: turn right off the St Florent to Oletta road, just before Oletta. ☎ 04 95 37 00 72; Clos Arena by the junction of the D81 and D 80 Cap Corse road ☎ 04 95 37 08 27

AOC Coteaux du Cap Corse & Muscat du Cap Corse: Cave Pieretti, Santa Severa ☎ 04 95 35 01 03; Clos Nicrosi, Rogliano ☎ 04 95 35 41 17; Domaine de Pietri, Morsiglia ☎ 04 95 35 60 93

Beer

Corsican beer is one of the island's surprises. *Pietra* is made using chestnut flour and at 6% is strong. *Colomba* from the same brewery is lighter, but not as widely available. *Torra* brands itself as the beer of the *maquis*, with a taste of myrtle and arbutus. All are delicious.

1. Calvi and the Balagne

Balagna

Tucked into the island's north-west corner, the Balagne is in many respects the quintessential Corsica. Its beach-studded coastline is backed by per-fumed hills, where timeless villages lie stacked up in the shadow of the ridges spilling off the north end of the central dividing range. Nowhere else on the island are the 2,000m (6,500ft) high peaks closer to the coast, their serrated profile dominating the view to the south. Deep in the mountains, secluded valleys shelter the majestic forests of Bonifato and Tartagine, where some of the island's most elusive wildlife can be observed.

From Corsica's earliest history, settlers and plunderers alike were drawn by the Balagne's fertile soil, which yielded oil, fruits and cereals and supported grazing herds and flocks. In the wake of Saracen raids, papal authority granted Pisa domination and its feudal overlords ejected the last of the Moors, bringing relative peace and prosperity. From the eleventh to thirteenth centuries many fine churches were built, including Balagne's architectural masterpiece La Trinité d'Aregno. During the second half of the thirteenth century, tired of the power-grabbing tactics of the local nobles, the inhabitants appealed to the Genoese. Ever at the ready to further their interests in Corsica,

Genoa's response was to fortify the repeatedly sacked site of Calvi and in doing so secure its second powerbase on the island.

Calvi

The Genoese placed their imposing, angular citadel strategically on a rocky headland, guarding a perfect semicircular bay and 4km (2.5 mile) long sandy beach, which shelves gently and is ideal for families. Hotels and campgrounds are discreetly hidden among the pinewoods behind the beach and flank the long approach road to the town from the east. Running parallel is the railway,

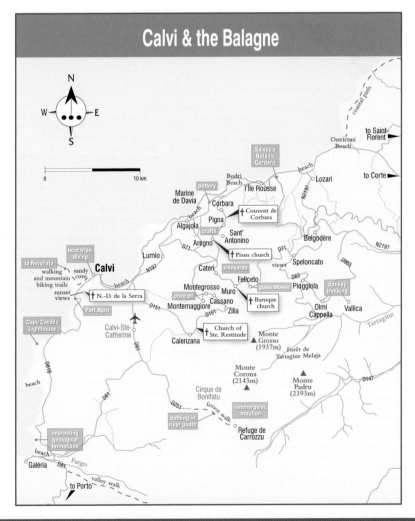

Calvi & the Balagne

to Saint-Florent

to Corte

Ostriconi Beach

Saleccia Botanic Gardens

coastal path

Bodri Beach
I'le Rousse
Lozari
Marine de Davia
pottery
Corbara
Couvent de Corbara
Pigna
Algajola
crafts
Sant' Antonino
Aregno
Belgodère
boat trips, diving
Lumio
Pisan church
la Revellata
walking and mountain biking trails
Calvi
sandy cove
Cateri
vineyards
views
Speloncato
Feliceto
Pioggiola
sunset views
beach
Montegrosso
Muro
glass blower
donkey trekking
N.-D. de la Serra
olive oil
Cassano
Baroque church
Capu Cavallu Lighthouse
Port Agro
Montemaggiore
Zilia
Olmi Cappella
Vallica
Calvi-Ste-Catherine
Church of Ste. Restitude
Monte Grosso (1937m)
Forêt de Tartagine Melaja
Tartagine
Calenzana
Monte Corona (2143m)
Monte Padru (2393m)
interesting geological formations
Cirque de Bonifatu
lammergeier, moufion
beach
bathing in river pools
forest walk
Refuge de Carrozzu
Galéria
Fargo
valley walk
to Porto

with stops conveniently placed along the coast, which links in with the main Ajaccio to Bastia line at Ponte Leccia. But Calvi is at its most striking when approached from the sea and, plying the 180km (112 miles) of water that separate Corsica's north coast from mainland France, ferries dock at the foot of the citadel. Many visitors also stream in through the airport, making Calvi, with 5,270 inhabitants, one of the island's holiday hotspots. Packed out in high summer and all but deserted in winter, the town retains its appeal whatever the season, with accommodation to suit all budgets.

The port and the lower town, where most of the shops and restaurants are located, are set at the foot of the citadel. The broad, palm-lined promenade of **Quai Landry**, with its bars and restaurants shaded by bright awnings, is the perfect place to relax after a day out. As the sun goes down, the jagged summits of Monte Grosso and Capo a Dente glow gold and then pink, while row upon row of gleaming yachts nudge one another in the marina. On the hillside behind, traffic clogs the **Boulevard Wilson**, where the bank, post office and launderette are found. The narrow streets between here and the marina, linked by steps and alleys, form the heart of the lower town, and are sensibly a pedestrian zone. Shops and restaurants spill out onto the streets and squares either side of the main thoroughfare of **rue Clemenceau** and the place buzzes both day and night. The railway station, tourist office and taxi rank are all located just off **Avenue de la République**, at the south end of the lower town. Parking is available at the south end of the marina and off Avenue de la République, where the two main supermarkets are also to be found. Located by the marina, the tourist office rents out an audio-guide in English for those wanting a comprehensive tour of the citadel.

At the foot of the citadel the thirteenth-century round tower known as the **Tour du Sel**, though built as a watchtower, was later used to store salt. From here it is a steep haul up to the Place Christophe Colomb, where steps lead to the single entrance through the ramparts to the fifteenth-century **citadel**, which towers 80m (250ft) over the sea. Above the entrance is placed a stone inscription, *Civitas Calvi Semper Fidelis*, awarded to the town in recognition of Calvi's loyalty to Genoa, for which its citizens enjoyed special privileges.

Once inside the walls, which protect it from all four sides, the citadel is easily explored on foot. A walkway, following the ramparts from bastion to bastion, offers memorable views of the port, the coast and mountains that will make you linger, even under the midday sun. Some of the tall, red-roofed houses within the walls are still dwellings but unlike Bonifacio, there are few shops or restaurants in the citadel and the place has a quiet, almost sombre feel to it. At its heart is **place D'Armes**, presided over by the fifteenth-century **Palais des Gouverneurs Génois**, built as the residence of the Genoese governors but today the French Foreign Legion's **Caserme Sampiero**, which is closed to the public.

Across the square and up the steps is the **Cathédrale Saint Jean-Bap-**

tiste. The original church, possibly erected in the thireenth century, was burned down in 1481, subsequently rebuilt but damaged again in 1553 and 1567. In its present form, the domed cathedral dates from 1570 and contains several important works of art. Behind the ornate, polychrome marble altar is a late-fifteenth-century triptych by the Ligurian Barbagelata but for the Calvesi it is the ebony Christ, above the altar to the right of the choir, who holds special significance. Known as the **Christ des Miracles**, legend has it the statue was paraded above the ramparts to repel the forces of Sampiero Corso and the Franco-Turkish alliance, during the siege of August 1555. The statue, like that of the **Virgin of the Rosary**, is carried by members of the brotherhoods during the Holy Week processions.

Tucked down an alley east of place d'Armes is the **Oratoire de la Confrérie Saint-Antoine**, whose carved door lintel features the saint with his piglet. Inside are a small collection of art treasures and a series of rather damaged frescoes. Further down the street to the right **Chez Tao** occupies the cellars of the bishops' palace, **Palais des Evêques de Sagone**. Founded in the 1930s by a Russian immigrant (no Chinese connection here) who fell for Calvi and its citadel, this upmarket restaurant, piano bar and nightclub is still in the same family and enjoys almost legendary status for its ambience and panoramic views of the town.

Also the stuff of legends is Calvi's claim to **Christopher Columbus**, whose supposed birthplace is marked by a plaque on a house on the north side of the citadel. The hypothesis is argued in a booklet available at the tourist office but the supporting evidence, if it can be called that, is at best circumstantial and tenuous and is vehemently disputed by historians.

In the lower town, set in a compact square just off rue Clemenceau, is the domed baroque church of **Sainte Marie-Majeure**, housing a statue of St Erasmus, patron saint of fishermen.

Things to see and do around Calvi

Boat trips south to the Scandola Reserve, Girolata and Porto or east to the Agriates coast depart from Quay Landry. Both will tempt you with breathtaking, unspoiled coastal scenery, largely due to their inaccessibility by road, but pick a calm day for the ride. **Scimia Calvese**, in the pinewoods behind the beach, is an **aerial adventure course** aimed at adults and older children.

There is some excellent **scuba diving** in the vicinity of Calvi around the rocky coast of the Revellata Peninsula, which is peppered with underwater marvels. The top site, but one for experienced divers only as it lies in 27m (90ft) of seawater, is the wreck of a B-17 US bomber, which crashed just off the citadel as its pilot attempted an emergency landing at Calvi airport in 1944. Diving and snorkelling trips depart from the marina and port.

The Revellata Peninsula and hills behind Calvi offer a range of tracks suitable for cycling. **Mountain bikes** can be hired by the day, with advice given on suggested routes. A folder of route cards in a handy plastic pouch is on sale

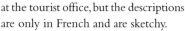

at the tourist office, but the descriptions are only in French and are sketchy.

Watersports enthusiasts will find plenty to occupy their time at the Calvi Nautique Club at the north end of the beach, where sailing dinghies and kayaks can be hired. Motorboat hire is available at Tra Mare e Monti, by the tourist office.

Coastal Walk to the Revellata Peninsula

Distance: 12km (7.5 miles) but shorter if you drive part of the way
Duration: allow 5 hours (including swim stops)
Ascent & Descent: 150m (500ft)
What to take: water, sunhat, sun-screen, swimwear, mask and snorkel. There is almost no shade on this walk.

Lying west of Calvi, the rocky Revellata Peninsula offers spectacular coastal scenery and sheltered coves for swimming and snorkelling. From Place Christophe Colomb, walk out of town on the D81b past the Balkan Cross, a monument to the 400 passengers and crew who lost their lives when the *Balkan* was torpedoed by a German submarine off Calvi on the night of 15 August 1918. After 1.5km (1 mile) turn right past the entrance to the residence Tramariccia and walk down a lane. Where it divides shortly after, bear left down a shady lane until you reach a broad trail to the left, with open views over scrub down to the coast. Follow this trail, which from now on is marked by splashes of red paint, and descend after 1.5km (1 mile) to the sheltered sandy bay of Alga. The path now hugs the coast of the Revellata Peninsula, past several coves, and climbs steeply to meet the dirt track that leads to the lighthouse. Below you is the marine research station of Stareso. Backtrack on the dirt road, staying on the main track, which follows left of the crest of the ridge. Every so often, the view to the south opens up, revealing the cliffs of a wild, surf-lashed coast. The track loops down to a saddle, where the red paint splashes guide you back down to the bay of Alga. From here follow the same route back to Calvi. To shorten the walk by half you can drive on the D81b as far as the turn-off to Revellata, park and walk down the dirt track to the bay of Alga to join the trail.

Exploring the Balagne

The Balagne offers such a showcase of Corsican experiences that you will probably still find plenty to keep you amused, even after a week's stay. Unless you're planning to walk one of the long-distance routes, or stay glued to the beach, a car is useful as many bus routes only operate once a day, even in high season.

The region's most scenic drives, the Balagne mountain village routes and the Calvi to Porto road, are narrow and winding and may take far longer than expected. For those happy to tackle longer drives, the interior and high valleys of Tartagine, Asco, Restonica, Tavignano and the Niolo offer mouth-watering mountain vistas, while the picture postcard hill villages of Castagniccia, set among chestnut forests, are in a world of their own.

Sunset at Notre Dame de la Serra

This little church lies up a steep lane, which turns off the D81b, 4km (2.5 miles) southwest of Calvi, opposite the track to Pointe de la Revellata. The nineteenth-century chapel is of little architectural interest but it stands on the site of a fifteenth-century sanctuary, destroyed in 1794 when Nelson's forces and those of patriot Pascal Paoli laid siege to Calvi. The real reason to come here is evident when you arrive – the breathtaking view over the town and bay, which is at its most sensational as the last rays of sun catch the citadel. It's also worth taking a look at the strange eroded granite *tafoni* which dot the surrounds of the chapel.

The Balagne Coast

Up to nine trains a day meander along the coast between Calvi and Île Rousse, stopping at beaches, towns and villages along the way. The first, **Lumio**, is more easily accessed by road, its tall houses stacked up against the hillside. There's a short but spectacular walk to the abandoned village of **Occi**, sited atop the hill behind Lumio. The path starts from the north end of the village by a little turning off the N197, near restaurant Chez Charles. It's quite a steep climb but in 30 to 45 minutes you'll reach a stunning viewpoint over the Bay of Calvi and the ruins of a safe retreat from Saracen attacks. Occi's last inhabitant, Félix Giudicelli, died in 1927. If you're feeling energetic, from Occi the trail climbs another 200m (656ft) to the summit of Capu D'Occi, for an even more mouth-watering panorama.

Algajola (Algaghjola) is a compact little town, hemmed in by the fortifications built by the Genoese in response to Saracen harassment. You can walk through its quiet, narrow streets and soak up the atmosphere, but the citadel itself is privately owned. There's a gorgeous long sandy beach to the east and a couple of laid-back hotels, bars and restaurants.

Development has been quite extensive along the coast so don't expect to find deserted beaches, though there are a couple of nice ones. Pick of the bunch is **Bodri**, accessible by train and by a signposted dirt track off the N197, 2km (1.25 miles) east of Île Rousse. **Île Rousse (Isula Rossa)**, a busy coastal town of 2,800 inhabitants, dates back to Phoenician and Roman times. Thrust into the spotlight in 1758, when Pasquale Paoli chose it because of its potential as a port to rival Genoese Calvi, this one-time fishing village is today a bustling resort town, in spite of being eclipsed by the architectural heritage of its rival. The port, sited by the offshore red granite islet, from which the town gets its name, competes with Calvi for the ferry traffic from the mainland and services run to Marseilles, Nice and Toulon. Beyond the port, a **lighthouse**, dating from 1857 and housing an exhibition, and a ruined **Genoese tower** are a popular viewpoint at sundown. Another tower, adjacent to the town hall, was part of the defences erected by Paoli in 1765.

The town's centerpiece is **Place Paoli**, an unpretentious shaded square, flanked by shops and cafés, with predictably a statue of the national hero, who is reported to have built the town as 'a gallows on which to hang Calvi'. At its north-east corner a colonnaded **covered market**, dating from around 1850, is packed with stalls selling local produce. Behind the market, a web of narrow streets forms the town's compact historic centre. The tourist office is just east of the square, while

> ## Nelson's eye and the siege of Calvi
>
> In 1794 Horatio Nelson's forces besieged Bastia, then Calvi, supporting Pascal Paoli's second bid for Corsican independence. From a gun emplacement on the hillside behind Calvi, Nelson was injured in the face by stones and sand dislodged by enemy fire on 12 July. Writing of the injury in a letter to Lord Hood, Nelson remarked: 'I got a little hurt this morning: not much as you may judge by my writing.' But ten days later the wound had deteriorated, leading to the loss of sight in his right eye. On 10 August, Calvi capitulated after 51 days of siege and Corsica came fleetingly under British rule.

banks, post office, bus station and other services lie on and either side of the main Calvi to Bastia road, south of the old town.

The beach at Île Rousse, backed by the **Promenade A Marinella**, struggles to cope with the crowds in high summer but there is another stretch of sand a little further to the east.

On the main road east of Île Rousse is the **Parc de Saleccia**, a beautifully designed botanic garden on a private estate. The original olive grove was ravaged by fire in the 1970s. Replanted with olive and other trees and shrubs from all over Corsica, the 7-hectare (17-acre) park showcases the island's native vegetation, with thoughtful insights into plant mythology and the medicinal and culinary use of species.

Where the railway turns south into the hills, the road continues around a rocky coast to **Lozari**, a coarse shingle beach with a large holiday complex at its east end. Here the old N197 heads inland, but for the coast you should continue on the fast new road, 'La Balanina'. After a few minutes' drive, **Ostriconi Beach**, accessed by a turning to the left, comes into view. This gorgeous, deserted stretch of sand, backed by dunes and wetland, gives a foretaste of the even wilder landscapes to the north. There's no proper parking so cars are strung out along the access road, from where it is a very steep descent on a rocky path. The beach is exposed and bathing is not advisable once the waves start to pound the shore. Instead, hike to the end of the beach and follow the path into the uninhabited **Désert des Agriates**. Take plenty of water and protection from the sun as there is no shade.

About 18km (11 miles) inland the N1197 passes the village of **Lama**, which looks set to topple from its rocky spur guarding the Ostriconi valley. In 1970, a catastrophic fire destroyed its 50,000 olive trees but recent low-key tourism ventures, including a summer outdoor film festival, have brought a new lease of life to this perky little village in an undeniably picturesque setting.

Strada di l'Artigiani (The Artisans Route)

If you're interested in small-scale local production of wine, honey, biscuits and olive oil and crafts such as pottery, musical instruments, glassware, leather goods and jewellery, the mountain villages of the Balagne are the place to seek out and enjoy them as well as meet local Corsicans. In doing so, you'll also be supporting the rural economy and helping keep these villages and their traditions alive. All the producers' details and a map of the route are found in a booklet available at the tourist office.

Balagne Mountain Village Drive

Visible from the Calvi to Île Rousse coast road, a cluster of perfect little Corsican villages sit perched 300m (1,000ft) up in a natural amphitheatre flanking the foothills of towering Monte Grosso. Linked by what is arguably the Balagne's most picturesque road, each has its own character and history. Those willing to invest a bit of time and effort can track down some real architectural gems in the region's olive oil mills, fountains, Baroque churches and Romanesque chapels. Many of the villages are closed to vehicles but parking is often available as you enter, for which you may be expected to pay. You could do the drive in a morning or afternoon, but a whole day allows a much more relaxed pace as the road is very, very twisting.

The route starts just west of Île Rousse, where the D151 turns off, passing a traditional pottery, and leads to **Corbara (Curbara)**, a sizeable village spread over Monte Guido, whose splendid eighteenth-century Baroque Church of the Annunciation may draw you to halt. Just beyond the village is the working Dominican monastery and spiritual retreat of **Couvent de Corbara**, set around a peaceful courtyard and overlooking the Balagne coast. The next village, **Pigna**, is a compact cluster of red-tiled houses with smart blue shutters, set among olive groves and fruit trees. With funding, the place has become a beacon of rural develop-

Davia – Empress of Morocco

At the end of the eighteenth century, the poverty-stricken Franceschini family from Corbara set sail for the continent in search of a better life. The day before, Davia, their eight-year-old daughter, had given alms to a beggar woman, who handed her a talisman, which she hung from her neck. Blown off course in a gale, the family were shipwrecked on the coast of Morocco and taken into captivity. When Davia's talisman was identified as the valuable 'main de Fatma', the family's luck changed and they were brought to the sultan's court. As Davia recounted how she had obtained the talisman, the beggar was recognized as none other than the sultan's sister, who had run away years before. Davia grew up at the palace, under the sultan's watchful eye, and in due course they were married. When her family yearned to return to Corsica, Davia built a house for them in their village, which still stands and is known as 'Casa dei Turchi'. That, at any rate, is the legend. The other version has it that Davia was born in Tunis to Corsican parents, who had been captured by pirates. She did become a sultan's favourite, but probably never set foot in Corsica. Marine de Davia, on the coast, is named after her.

ment, and as you wander among its narrow cobbled streets, you'll come across potter, flute maker, lute maker, engraver, sculptor, a fine selection of local food and drink products and the exquisite little painted music boxes for which the place is world famous. In fact the village has taken things a step further and its delightful little guesthouse, **La Casa Musicale**, hosts music events and workshops, including the 13 July 'Paese in Festa', which offers a rare chance to hear the traditional *chjam'e rispondi*, singing dialogue. You don't have to be a musician to stay or eat here but reservations are recommended as the view from its panoramic terrace is sublime.

Aregno, situated among citrus and almond orchards, boasts the splendid twelfth-century **Église de la Trinité et de San Giovanni**. This masterpiece of Pisan Romanesque architecture is set back from the road among the gleaming white tombs of its cemetery, as you leave the village. Its fine polychrome granite in dark green, beige, pink and ochre is embellished with a number of enigmatic sculptures: above the left of the door a woman with hands on her hips; to the right a man; above them, adorning the four blind arches, a row of exotic animals; and under the apex

Speloncato, a village with fine views and interesting architecture

Laricio pines

of the pediment a male figure, seated as if perhaps examining his foot for thorns. Inside the church are fifteenth-century frescoes, one of which depicts St Michael slaying the dragon.

Visible from afar, the hill-top village of **Sant'Antonino** may be one of Corsica's oldest, probably dating back to the ninth century. Vestiges of fortifications, including a ruined keep, are visible on its summit, suggesting it may have been a safe retreat for the inhabitants of the surrounding valleys when Saracens appeared on the horizon. Being acknowledged as '*un des plus beaux villages de France*' carries a price and Sant'Antonino is today invaded by coachloads of visitors. To appreciate the peaceful labyrinth of stepped alleys and vaulted archways and for the breathtaking views of the Balagne coast to the north and rugged mountains to the south, aim for sunrise or sunset. Access to the village is via a narrow lane that takes off just south of Aregno. Park by the church and walk from there, perhaps stopping for a freshly-squeezed lemon juice at Maison du Citron. A bargain Corsican menu of local produce is on offer at Le Bellevue, a family-run restaurant in the village. In late June and early July Sant'Antonino hosts a contemporary arts festival, known as *Île Mouvante*.

From Cateri, the D71 swings around the lower slopes of 1,938m (6,356ft) Monte Grosso, hanging high above the plain as it strings together one picture postcard village after another. If you can face yet another priceless Baroque church, that of **Muro**, with its ornate marble altar, will not disappoint. Inside, an inscription recalls the tragedy of 4

Colourful Kites

Red Kite *Milvus milvus*
Look for the long, deeply-forked rust-red tail and white patches on the underwings of this elegant, slender-winged raptor. Red kites hunt small rodents and birds over hilly, open terrain with patchy woodland. They are fairly common throughout and readily observed in the Regino Valley, near Calvi.

March 1798, when the roof collapsed, killing 59 churchgoers. It's not hard to be charmed by **Feliceto (Filicetu)**, whose chestnut groves are a welcome contrast to the scorched slopes so prevalent in this fire-prone region. At the bottom end of the village past the church and cemetery is the renowned glass-blowing workshop **Verrerie Corse**. If you feel like an overnight stay here, the **Hotel Mare e Monti** has heaps of character, occupying a grand old mansion built by the present owner's ancestor, who made his fortune in Puerto Rico. The same family owns the local Domaine Renucci vineyard, which offers wine tasting. The village restaurant, **U Mulinu**, is housed in a restored olive mill and does a roaring trade thanks to its good food and the theatrical antics of the proprietor.

Past the village of Nessa, bear right on the D663 for **Speloncato (Spelun-catu)**, a neat little village of tall granite houses, defiantly clinging to a rocky spur 550m (1,800ft) above sea level and offering marvellous views. The square, as in most Corsican villages, is where everything (or nothing!) happens. For Speloncato the all-important dates are 8 April and 8 September, when each year at 6pm the sun drops behind a rock on the flank of the hill to the west. Then seconds later it magically reappears, illuminating the square for a moment or two as it shines through a hole in the pierced rock, *Petra Tafunata*. The village owes its name to caves (*spelonche*), one of which lies below the church, serving as an ossuary in Medieval times.

Facing the square the historic **Hotel Spelonca** was the nineteenth-century summer residence of Cardinal Savelli

and it has been carefully restored to retain its original features, among them a splendid staircase.

Rejoining the D71, the road twists tortuously around the flank of the hill to reach **Belgodère (Belgudè)**, the final village of note on this tour. Perched around a natural rock balcony, it more than lives up to its name, which means 'pleasant place', and the views are breathtaking. In the square, the sixteenth-century church of St Thomas has a painting on wood of the Virgin and Child.

The Calenzana and Montegrosso Loop

If you don't have the time or inclination for the Balagne Mountain Village Drive, this shorter alternative explores a cluster of gorgeous villages before the long haul up to the scenic Col de Salvi. East of Calvi take the D151 to the flourishing town of **Calenzana (Calinzana)**, the trailhead for the famous GR 20 and Mare e Monti long-distance walks. There are a couple of small hotels and the reputable restaurant **Chez Michel** on the main street opposite the church, which does a good-value Corsican menu. The monumental early-eighteenth-century **Église Saint Blaise** is packed with polychrome marble but its most striking feature is the tiled floor, which gives the impression of sloping and indeed it does. An inscription on the clock tower relates to the 1732 battle, when 500 German mercenaries, enlisted by the Genoese to put down the Corsican revolt, were hacked to death by the citizens of Calenzana. One popular version has it that the locals hurled

Saint Restitude, patron of Calenzana

Just east of Calenzana on the D151 is the little church of Saint Restitude, an obscure third- or fourth-century Corsican martyr, born into a pagan family but converted as a young woman. She was tortured and then burned, but survived to be taken out to sea and drowned. Clinging to a piece of cork, she floated ashore while her captors perished instead. Finally she and five others were decapitated. In 1951 her marble sarcophagus, now on display in the church, was found behind the altar, containing the remains of six people. On Easter Monday and 21 May, her saint's day, there are processions through the village, which is decorated with flowers and garlands. Among the miracles attributed to her is the ousting of the Black Death from the village, which is still commemorated on 5 August.

beehives from their windows and the bees stung so mercilessly, the soldiers were unable to defend themselves.

A trio of delightful little villages is strung out along the foot of Monte Grosso: **Zilia**, known for its mineral water, which is bottled on site; picturesque **Cassano**, its square accessed by an archway and **Montemaggiore**, which affords a splendid view over the valley. You will have passed a working **olive mill**, to the right of the road, where there is no doubt who does the donkey work – one or two are usually tethered outside. You can visit the mill and sample the different grades of fine oil. The village hosts an olive festival, *A Fiera di L'Alivu*, in July.

The road now climbs high above the valley, over a fire-scorched hillside to the 509m (1,670ft) **Col de Salvi**, another great viewpoint. From here it drops to the crossroads at Cateri, where you can join the D151 to descend via Aregno, Pigna and Corbara to the coast (see Balagne Mountain Village Drive) or take the more direct D71 to Lumio.

Cirque de Bonifato (Bonifatu)

From Calvi take the D81 past the airport and then the D251. The narrow road winds above the Figarella River for 10km (6 miles), ending at the Auberge de la Forêt, worth a stop for coffee and cake or even a meal. From here there is a choice of walking trail, from easy stroll to full-day hike into the rugged cirque.

Hike to the Refuge de Carozzu & Spasimata Bridge

Distance: 5.5km (3.5 miles) each way

Duration: 2.5 hours ascent and 2 hours descent

Ascent & Descent: 730m (2,400ft)

What to take: walking boots, warm clothing and rain jacket (as well as shorts); water and packed lunch; sunscreen and sun hat; walking poles can be helpful

The classic walk leads up a deep valley, flanked by colossal, serrated 2,000m (6,500 ft) high mountains and gorgeous tracts of Laricio pine forest. It's an immensely popular walk in summer, not least for the chance to bathe in the refreshing river pools, set among giant granite boulders. Start early to avoid the crowds and the heat. The trail begins at Auberge de la Forêt and the first 30 minutes is on a broad and easy track, which you can do even in sandals. When this turns to a path, which continues on the same side of the river and is marked with yellow splashes of paint, it soon becomes obvious why walking boots are a must – the trail is rocky and uneven, though well trod. After a further 30 to 40 minutes, it crosses the river by a bridge, where there are several bathing pools. Climbing more steeply, the trail weaves in and out of the forest and is punctuated by glimpses of the STET, which closes in on all sides. After an hour, or more, cross a side stream – in spring or with heavy rainfall it may become tricky or even dangerous, so care is needed. Shortly, you will arrive at an abandoned *bergerie*, a cluster of stone huts, where the path continues directly above the huts for a further 10 minutes to reach the Refuge de Carozzu, at 1,270m (4,165ft). From its panoramic decked terrace, a perfect place to relax over a cool drink, the view stretches back to Calvi, if you

Left: The walking trails of the Forêt de Bonifato are just a short drive from Calvi
Opposite: hiking near Galéria

The Giunssani (Ghjunsani)
– the hidden valley

Wedged between the massifs of Monte Grosso and Monte Padro, the Tartagine River roars off the dividing range into a deep secluded valley that is as beautiful as it is inaccessible. Legend has it a hunter once found a golden mouflon there but was so taken aback that he did not shoot it. Next day he regretted not having added it to his trophies so he returned to kill it. As he did so, an old woman appeared from nowhere and in fury at what he had done, ordered the hunter to throw himself into the ravine. It's said an eerie wailing can be heard in the vicinity. It's more likely to be your car that wails and groans on the narrow potholed road up the valley, which requires your full concentration – ask in one of the villages before you set out.

In its narrow inner reaches the Tartagine is densely wooded with pines, but where the valley broadens these give way to holm oak and chestnut groves, planted around the four little villages that make up the micro-region of the Giunssani. Some rather grandiose baroque churches suggest this was once a wealthy region but it is the village of **Vallica** that is most striking, having perfectly preserved its feudal ambience. From the village a path descends to the river and a beautiful and ancient bridge over the Tartagine, taking about one hour each way. There are many other walking trails in the area, including an access route to the GR 20 and a new long-distance path from Île Rousse to Corte, which traverses the Giunssani. For families or those who don't want to carry a pack, Balagn'ane, based in Olmi Capella offer the solution – trekking with a pack donkey.

Access to the region is from the Balagne village of Speloncato, taking the winding D63 over the 1,100m (3,600ft) Col de la Barraglià, where a little café (open summer only) invites you to linger over the view. There's also a gem of a village *auberge* and restaurant at Pioggiola and plenty of idyllic picnic spots.

can take your eyes off the mountains around you. Mouflon are sometimes spotted on the rocky slope behind the *refuge* among the pines stubbornly clinging to precipitous rocky outcrops. It is also worth looking out for bearded vultures (lammergeier), soaring effortlessly above the peaks to the north. Time permitting, you can drop back down to the river from here by following the red and white markings of the GR 20 to the famous suspension bridge, but the trail becomes appreciably more challenging, with rocky slabs to negotiate, which can be very slippery when wet.

Coastal Drive South of Calvi

The 34km (21-mile) drive from Calvi to Galéria on the old road to Porto presents a startling contrast to the gentle landscapes of the north coast of the Balagne. As Calvi fades from view, the road climbs and hangs above the coast, narrow and eternally winding from one spine-chilling viewpoint to the next, the steep, barren rocky slopes plunging to the sea below. Not surprisingly, this whole coast is practically uninhabited. The bay of **Agro** was where Nelson discharged his cargo of cannons, which were then arduously hauled overland by his men to their vantage point overlooking Calvi. On the next rocky headland, a rough track leads down to **Capu Cavallu**, where the oldest granite on Corsica is found, dating back around 340 million years.

The road does not drop to sea level until you reach the Baie de Crovani and abandoned mine at **Argentella**, whose rather grand but crumbling

Calvi/Île Rousse to Corte by train

For a change, take a day trip on Corsica's scenic narrow-guage railway, which links Calvi and Île Rousse with Corte, winding through splendid coastal and mountain landscapes. It's a full day trip with an early start, taking three hours each way, but allows plenty of time to explore Corsica's famous mountain town.

buildings are clustered in the *maquis* behind the south end of the beach. Argentiferous galena, or silver-bearing lead was extracted and worked here until about a century ago and in the 1960s de Gaulle had plans for nuclear testing here, vigorously opposed by Corsicans. The area south of here is one of Corsica's top geological sites and progresses from granite through metamorphic amphibolites to the volcanic rhyolite of Galéria. Little pebbles of this red volcanic rock are scattered on the beach at the mouth of the Fango River, just north of the town. You can access the beach from the north end via a track but it is easier to continue over the river and park by the ruined tower at its south end.

The small town of **Galéria** has a cluster of bars and restaurants and was at the end of a transhumance route used by the shepherds of the mountainous Niolo region to take their flocks to the winter pastures on the coast. Walkers can follow a part of this route inland up the beautiful Fango Valley. The trail is marked with the characteristic orange splashes of the Mare e Monti route.

Places to Visit

Calvi

Calvi Tourist Office
By the marina
Open 8.30am–1pm and 2.30–7pm daily, June to Aug; out of season 9am–12pm and 2–5pm Mon to Fri and on Sat from Easter
☎ 04 95 65 16 67
www.balagne-corsica.com

A Scimia Calvese – aerial adventure course, Calvi
In the pine woods behind the beach Challenging and fun for adults and older children. Open June to Oct
☎ 04 95 61 80 08, www.altore.com

Colombo Line – boat trips from Calvi to Scandola and Porto
Daily departures from the port, late March to mid-Nov, half and full-day trips to the spectacular coast south of Calvi. Reservations essential.
☎ 04 95 65 32 10
www.colombo-line.com

Diving Calvi Castille
Operates diving and snorkelling trips all year on demand, from the port by the citadel
☎ 04 95 65 14 05
www.plongeecastille.com

Bicycle hire
At Garage d'Angeli just off place Christophe Colomb. Open all year
☎ 04 95 65 02 13
www.garagedangeli.com

Boat hire
At Tra Mare e Monti, by the Tourist Office
☎ 04 95 65 21 26
www.tramare-monti.com

Around Calvi

Île Rousse Tourist Office
on Place Paoli
Open: 9am–8pm daily (Sun 10am–12pm and 5–7pm) in July and Aug; out of season 10am–12pm and 2–7pm Mon–Fri
☎ 04 95 60 04 35
www.ot-ile-rousse.fr

Horse riding on the beach, east of Île Rousse
Ostriconi Beach, 5km (3 miles) east of the town
Riding tours of an hour or longer in summer; telephone out of season
☎ 06 16 72 53 12

Parc de Saleccia, Île Rousse
3 km (2 miles) east of the town
Botanic garden, focusing on the *maquis*
Open April to Oct, 9.30am–12.30pm and 4–8pm daily (but all day on weekends and slightly reduced hours out of high season)
☎ 04 95 36 88 83
www.parc-saleccia.fr

Balagn'ane – Donkey Treks, Olmi Capella
☎ 04 95 61 80 88
www.rando-ane-corse.com

Corbara Pottery
Corbara
By the junction of N197 and D313 to Corbara
Simple, glazed functional pottery in natural colours
Open 10am–12pm and 3–6pm daily (not Sun out of season)
☎ 04 95 60 23 37

The busy seaside resort of St Florent is bounded by Cap Corse to the north and the uninhabited Agriates, with its gorgeous beaches, to the west. Inland, touring the vineyards of Patrimonio and hilltop villages of the Nebbio, there are beautifully proportioned Romanesque churches to admire, top-quality wines to taste and seductive views to detain you in an easily explored enclave that is compact yet diverse.

Saint-Florent (San Fiurenzu), with a population of 1,500, is a pleasant town sited at the estuary of the Aliso. Its historic hub fronts the port and marina, where an eye-catching promenade of cafés, shops and restaurants invites you to linger over a sunset drink or dinner.

La Gaffe, on the quayside, is a popular fish restaurant. For fresh pasta, head for **U Troglu** on rue Principale, behind the quay.

There's not a lot to visit in town. The **citadel**, built by the Genoese in 1439, was scarred by repeated attacks,

Opposite: The Mortella tower of the Agriates coast was destroyed by the English in 1794

including that of Nelson's forces in 1794. North-east of here, a narrow strip of shingle is flanked by the main road and tourist development, but the best beach is to the west of town, accessed by a turning off the D81, once over the bridge. Several pleasant campsites are located in the woods behind **Plage La Roya**. With the full range of watersports on offer there's enough here to keep sun and sea enthusiasts happy.

Don't miss the wonderful **Cathédrale du Nebbio**, situated 1km (half a mile) down the D238, on the site of an earlier Roman settlement, which was placed inland away from the marshy,

mosquito-infested estuary. A former bishopric, the twelfth-century Pisan Romanesque church of Sta-Maria-Assunta is built of pale limestone, its exterior adorned with tiers of blind arches and a strange beast and serpents in relief above the pilasters of its facade. The interior (ask for the key at the Tourist Office if it is closed) is also embellished with fine stonework on the capitals of the pillars dividing the aisles and nave, which lead to a vaulted apse and gilded wooden statue of St Flor, a third-century young Roman soldier, martyred for his beliefs. The youth's mummified remains are displayed in

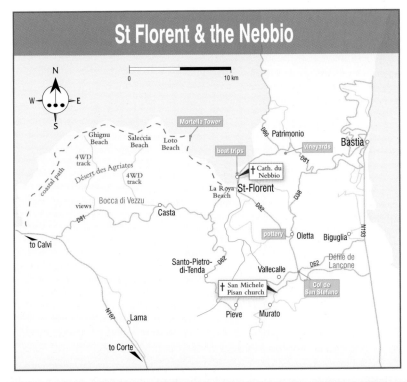

St Florent & the Nebbio

the church, having been taken from the catacombs of Rome to Corsica by order of Pope Clement XIV in 1771.

Patrimonio and La Route des Vins

Sited on the main St Florent to Bastia road, this prosperous hillside village overlooks the Golfe de St Florent and the chalk ridge of Monte Sant'Angelo, a geological oddity in this transition zone between the schist and granite regions. Just above the village, the imposing church of St Martin was built in the sixteenth century, though the tower is a later addition, erected when it was restored in the nineteenth century. Left of the lane leading to the church is a 3,000-year-old limestone statue-menhir, unearthed in 1965, during the planting out of a vineyard. If you're a music fan, it's worth knowing that Patrimonio hosts the annual music event **Les Nuits de la Guitare** each year during the second half of July.

Exploring the villages of the Nebbio

The Aliso valley is flanked by a semi-circle of hills, on whose ridges a dozen or more defiant villages are perched. As the bread-basket of Corsica, the Genoese grew wheat in the fertile valley, while the Nebbio hills were given over to fruit and olive trees.

This circular 48km (30-mile) drive is best done early in the morning or late in the day, when the light is mellow. From St Florent, take the D82 towards **Oletta**, a picture postcard village of tall red-tiled houses stacked up against the hillside. It's worth stopping at the **Poterie d'Oletta** en route to admire their beautiful blue, green and brown-glazed ceramics. The road contours above the valley, climbing steadily to 350m (1,148ft) and the **Col de San Stefano**, a fine viewpoint over the Nebbio hills, Golfe de St Florent and the natural amphitheatre of the Aliso Valley.

From the crossroads on the pass, the D62 plunges to the east coast through the precipitous **Défilé de Lancone** while the D5 leads to one of Corsica's most beautiful churches, the twelfth-century Pisan masterpiece of **San Michele de Murato**. Standing in splendid isolation on a grassy plateau, legend has it the church was built overnight by angels, who chose a forested site so as to keep their work secret. In the morning the trees were felled to reveal the church. Divine or not, the two-tone stonework in dark green serpentine marble from the nearby Bevinco river and pale limestone from St Florent is as eye-catching as it is chaotically irregular. Take time to discover the exquisite carved reliefs on the arcading, windows and blind arches, depicting enigmatic faces and figures, animal, bird and flower motifs, a pair of entwined snakes and Eve, tempted by the serpent.

Murato (Muratu) village, 1km (0.5 miles) further on, overlooks the Bevinco valley and was chosen by Paoli as his headquarters when he installed his troops in the local monastery in 1755 and minted Corsica's first currency, '*a zecca*'. This unassuming village has a further claim to fame as birthplace to

Wines of Patrimonio

Surrounded by vineyards, Patrimonio is one of Corsica's premier wine-producing regions and was the first to receive its own AOC. With 21 of the 32 producers located in and around the village, Patrimonio is perfect for a wine-tasting tour. Its *Appellation d'Origine Contrôlée* spans the full range of red, white, rosé and muscat wines, produced from *Nielluccio*, *Vermentinu* and *Muscat* grapes that thrive on Corsica's only chalk-clay soils. With barely 500 hectares (1,235 acres) under cultivation, production is limited but sought after as much of it is organic. Pick up a leaflet from the tourist office, which gives details of the vineyards and their location. It's best to ring ahead to check opening hours as most are small, family-run vineyards.

Clément Leoni, father of Raúl Leoni, who was elected president of Venezuela in 1963. By strange coincidence, his opponent was a Pietri and the descendant of a Cap Corse family.

If you want to combine this drive with a Corsican feast, then head for the worthy **Restaurant Le But**, in Murato itself, or the **Ferme Auberge Campu di Monte**, on the opposite side of the valley up a dirt road off the D305 by the bridge. It's a little off the beaten track but worth it for authentic cuisine and ambience in a traditional stone farmhouse.

Backtracking to the church, the circular drive continues on the D162 and D62 passing a cluster of villages, among them **Pieve**, whose church has two weathered menhirs on display in its grounds. Once past **Santo Pietro di Tenda**, the landscape turns rocky, bare and less suited to cultivation. Set among the scattered olive trees are curious drystone shepherds' huts, built of flat stone slabs. Though square-walled, the roof is rounded and slightly domed. Roughly 24km (15 miles) from San Michele, the winding D62 meets the D81 to return to St Florent.

Exploring the Désert des Agriates

Dividing the Balagne coast from Cap Corse, the Agriates covers an area of roughly 155 square kilometres (60 square miles) of rocky scrub-clad hills and valleys and 40km (25 miles) of protected coastline, to the north of the D81. Though hardly a true desert, the overwhelming aridity and harshness of the landscape today make it hard to imagine that under the Genoese, this was the bread-basket of Corsica, and as recently as 150 years ago, one fifth of the land was under cultivation. The people of Cap Corse grew wheat along the river courses, planted vineyards on the hills, sharing the land with the shepherds and their flocks. In time, through overgrazing and erosion, the land became unusable and was abandoned. Neither shepherds nor farmers lived here year round, which explains why today there is only one village, **Casta**, but hidden in the valleys are remains of their stone dwellings, known as *pagliaghji*.

Above: Patrimonio is famous for its wine

Left: 12th century Romanesque church of Santa Maria Assunta at St Florent

Below: The Agriates coast has many fine beaches and turquoise seas

Above: St Florent, a resort town backed by the fertile Nebbio hills

Left: One of Corsica's finest Pisan churches is that of St Michele at Murato

Developers have long had their eyes on the spectacular unspoiled Agriates coastline of rocky headlands and pristine white sand beaches lapped by azure seas. Now that it is safely in the hands of the Conservatoire du Littoral, today's main threat is fire. For visitors, the main challenge is getting there. Road access is limited to two bumpy dirt tracks that descend to the coast from the D81 at Bocca di Vezzu and Casta. These are for four-wheel-drive only and vehicles can be hired by the day at St Florent. An alternative is an excursion by quad bike but it's best to avoid the fearsome summer heat. Several companies offer boat trips from St Florent, Calvi or Île Rousse – day walkers can take the boat as far as Saleccia and return to St Florent on foot. Boat rental is also possible for those who prefer to be independent. It is not advisable to walk or cycle down from the D81 because of the heat, lack of water and fire risk.

The Agriates Coastal Trail

Duration: two days (8 hours and 6 hours)
Ascent & Descent: mostly level walking
What to take: food, water, sunscreen, sunhat, sleeping bag, insect repellent
Highlights of the walk: uninhabited coastline, beautiful beaches, spring flowers

This is a relatively easy walk, but the terrain is often rugged underfoot. The main challenges are taking all your own food and water, and with the heat and lack of shade it is best to avoid July and August. It is possible to do day hikes into the Agriates from St Florent or Ostriconi, at the western end. The *Gîtes* at Ghignu must be reserved at least a month in advance and are open from April to October.

Day 1: St Florent to Plage de Ghignu (about 8 hours)

From the end of Plage de Roya at St Florent follow the road, which soon turns to a dirt track, for 2km (1.25 miles) to a parking area. A sign marked *'Sentier du Littoral'* marks the start of the trail, which is marked by red and white plastic tags and arrows. Descend on foot to a cove, and continue around the coast through three gates and past several villas and pretty sandy bays and coves. In 2.5 hours, reach the ghostly silhouette of the **Mortella Tower**, built in 1555 but destroyed by the English in February 1794. Nelson was said to be so impressed by the solidity of the tower that features of the design were adopted for the defensive towers built along the English coast from Suffolk to Sussex, which became known as Martello (a misspelling of Mortella) towers.

Continue around the coast to the gorgeous **Plage de Loto**, which is backed by two lagoons. Heading briefly inland, cut through *maquis* and marshland or follow the coast around to the even more arresting pine-fringed **Plage de Saleccia**, reached after about 5 hours from the start of the walk. There now follows an easy walk of about 3 hours following a rocky section of coast to **Plage de Ghignu** and **Plage de Malfalcu,** both less frequented than the others.

Day 2: Plage de Ghignu to Plage de l'Ostriconi (6 hours)

Rocky coves and tiny sandy beaches punctuate the wild stretch of coast as far as Baie de L'Acciolu, where the path bears inland briefly before meeting the sandy bay of Vana. Just south of here the splendid **Plage de L'Ostriconi** comes into view, backed by dunes, wetland and a hotel and restaurant. After about six hours' walk, the coastal trail ends here and you can pick up the bus west to Calvi or east to Bastia.

Places to Visit

San Florent

Tourist Information

On the left side of the Bastia road, 200m (200yds) from the town centre in the same building as the town hall and the post office
Open 9 am–7pm Monday to Saturday and Sunday mornings, July and August; 9 am-12 pm and 2–5 pm Monday to Friday and Saturday mornings during the rest of the year

Boat Rental

To the right of the road by the river leaving the centre of town in the direction of Calvi, Dominique Plaisance rent out inflatable ribs, kayaks and canoes
Open April to October
☎ 04 95 37 07 08
www.dominiqueplaisance.com

4x4 rental and excursions

St Flo 4x4, on the road to La Roya beach, rent out jeeps and do escorted trips into the Agriates and beyond
Open all year
☎ 04 95 37 06 42
www.stflo4x4.com

Adventure Sports

Altore, based on La Roya beach, do paragliding, canyoning and sea kayaking
☎ 04 95 37 19 30
www.altore.com

Sailing and Diving

On La Roya beach, CESM offer sailing and diving
Open April to October
☎ 04 95 37 00 61
www.cesm.net

Sea Kayaking

On La Roya beach by U Pezzu camping
Kayak hire and short and longer guided tours
☎ 06 12 10 23 27
www.corskayak.com

Patrimonio Wine Tasting

Here is a selection of places to taste the famous AOC Patrimonio wines:
Orenga de Gaffory & San Quilico: on the Patrimonio to St Florent road Tel. 04 95 37 45 00
Domaine Giacometti: turn right off the St Florent to Oletta road, just before Oletta Tel. 04 95 37 00 72
Clos Arena: outside Patrimonio by the junction of the D81 and D 80 Cap Corse road. ☎ 04 95 37 08 27

3. Cap Corse

Shaped like a rabbit's ear, the 40km (25-mile) long peninsula of Cap Corse (Capicursu) thrusts into the Ligurian Sea off Corsica's north shore. Geographically closest to Italy and France, the Cap's architecture would not look out of place on the mainland, with whose merchants the peninsula traded its wine, olive oil and cork. From the outset, the inhabitants of Cap Corse were at ease with the sea and became skilled fishermen, one of several subtle differences that distinguish the region from the rest of the island.

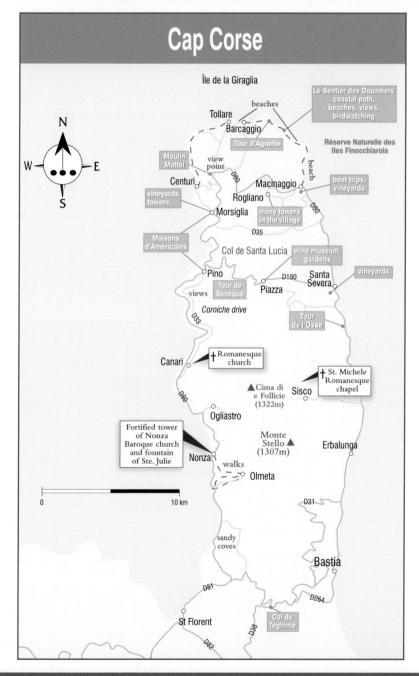

Cap Corse

Île de la Giraglia

Le Sentier des Douaniers coastal path, beaches, views, birdwatching

beaches

Tollare

Barcaggio

Tour d'Agnello

Réserve Naturelle des Iles Finocchiarola

N
W E
S

Moulin Mattéi

view point

D80

Centuri

Macinaggio

beach

boat trips, vineyards

vineyards towers

Rogliano

Morsiglia

many towers in the village

D35

D80

Maisons d'Américains

Col de Santa Lucia

wine museum, gardens

Pino

D180

Santa Severa

vineyards

views

Tour de Sénèque

Piazza

Corniche drive

D33

Tour de l'Osse

Canari

✝ Romanesque church

D80

✝ St. Michele Romanesque chapel

▲ Cima di e Follicie (1322m)

Sisco

Ogliastro

Fortified tower of Nonza Baroque church and fountain of Ste. Julie

Monte Stello (1307m) ▲

Erbalunga

Nonza

walks

Olmeta

0   10 km

D31

sandy coves

Bastia

D81

D264

St Florent

D82

D38

Col de Teghime

Les Maisons d'Américains

When their vineyards were wiped out by phylloxera in the nineteenth century, many Cap-Corsins left to seek their fortune in Santo Domingo, Puerto Rico and Venezuela, where they set up coffee and sugar plantations. Fortunes made, they returned home, building sumptuous mansions, quite out of keeping with the modest villages they are situated in. Over 150 in number, these 'palaces' are built in a mish-mash of Spanish colonial, Tuscan and American architectural styles and as often as not their present owners may speak only Spanish and visit but once a year. Intriguing though they may be, none are open to the public, but in villages like Pino, Morsiglia and Rogliano, you can hardly miss them. Look out too for their ornate family tombs, often sited on the outskirts of the villages and in similarly ostentatious style. Former Venezuelan president Raúl Leoni was of Corsican descent, while one third of Puerto Ricans are said to have island blood.

The mountainous backbone of the peninsula culminates in 1,324m (4,342ft) Cima di e Follicie, dropping steeply to the west coast, but more gently on the east side. Hot and sun-baked in summer, wind and wave-lashed in winter, Cap Corse has produced some of the island's best wines and its most affluent citizens. In contrast to the rest of the island, settlements sprung up along and near the coast, among them fishing villages. Nowhere else in Corsica is there such a concentration of Genoese towers, standing sentinel along the shore at 6km (4-mile) intervals.

The 122km (76 miles) circular route around the Cap can be driven in a day, but a long day as there is a huge amount to see and the roads are very slow. In particular, the section between Nonza and Macinaggio is a real twister and demands concentration, but it is worth it for the views. Macinaggio on the east coast has a bus link with Bastia but otherwise public transport is poor and visitor services are notably absent outside the summer months.

The real reason to make the long trek to the tip of the Cap is for the eye-catching coastal scenery, the pick of the beaches and one of Corsica's best shore walks.

East Coast of Cap Corse

Leaving the last of Bastia's suburbs, the traffic thins out on the approach to **Erbalunga**, a dreamy little village with its feet in the sea. The port and historic hub are a compact maze of narrow alleys and archways, hugging a rocky promontory and guarded by a Genoese tower. Some years back artists were drawn to the place but today it is more chic than bohemian. If you're curious to discover what lies inside those grandiose *Maisons d'Américains* (see feature box), make for the gorgeous Hôtel Castel Brando, meticulously restored and furnished in period style. At Easter, don't miss the Maundy Thursday and Good Friday processions, which culminate in the mysterious

Granitula, whose white-clad penitents form a human coil that appears to move of its own volition.

The main D80 road continues to hug the east coast of the Cap, at times high above it, affording views of the Tuscan isles of **Elba** and **Capraia**, then dipping down to where the tight little valleys meet the shore and the fishing ports for the inland villages are located.

The Cap Corse villages are perched up secluded side valleys, and consist of several hamlets, each with its own name, though the *commune* as a whole may be known by a quite different name. If you have time for a detour, the lush valley of **Sisco**, made up of 17 tiny hamlets, is a worthwhile side trip. At its head, 9km (5.5 miles) inland, is **San Martino**, whose parish church of the same name conceals some unusual relics, originally donated to the nearby convent of Santa Catalina by sailors, who had promised a reward if they were delivered safe from a terrible storm. Among them are a piece of the Virgin's coat, one of Enoch's fingers and the gilded copper mask of St John Chrysostom, believed to have been locally crafted in the thirteenth century.

Turning right at the church, the D32 continues around the flank of the hill. Above and to the left, the Romanesque chapel of **St Michele**, sited on a rocky buttress, can be reached by a footpath off the road. Walkers may also be tempted by the dirt track winding up from the D32 to the Col St Jean, which gives access to the crest of peaks forming the backbone of the Cap. The views are outstanding but fog and high winds can make walking hazardous and great care is needed once you are off the track.

The road passes a string of Genoese towers, sited at roughly 6km (4-mile) intervals along the Cap coast, bearing testimony to the economic and strategic importance of the peninsula as well as its vulnerability. The **Tour de L'Osse**, 4km (2.5 miles) north of Marine de Pietracorbara, is among the best preserved. North of here at Santa Severa, the **Domaine Pieretti** vineyard is worth a stop for the chance to taste its exquisite *Muscat* and also very drinkable red, white and rosé.

The Luri Valley

Turning left on the D180, the forested **Luri Valley** invites exploration and makes a convenient short cut to the Cap's west side. **Piazza**, the main village, hosts a **wine festival (Fiera di u Vinu)** on the first weekend in July, attracting producers from all over the island. There's also a small wine museum here and, along the D180 east of Piazza, an organic fruit and vegetable garden, open to visitors, **Les Jardins Traditionnels de Cap Corse**. Nestled in the upper reaches of this fertile and leafy valley is the wonderful country guesthouse I Fundali, 3km (2 miles) from Piazza, up the very narrow D 532. It's built on the site of a fortress-like tower and run by a very hospitable family, renowned for their local knowledge, good food and wine.

The D180 climbs out of the densely forested valley to the **Col de Santa Lucia**, where a side road bears south and after 1.5km (1 mile) reaches a cluster of derelict buildings, once a children's home and school. A path leads uphill from here and in 30 minutes

Nonza is perched on a rocky bluff above the coast

Flight of Fancy

Hoopoe *Upupa epops*
They look like giant fanciful butterflies in flight but hoopoes spend most of their time on bare or grassy ground in open forests, hunting out worms and insects. When startled, they take flight, their beige, black and white markings designed to confuse and disconcert sparrowhawks and other predators. Hoopoes arrive in March to breed, but leave again in September.

Success Story

Audouin's Gull *Larus audouinii*
This was once the world's rarest gull, when in the 1960s only 1,000 birds were left. Today there are 10,000, but they are only found in the Mediterranean and off Saharan Africa, breeding on small offshore islands. Look for them on the islands off the tip of Cap Corse, where they are easily recognised by their red bill.

arrives at the imposing ruined **Tour de Sénequè**. Exiled by the emperor Claudius to Corsica in 41 AD, Spanish-born Roman philosopher, dramatist and statesman Seneca is said to have lived here. It is all a bit implausible as the fortress was probably erected a thousand or more years after his death, but it makes a good story. Later, the site became a stronghold for the Da Mare nobles, whose Genoese ancestry helped them dominate the north of the peninsula's politics and economy for centuries. In any event, perched on its rocky platform at a height of 580m (1900ft), the tower commands a mesmerising view of the rugged west coast of the Cap.

Tip of Cap Corse

The unassuming little port of **Macinaggio (Macinaghju)** is popular with yachters and the closest you will find to a tourist resort on Cap Corse. First the Romans, and later the Genoese developed it for shipping out the valuable olive oil and wine. Today, the vineyards of Clos Nicrosi, on the slopes inland, produce one of Corsica's best dry whites – you can taste and buy it at their outlet in Macinaggio, opposite Hotel U Ricordu. In 1790, defeated independence hero Pasquale Paoli set foot again on Corsican soil after exile in England declaring 'O ma patrie, je t'ai quitté esclave, je te retrouve libre' ('Oh my country, I left you as a slave but return a free man'). A string of eateries line the waterfront, among them the Osteria di U Portu, which does copious Corsican and seafood menus and also has a few rooms for rent.

Dotted over the hillside behind the port are the seven hamlets of **Rogliano**, whose inhabitants once topped 4,000 but today number just 465. This one-time regional capital is noted for its contrasting architectural styles, which include a ruined castle, several fortified houses, two Genoese towers, splendid baroque churches and simple schist-tiled village homes.

The real reason to drive all this way can only be discovered if you're prepared to walk at least a part of *Le Sentier des Douaniers* (the customs officials' path), the 19km (12-mile) trail that hugs a deserted coastline of beaches, dunes and cliffs, backed by the heady scent of the *maquis*. At its best in spring, when the birds and flowers are prolific, the path can be accessed from Macinaggio, Barcaggio and Centuri.

The attractive little port of **Barcaggio (Barcaghju)**, on the north shore of the Cap, is reached by a loop road off the D80 and boasts a reputable fish restaurant, U Fanale. East of the village the beach is backed by sand dunes and a lagoon, where the rare plants *Lippia nodiflora*, *Cressa cretica* and *Vitex agnus castus* thrive. Between Barcaggio and Tollare to the west, curious eroded limestone formations line the shore, a geological oddity among the largely schist rocks of the Cap.

The D80 loops over windswept hills densely shrouded in *maquis* to reach the Col de la Serra and **Moulin Mattei**, a restored windmill and panoramic viewpoint. Once used to mill wheat from the Balagne and Italy, which was traded for olive oil, the windmill no longer works, but its modern counterparts line the ridge behind, testimony to the strength of the wind in these parts. West of the saddle is a worthwhile detour on the D35, which drops to the coast and what some consider to be Corsica's most picturesque fishing village, **Centuri**. Lobsters are the big draw here and are on offer at several of the eateries clustered around the port, but at a price. There's no beach here, but sunsets are memorable.

The Towers of Cap Corse

Of Corsica's one hundred defensive towers, a quarter are found in Cap Corse. Built from the fourteenth to eighteenth centuries, those located along the coast were mostly round and owned by the community. Their purpose was to warn of and defend against Barbary pirate attacks. If suspicious vessels were spotted a fire would be lit as a warning. The next tower along would light their fire and in this way news of an impending attack would work its way around the whole island. Square village towers are also a special feature of many of the Cap villages. Privately owned, they were built to shelter the inhabitants in case of attack. The commune of Rogliano has no fewer than ten towers within its boundaries.

The Tower of Nonza

Unlike most of the Cap's towers, Nonza's is square and was built by order of Paoli in 1760. After Genoa ceded Corsica to France in 1768, those loyal to Paoli resisted the French forces and pockets of resistance sprang up around the island. When 1,200 French soldiers laid siege to Nonza, they found it impossible to take the tower, whose volley of fire was unremitting. Offering safe passage to rejoin Paoli to those who would surrender, the French troops were astonished when one man alone emerged from the tower. Ingeniously, Jacques Casella had succeeded in deceiving the French into believing the tower was occupied by a large force.

Le Sentier des Douaniers

Distance: 19km (12 miles) but conveniently divides into two shorter walks

Duration: allow 8 hours (not including swim stops)

Ascent & Descent: several short sections of around 500ft (150m) each

What to take: water, picnic, sunhat, sunscreen, swimwear, mask and snorkel

Highlights of the walk: sandy beaches, turquoise sea, Genoese towers, birds and the maquis in all its scented glory

Important note: high winds can make this walk hazardous in the event of forest fires

There is almost no shade on this walk so July and August are best avoided because of the heat. Unless you have two cars, you will need to arrange a taxi from Macinaggio or Centuri or use the boat service between Macinaggio and Barcaggio. The walk can be done in two sections, from Macinaggio to Barcaggio and from Barcaggio to Centuri – a route map is available at the Macinaggio Tourist Office or you can download a pdf version from www.karibu.fr. The path is marked by yellow paint splashes, posts with green markers and small cairns.

Macinaggio to Barcaggio (3 hours)

Start the walk heading north along the beach at Macinaggio then around the headland to **Plage de Tamarone**. Continue following the coast around a second headland. Just offshore are the **Îles Finocchiarola**, a sanctuary for a few breeding pairs of **Audouin's gull**, a declining species confined to the Mediterranean. Access to the islands is forbidden from 1 March to 31 August. They form part of the **Capandula Reserve**, protecting the whole coast between Tamarone and Barcaggio, which is an important staging point for migrant birds returning from Africa in spring. Some incredibly rare plants have also made their home on the islands of the Cap – among them *Nananthea perspusilla*, a tiny member of the daisy family. Along this protected coast Phoenician juniper is unusually abundant in the *maquis*, along with cistus, arbutus, tree heath, rosemary, myrtle and lavender. Continue around the coast to the nineteenth-century chapel of Santa Maria, and a ruined tower, dating from 1549 but recently reinforced, sited on a spit of land west of a vibrant turquoise bay. Just beyond are two lovely sandy coves, perfect to cool off before the climb to the clifftop perch of the Tour D'Agnello, near Corsica's most northerly point. From here there is a view of **Île de la Giraglia**, where Cory's shearwaters, Audouin's gulls and shags breed. Past a sandy beach backed by dunes is the pretty village and port of **Barcaggio** marking the end of the walk's first stage.

Barcaggio to Centuri (5 hours)

More strenuous than the first section, the route hugs the cliff tops and summits of the undulating western tip of the Cap with little access to the sea. With luck walkers may spot osprey on this section. Past the lighthouse at Capo Grosso, the terrain becomes more

Barcaggio, a small fishing village on the tip of Cap Corse

Above: Erbalunga, on the east coast of Cap Corse

Left: Grey, shingle beaches are typical of the dramatic west coast of Cap Corse

Below: Tour de l'Osse, one douzens of 16th and 17th century Genoese towers, built to protect the coast of Cap Corse

rugged and demanding. Splendid views open up to the south on the approach to the fishing village of Centuri and the end of the walk.

West Coast of Cap Corse

For most of its tortuous length, the D80 from Morsiglia to Patrimonio hangs high above a surf-pounded coastline that is rugged, precipitous and broken only by a handful of shelving pebble beaches. Strung out along this balcony drive are a string of affluent little villages, whose ostentatious *Maisons d'Americains* evoke the wealth their owners brought back from the Americas – at Pecorile, a hamlet of **Morsiglia (Mursiglia)**, admire the **Château Fantauzzi**, which cost 30,000 gold francs to build. There are no fewer than six fifteenth-century towers in this impressive village, which has a small shop, a fuel station and bar. The surrounding vineyards of **Domaine de Pietri** have produce one of the Cap's best examples of Muscat since 1786. Past the viewpoint of Capo Corvoli, **Pino (Pinu)**, set among pines, comes into view to the south. The two fancy village fountains and the restoration of its church were financed by absentee benefactor Antoine Piccioni, born there in 1819, while another saw to the building of the road over Col de Santa Lucia. Equally ornate are their mausoleums – that of the Franceschi family, just outside Pino, is particularly striking. South of the village a narrow road descends to the coast, where a Genoese tower guards the fifteenth-century **Couvent St François** on a rocky promontory. The village has a small supermarket and fuel station.

There is now a choice of route: the D80 continues along the coast, while snaking high above it on a *corniche* is the D33, an even stronger contender for the most hair-raising drive on the island. Both demand concentration as the views, plunging to the coast below and to the snowy summits of the central range, are a constant distraction. The upper road ends near **Canari**, a cluster of hamlets whose main square, dominated by a white tower resembling a lighthouse, has a superb view of the coast below and is the perfect place for a sunset vigil. While you're here, take a look at the well-preserved twelfth-century Pisan **church of Santa Maria Assunta**, whose cornice is embellished with animal heads, masks and human figures. For an overnight stay, head for **Résidence I Fioretti**, housed in the former Couvent Saint François, where you can sleep in the monks' cells or rent a self-contained cottage by the week.

South of Canari, an unsightly gash in the flank of the mountain marks the site of a quarry, where amianthus, a form of asbestos, was extracted until 1965. Debris from the 15 million tons a year of quarried rock formed the beaches along this stretch of coast, which are tinted grey-green. Past the mine, the D233 invites you to explore the lush, forested Olcani valley, guarded by the defiant little hamlet of Ogliastro, at the foot of the rocky west face of 1,250m (4,100ft) Monte Caneto.

The D80 continues around the coast to Nonza, whose compact pink and ochre houses are wedged tightly on a bluff, topped by a square tower strategically placed 150m (492ft) above the sea. The gaudy orange-façaded baroque church of St Julie houses an impressive polychrome marble altar from the seventeenth century, above which hangs a painting of the saint, who was martyred in AD 303. At the north end of the village, steps lead down to the beach past the Fontaine St Julie, which sprang from the spot where the saint's breasts were cast after her torture.

An easy trail climbs around the flank of the hill to the south of Nonza, contouring high above the road before heading inland to the pretty village of **Olmeta**. This can be a circular walk by following the trail from the Olmeta cemetery down the valley to the coast at Marine de Negru and returning along a particularly scenic stretch of road to Nonza.

Marine de Farinole, south of Nonza, is dominated by its tower, set on a rock outcrop between two sandy coves. Another beach to the south offers the last chance for a dip, before the road heads inland to Patrimonio at the junction of the D81.

Places to Visit

Macinaggio Tourist Office
By the port
Information on local footpaths – ask for a map
Open 9am–12pm and 2–7pm (until 5pm out of season) Monday to Saturday and 9am–12pm on Sunday; out of season 9am–12pm Saturday and closed Sunday

Macinaggio Boat Trips
U San Paulu do boat trips from June to September along the tip of Cap Corse, leaving Macinaggio at 11am and returning from Barcaggio at 4.30pm, with stops at beaches along the way. Walkers on the *Sentier des Douaniers* can use it as one-way transport
☎ 04 95 35 07 09
www.lebateau.fr.st

A Mimoria di U Vinu - Luri Wine Museum
Small museum in village of Piazza dedicated to vine cultivation and wine production

Open 10am–1pm and 4–6pm Wednesday to Saturday in July and August and 10am–12.30pm and 2–5pm Tuesday to Friday in June and September
☎ 04 95 35 06 44

Les Jardins Traditionnels du Cap Corse – Organic Garden
Situated south of the D 180 between Campu and Piazza in the Luri Valley, this organic garden seeks to preserve and encourage the cultivation of local fruit and vegetable varieties.
Open 10am–12pm and 2–5pm, Monday to Friday in April, May, June, September and October; 9am–12pm and 4–7pm Monday to Friday in July and August
☎ 04 95 35 05 07

Domaine de Pietri Vineyard, Morsiglia
Visits can be arranged to taste and buy the excellent local *Muscat*.
☎ 04 95 65 64 79

Bastia

With 39,000 inhabitants, Bastia is second in size to Ajaccio but as capital of the Département de Haute-Corse it enjoys equal status. Traditional rivalry between the two has led some to insist that Bastia is more authentically Corsican, while others liken its architecture to that of Liguria on the Italian coast. In any event, this essentially industrial and commercial hub of the island is also its chief maritime gateway, bringing in ferries from France and Italy as well as container ships for the export of the island's agricultural produce.

Wedged on a narrow strip of flat land at the foot of 960m (3,150 ft) Serra di Pigno, facing the Tyrrhenian Sea, the **Vieux Port** (old port) sits on the site of a 2,000-year-old Roman settlement, which became the port for the hillside village of Cardo. Then in 1378, the Genoese governor abandoned his residence in Biguglia and built a fortified site (a *bastia*) on the hill above Vieux Port. By 1480, ramparts were in place to protect the little Genoese colony that became known as *Terra Nova*, as opposed to the port, which was *Terra Vecchia*.

With the completion of the **Palais des Gouverneurs** in 1530, Bastia became the Genoese capital and remained the chief town until 1791, when the French divided Corsica into two *départements*, each with its own capital. Worse still, in 1811 Napoleon moved Corsica's administration to Ajaccio.

The historic heart of the town, taking

in Place St Nicolas, Terra Vecchia and the Vieux Port, and the Citadel and Terra Nova, is best explored on foot. The vast palm-lined **Place St Nicolas** faces the sea and is the perfect place to sit over a drink or ice cream and watch Bastia life go by. Improbably, its centrepiece is a statue of Napoleon, dressed as a Roman emperor, while at the north end is the tourist office. On Sundays there's a lively flea market in the square. Notable among the elegant mansions flanking the square is the **Maison Mattei** shop, selling the famous aperitifs and liqueurs of which *Cap Corse* is the best known. Bastia's main shopping district spans the two parallel streets west of the square.

At the south end of Place St Nicolas, rue Napoléon leads to the narrow streets and stairways of Terra Vecchia. On its east side is the **Oratoire de l'Immaculée Conception**, the chapel of a still active brotherhood, one of several founded in the sixteenth and seventeenth centuries. Richly decorated in red and gold, it was here that the Anglo-Corsican parliament convened in 1795 under Sir Gilbert Elliot. On the pavement outside, a pebble mosaic of a face ringed by radiating sunbeams suggests a sundial. Close by is the peaceful **Place du Marché**, at its liveliest during the morning market, which runs Tuesday to Sunday. Off the square, the seventeenth-century baroque **L'église St Jean-Baptiste** contains an ornate polychrome altar and is an unmistakeable landmark, with its twin towers overlooking the **Vieux Port.** Clogged with yachts and fishing boats, the horseshoe-shaped port is traffic-free and less touristy than might be expected. Walk out along the **Môle Génois** or **Jetée du Dragon** piers for the best view of the city, at its most atmospheric at sunrise. Several tiers of tall, stark buildings rise from the port, some pock-marked from the pounding they received in 1943 by American bombers, which badly damaged much of Bastia. Evidently these crumbling giants are still lived in because strings of laundry hang over the narrow alleys that divide them. **Quai des Martyrs** heads along the seafront back to Place St Nicolas and its broad terrace is a popular place to eat in the evening. In contrast to more tourism-oriented seaside towns, there are some good eateries along here.

South of the old port, a monumental staircase climbs through the **Jardins Romeu** to the **citadel**, whose compact grid of tight alleys is today a quiet residential area. If this sounds all too energetic, the **Petit Train**, departing from outside the Tourist Information office on Place St Nicolas, will take you there effortlessly. Once inside the massive ramparts, there are several interesting places to visit. **Palais des Gouverneurs**, in distinctive Genoese style, was completed in 1530 with the addition of the *campanile* but the oldest surviving part is the round tower or *bastiglia*, from which the town draws its name. When Napoleon chose Ajaccio as capital, it was turned into a barracks. Badly damaged in World War II, the

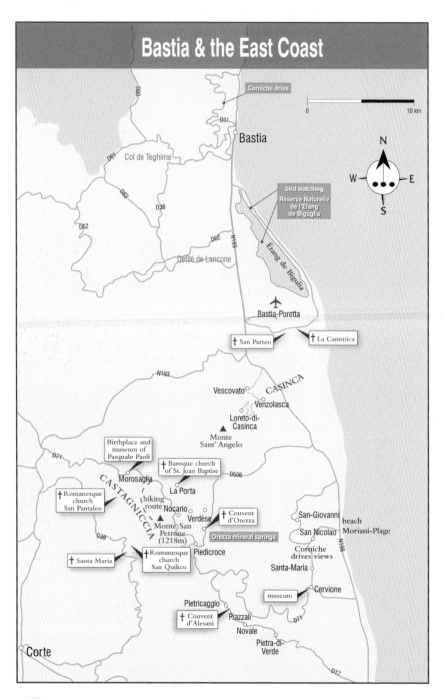

Bastia & the East Coast

Corniche drive

0   10 km

D80

D31

Bastia

N

W   E

S

D81

Col de Teghime

D62

D38

bird watching
Réserve Naturelle
de l'Étang
de Biguglia

D62

D62

N193

Défilé de Lancone

Étang de Biguglia

Bastia-Poretta

† San Parteo   † La Canonica

N193

CASINCA

Vescovato

Venzolasca

Loreto-di-
Casinca

Monte
Sant' Angelo

Birthplace and
museum of
Pasquale Paoli

D71

† Baroque church
of St. Jean Baptise

D506

CASTAGNICCIA

Morosaglia

La Porta

† Romanesque
church
San Pantaleo

hiking
route   Nocario

Verdèse

† Couvent
d'Orezza

San-Giovanni

beach

Monte San
Petrone
(1218m)

Orezza mineral springs

San Nicolao   Moriani-Plage

D39

† Santa Maria

† Romanesque
church
San Quilico

Piedicroce

Corniche
drives views

N198

Santa-Maria

museum   Cervione

Pietricaggio

† Couvent
d'Alesani

Piazzali

D71

Novale

Pietra-di-
Verde

Corte

D17

palace has now been restored to house the **Musée d'Ethnographie Corse**, worth a visit for its insightful exhibits on Corsican culture and way of life.

Also in the citadel is Bastia's original cathedral, the baroque church of **Sainte-Marie**, containing a silver statue of the Virgin weighing nearly a ton. In the street opposite is the childhood home of **Victor Hugo** and just around the corner the splendidly ornate **Oratoire Sainte-Croix**, built in 1543 by one of Bastia's most influential brotherhoods. To the right of the altar is the famous *Christ des Miracles*, a blackened oak statue reputedly found floating in the sea by fishermen in 1428 and paraded through the streets in the procession on 3 May each year. Chil-

dren and adults alike will be fascinated by the **Paisolo**, a miniature Corsican village, complete with church, Genoese tower and chestnut flour mill, housed in the old powder magazine on the southern tip of the citadel.

Exploring around Bastia

If you have time on your hands, take the **corniche drive**, which winds along the slopes of Serra di Pigno above Bastia, with breathtaking views of the town, the Cap Corse coast and the Italian islands of Elba and Capraia. The D64 route turns off the St Florent road, passing the pretty village of Cardo

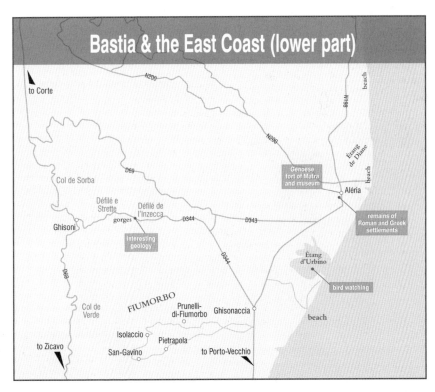

Bastia & the East Coast (lower part)

to Corte

N200

beach

N198

Col de Sorba

D69

Étang de Diane

Genoese fort of Matra and museum

Aléria

beach

Défilé e Stretto

Défilé de l'Inzecca

gorges

D344

D343

remains of Roman and Greek settlements

Ghisoni

Interesting geology

D344

Étang d'Urbino

D69

bird watching

Col de Verde

FIUMORBO

Prunelli-di-Fiumorbo

Ghisonaccia

beach

Isolaccio

Pietrapola

to Zicavo

San-Gavino

to Porto-Vecchio

Above: Aléria, Corsica's most important Roman remains

Below: Attic vessel in the museum at Aléria

Opposite page: Bastia, view from the Citadel over the port

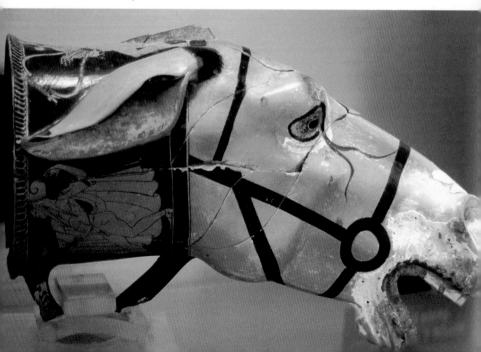

Fast Food Fan

European bee-eater *Merops apiaster*
With its elongated tail feathers and brilliant plumage, this is one of Corsica's most attractive birds; unless you're a bee that is. Perched on branches or wires, they dart out to catch bees and wasps on the wing. Before eating, they return to their perch and remove the poisonous sting by hitting the bee on a hard surface. Look for them on the east coast plain, sometimes soaring high in the sky, catching their prey as it gets sucked up on thermals.

and several others before joining the Cap Corse road at Miomo, north of Bastia.

If you continue instead on the D81 St Florent road, it climbs to the 570m (1,870ft) **Col de Teghime**. On 3 October 1943 the strategically important pass was taken from the retreating Germans, proving a decisive battle in the liberation of Bastia and Corsica next day. There is a memorial to the Moroccan soldiers who were instrumental in securing victory on this bleak and windswept spot.

South of Bastia, the industrial suburbs flanking one of Corsica's few stretches of dual carriageway road thin out on the approach to Bastia Airport, 18km (11

Cap Corse Mattei

If your curiosity is aroused by an unusually shaped red-labelled bottle on the shelves of most Corsican bars, you are about to discover a phenomenal success story that put the island on the world map. Cap Corse is an aperitif laced with quinine that gained popularity a century ago with exports to North Africa and Indochina. The business was founded by Louis-Napoléon Mattei who had a citron pressing plant and distillery, and became so hugely successful that many tried to imitate his products. The aromatic vermouth-style drink is for most people an acquired taste, but worth a go! You can visit the Mattei shop on Place St Nicolas in Bastia.

miles) south of the town. Turning east on the D107 by the airport junction brings you to the beautiful church of **La Canonica**, on the banks of the Golo River. Consecrated by the archbishop of Pisa in 1119, **Santa Maria Assunta**, as it is also known, is considered the prototype of Corsica's Pisan churches. Austere in its simplicity, the church's 35m (115ft) long nave is flanked by two aisles ending in a semicircular apse. Above the portal, a frieze depicts griffins, a lion, wolf, stag and lamb, exquisitely carved from Cap Corse stone. Nearby excavations have revealed traces of a fourth-century cathedral with a beautiful mosaic floor, while a third

church, that of San Parteo, stands a little further away. This important site had been first settled in Roman times, when the general Gaius Marius founded a military colony there around 100 BC. **Mariana** flourished as a port on the Golo river, in spite of harassment from the Corsicans, but by the sixth century it was all but abandoned because of malaria and Vandal attacks.

Castagniccia

The verdant, hilly region lying south of Bastia is one of Corsica's best-kept secrets and is likely to remain so. Though one of the most widely popu-

Religious Brotherhoods or Confraternities

Many Corsican towns have one or more active religious brotherhoods, who are instrumental in organising religious processions on saints' days and particularly at Easter, providing the polyphonic chants accompanying them. Though often donning quite sinister-looking costumes, the lay brotherhoods, whose members are ordinary citizens, were set up in the sixteenth and seventeenth centuries amongst other reasons to meet the need for charitable support to the poor. Many have their own chapel, sometimes attached to or within a church but often, as in Bastia, built apart. Some contain precious works of art and are open to the public.

lated parts of the island, there are few facilities for visitors and almost none open out of season. The roads are endlessly winding, impossibly narrow and often pot-holed. On the face of it there seems little incentive to venture in here but this would be a mistake. Castagniccia, with its hundreds of villages, perched on the ridges and huddled in the brooding, forested valleys, is the quintessential Corsica.

With its proximity to Bastia, the Genoese exploited the economic potential of the region, encouraging the planting of chestnut groves, from which the name Castagniccia is derived. By the nineteenth century, it was the most densely populated rural area in Europe, but today many hamlets have but a handful of year-round residents and the chestnut forests are untended and in decline.

The austere, schist village houses, roofed in stone, have a character of their own and are often meticulously maintained by their absentee owners. Among the architectural gems tucked in the narrow streets you'll find fountains, bread ovens and splendid baroque churches. In Castagniccia you will also come across monasteries, both bastions of culture and hotbeds of dissent, and little Romanesque chapels secluded deep in the forests.

To explore the region, you need a car or to be prepared to walk. The *Mare a Mare Nord* trail traverses the southern hills of Castagniccia before heading into the Bozio region en route to Corte, while the central hills around Piedicroce and La Porta have mapped out and waymarked many of the original mule routes that linked the villages,

Réserve Naturelle de l'Étang de Biguglia

Corsica's largest coastal lagoon is a mix of fresh and salt water, creating habitats for a wide variety of wildlife. A nature reserve since 1994, it is home to a thriving population of mullet, eels, European pond turtles, Tyrrhenian painted frogs and Sardinian tree frogs. With over 200 bird species observed, among them purple heron, great crested grebe, reed warbler, Cetti's warbler, zitting cisticola, serin, European roller, hoopoe and marsh harrier, the area is one of Corsica's top birding spots, but access is frustratingly difficult. As well as the north end of the lagoon, where there is a car park and 1.5km (1 mile) walking trail, it is worth checking for sightings around Bastia airport to the south.

encouraging visitors to base themselves there for a few days.

Heart of Castagniccia drive

The route described penetrates the heart of the region, winding from village to village through the valleys, along the ridges and over passes. If you have time, take a detour and make your own discoveries.

From the N193 Bastia to Ponte Leccia road, there is a choice of route to **Morosaglia**, birthplace of the patriot Pasquale Paoli. The family house is today a small museum, furnished in period style, with a video in English shown on request. A chapel on the site contains Paoli's ashes, returned from

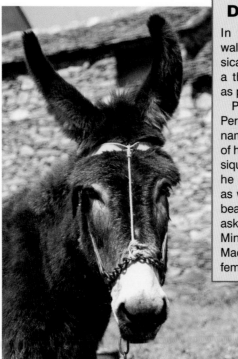

Donkey Work Done

In 1930 over 20,000 donkeys walked and worked in rural Corsica. Today there are fewer than a thousand and most are kept as pets.

Pietro Giovanni Ficoni, born in Perelli d'Alesani in 1715, was nicknamed 'Grosso-Minuto' because of his small stature but portly physique. Known for his quick humour, he travelled around by donkey, as was the norm. Once when his beast was heard braying, a woman asked if the animal was in love and Minuto replied: "You are wrong, Madame, it must have smelled a female donkey."

England, where he died in exile in 1804. In the hamlet of Terchjine the most photographed house in Corsica stands defiantly on a prominent ridge below the road. This fortified building may also be among the island's oldest and is believed to date from the tenth century.

The D71 climbs to **Col de Prato**, on the flank of Monte San Petrone. Just beyond the pass, the D205 descends abruptly to **La Porta (A Porta)**, a village dominated by its 45m (147ft) campanile, built in 1720, and flanked by the equally ostentatious (for a village of 200 inhabitants) late-seventeenth-century baroque church of **St Jean Baptiste**. Inside, the impressive concert organ was originally built for the

monastery at Rogliano on Cap Corse in 1780 but found its way to La Porta for 'safekeeping' following the French Revolution. North of the village in the now ruined Couvent St Antoine de Casabianda, Paoli was named General of the Nation in 1755, paving the way for Corsica's own constitution, government, currency and university.

Returning to the D71, continue around the rocky east face of Monte San Petrone to **Nocario (Nocariu)**, famous for its cabinet makers. The **Couvent D'Orezza** was the historic meeting place for two great Corsican chiefs, Paoli and Napoleon, in 1790, but was bombed to a shell by the Germans in 1943. Just before the convent, a tiny road leads up to the hamlet of **Cam-**

Réserve Naturelle de l'Étang de Biguglia

Corsica's largest coastal lagoon is a mix of fresh and salt water, creating habitats for a wide variety of wildlife. A nature reserve since 1994, it is home to a thriving population of mullet, eels, European pond turtles, Tyrrhenian painted frogs and Sardinian tree frogs. With over 200 bird species observed, among them purple heron, great crested grebe, reed warbler, Cetti's warbler, zitting cisticola, serin, European roller, hoopoe and marsh harrier, the area is one of Corsica's top birding spots, but access is frustratingly difficult. As well as the north end of the lagoon, where there is a car park and 1.5km (1 mile) walking trail, it is worth checking for sightings around Bastia airport to the south.

Beautiful animal friezes adorn the portal of La Conica, one of Corsica's finest Romanesque churches, located south of Bastia

Theodor, King of Corsica

The Franciscan Monastery of Alesani, near Piazzale, was founded in 1236 and became a hub of resistance against the Genoese. In 1736, a little-known German adventurer landed at Aléria and had himself crowned King of Corsica at the monastery. Born in 1694 in Cologne, Theodor von Neuhof had met Corsicans in exile, who had convinced him to seek finance to invade and take over the island for its own people. But money and guns ran out, within six months the venture had failed and Theodor was obliged to flee the island. He died penniless in London and on the wall of St Anne's church a tablet is incribed: 'Near this place is interred the King of Corsica, who died in this parish, December 11th, 1756, immediately after leaving the King's bench by the benefit of the act of insolvency: in consequence of which, he registered his Kingdom of Corsica for the use of his creditors.'

podonico, and a beautiful viewpoint over the region. The next village, **Piedicroce**, is strung out over a ridge with fine views and it has one of Castagniccia's few hotels, Le Refuge. From the village, the D506 plunges in eight hairpin bends to the Fium'Alto river. Across the bridge, the famous mineral springs of **Orezza** are unusually rich in iron and manganese. As if proof were needed of the health benefits, a sign explains how a local resident, Angèle-Marie Villa from Stazzona, drank a glass every week and lived to be 104. The water is bottled and sold all over Corsica but you can taste it for free at the fountain by the factory entrance. Crossing back over the river and continuing down the river valley brings you to the D48, which bears left to the village of **Verdèse**, where there is a delightful *chambres d'hôtes* in a restored eighteenth-century mansion.

A further 10km (6 miles) beyond Piedicroce, the **Col de L'Arcarotta** hosts a Sunday market in July and August, when local producers of honey, *charcuterie*, jam, cheese, fruit, vegetables and crafts set up stalls from 11am

onwards. **Auberge des Deux Vallées** does a bustling trade on market days and has a menu of local specialities.

The D71 now descends on the north side of the **Alesani Valley** to Cervione and the East Coast but the D17, hugging the mountainside south of the river, is a worthy alternative and passes a string of beautiful villages – **Pietracaggio**, **Piazzale**, **Novale** and **Pietra di Verde**.

Hike to Monte San Petrone – Castagniccia's highest mountain

Distance: 12km (7.5 miles) there and back walk on a mostly easy trail, marked by small cairns

Duration: 5 hours

Ascent & Descent: about 800m (2,624 ft)

What to take: walking boots, water, picnic, sun hat, sun screen

Highlights of the walk: beautiful beech and chestnut forest; wonderful views from the summit

This is an easy forest walk with a more challenging final section but start early to avoid the heat haze. From the Col de Prato the trail to the south up a dirt road, intermittently marked in yellow and then red. After 3km (2 miles) reach 1,200m and the trail divides. One branch descends to Saliceto village, the forest track continues straight ahead but the summit trail bears sharp left. It continues to climb, through splendid beech forest, with the odd opening for views, until it reaches an open ridge at 1,530m. The path now veers sharp left again, towards the summit, which is briefly in view. The last part of the walk is up a gentle gully, but this presents no real difficulty. From the rocky 1,767m (5,800ft) summit, a dizzying panorama takes in the whole of Castagniccia to the east and the central range to the west, with Monte Cinto, Monte Ritondo and Paglia Orba in view.

The East Coast

Extending 100km (63 miles) from Bastia to Solenzara, Corsica's eastern plains form the island's only significant lowlands. The gently undulating plain is backed in the north by the chestnut-clad hills of Castagniccia, while to the south the central dividing range rises abruptly from the vineyards and citrus groves that are the mainstay of the region's economy. While the scenery lacks the intensity and variety of the west and north, getting around is a lot quicker on the fast and straight N198, running the length of the coast. Mile upon mile of often deserted sandy beaches are broken only by the lagoons and estuaries of the rivers draining off the mountains and forming wetland nature reserves. If the summer heat gets too much, there are plenty of inviting country roads, winding into the forested mountains, where villages can be seen from afar, perched on inaccessible ridges.

In 1943 the retreating Germans and Italians blew up most of the bridges along the coast, destroying the railway link to Porto Vecchio, which was never rebuilt. In the aftermath of the liberation of Corsica, American forces stationed there set to ridding the coast of its malarial scourge, by liberally dousing the plains with DDT. This paved the way for a new lease of life for the plains.

The Casinca Villages

South of Bastia, the N198 hugs the base of the **Casinca** hills, where the villages hug the skyline like sentries. South of the Golo river, the D237 leads to **Vescovato (Vescovatu)**, meaning 'bishopric', where the bishops of Mariana moved in 1269 when the coast became unsafe because of Saracen attacks and malaria. The approach to the town from below suggests an impregnable fortress, its forbidding grey houses clumped together on the hillside. The houses are so tall they almost dwarf the church of St Martino, whose white marble tabernacle was the 1441 masterpiece of a Genoese sculptor. A stone eagle surveys the village square from his perch on a fountain. It is worth continuing to the ridge-top village of **Venzolasca**, past a cemetery of ornate family burial vaults. Along the way, look for Corsica's only organic restaurant, L'Ortu, which does a vegetarian menu although it is not exclusively vegetarian. Beyond Venzolasca, the D6 climbs to the equally picturesque

Loreto di Casinca, perched on a spur of Mt Sant'Angelo and at 600m (2,000ft) commanding an enviable view over the plains to the coast and out to sea.

If you're ready for more windy roads, then drive the **Castagniccia corniche route** (D330), which hangs above the plain passing St Giovanni, San Nicolao and Santa Maria and the **waterfall of L'Uccelluline**, set between two tunnels, to reach the town of **Cervione**. Above the huge church of St Erasme, the local history museum **Musée de L'ADECEC** offers an insight into everyday Corsican life through the centuries.

The Coastal Route

The N198 meets the coast at the resort of **Moriani Plage**, the main town on the Costa Verde and catering to the beach crowd, with hotels, restaurants and shops, but in itself a place of few obvious charms. There is a wilder stretch of beach to the south on the coastal side of the Étang de Diane, just north of the Tavignano River, at **Plage de Padulone**, reached from Cateraggio.

Unsurprisingly, the easily accessed eastern plain was an open invitation to invaders and settlers and Phocaean Greeks from Asia Minor established a colony there from 565 BC, building the town of **Alalia** (today **Aléria**). Conquered by Lucius Scipio in 259 BC, Aléria became a key military base and capital of Rome's Corsican outpost. With as many as 20,000 soldiers to feed, the plains were drained and cultivated, becoming Corsica's granary. As Rome's power dwindled, the cultivation of the land declined and the rivers reverted to marshland, attracting malarial mosquitoes. With the Vandal attacks, the remaining inhabitants fled to the mountains and for almost 1,500 years the plains were all but abandoned.

Aléria is one of Corsica's major historic sites and a worthwhile visit for anyone interested in the island's past. The site lies just off the N198 on an exposed plateau overlooking the Tavignano River on its south bank. The visit begins at the Genoese fort of **Matra**, built in 1572 and housing the **Musée d'Archéologie Jérôme Carcopino**, named after the Corsican scholar who did much to stimulate interest in the island's archaeology. The museum displays items unearthed and recovered from tombs on the site, which include priceless Greek, Etruscan and Roman ceramics, oil lamps, coins and weapons. Many of the items bear witness to the importance of trade in the western Mediterranean. Some of the pottery is exceptional in its form and detail: a wide-mouthed vessel or *crater*, decorated with a seated Dionysus, flanked by satyrs and a nymph, from around 425 BC; and two Attic vessels in the form of a dog's and mule's head.

A pathway leads to the site of the Roman city of Aléria, where excavations began in 1958. Information panels explain the layout of the city, with its Forum, flanked by shops, a temple at one end and *Praetorium* at the other and its baths, steam rooms and complex system of water storage and distribution.

South of Aléria, there is an interesting side trip on the D343 heading inland and joining the D344 to **Ghisoni**.

Left: Castagniccia gets its name from the chestnut forests that thrive in the region

Below: Morosaglia's grey schist houses overlook a brooding forested valley to the central mountains beyond

Penetrating the mountains, the road snakes above the Fium'Orbo through two spectacular gorges, the **Défilé de l'Inzecca** and **Défilé des Strette**. On the rock face to the right of the road some unusual volcanic features can be seen, among them pillow lavas and basalts. Once through the gorges, the small town of **Ghisoni** comes into view, nestled in an isolated valley, badly ravaged by fire in 1985. Here where the last of the heretic Giovannali sect were reputedly burned to death in the sixteenth century. As the fire gained strength, high in the sky its ashes were seen to form the shape of a dove. The villagers' chanting echoed back from the peak that towers over Ghisoni and in memory of the tragedy it became known as **Kyrie Eleison**, while the serrated pinnacles in front it were named **Christe Eleison**. Just off the main street is an ornate fountain presided over by a statue of Neptune, where a café and bakery might tempt you to linger.

To continue from here involves a long haul over either the 1,289m (4,227ft) **Col de Verde** to the Taravo Valley, or the even more tortuous route via the 1,311m (4,300ft) **Col de Sorba** to Vivario and Corte. Both routes may be impassable out of season – check locally. From Col de Verde, walkers can access the GR 20, which meets the road at the pass.

Villages of the Fium'Orbo

South of Ghisonaccia, the coastal plain narrows and the mountains meet the sea. At this point, the D145 cuts inland to a cluster of hill villages perched on

The Pieds-Noirs

When Algeria became independent in 1962, up to a million European Algerians left their country. Known as *pieds-noirs*, allegedly because they wore black boots, some bought land to farm on Corsica's recently reclaimed eastern plain. Subsidised by the government, their large-scale methods of farming and wine production were not always popular with the locals, who for centuries had cultivated the terraced fields around their mountain villages and produced high-quality food on a cottage industry level. Things came to a head on 21 August 1975, when protesters occupied a wine cellar in Aléria and in the skirmish that followed two policemen lost their lives.

the slopes of a hidden valley, linked by endlessly twisting single-track roads. **Prunelli di Fium'orbo**, presiding over the entrance to the valley, offers a splendid panorama of the east coast. In the inner reaches, with 2,042m (6,700ft) Punta di a Capella towering above, **San Gavino** and **Isolaccio** attest to the isolation of this micro-region. At **Catastaghju**, 2km (1.25 miles) from San Gavino, is a charming and rustic *gîte d'étape*, serving honest Corsican country food and with its own river pool for bathing. It's on the Mare a Mare Centre trail, which climbs from here to Col de Laparo in 4 hours to meet the GR 20 route on the dividing range. There are shorter walks in the area, between the villages, if you're feeling less energetic.

Places to Visit

Bastia

Tourist Information
Place St Nicolas
Open 8.30am–12pm and 2–6pm Mon to Sat; July and Aug 8am–8pm daily.

Paisolo Miniature Village
In the powder magazine at the south end of the citadel
Open 9am–12 pm and 2–6pm daily from Easter to Oct.

Musée d'Ethnographie and Palais des Gouverneurs
In the citadel
At the time of writing, still closed for renovations. Check locally.

Church of Sainte-Marie
In the citadel
Open 8am–12pm and 2–5.30pm (6.30pm in summer), daily except Sunday afternoons.

Oratoire Sainte-Croix
In the citadel
Open 9am–12pm and 3–7pm (summer) and 9am–12pm and 2–5pm (winter), daily except Sun and public holidays.

Petit Train
45-minute tour by miniature train of the most interesting sites in Bastia, including the citadel. Departs by the Tourist Office on Place St. Nicolas.

L'Église Saint-Jean Baptiste
By the Vieux Port
Open 8am–12pm and 3–7pm, daily except Sun afternoons.

Chapelle de l'Immaculée Conception
rue Napoléon, Open 8am–7pm daily.

The East Coast

Costa Verde Tourist Office
Moriani-Plage, town centre
Open 9am–12pm and 2–6pm Monday to Friday (all day, daily in high season)
☎ 04 95 38 41 73
www.otcostaverde.com

Castagniccia Tourist Office
At Folelli, at the junction of the N198 and D506
Open 9.30am–12pm and 3–6pm, Monday to Saturday, in season.
☎ 04 95 35 82 54

Musée de L'ADECEC
Cervione
Local history museum with displays on everyday Corsican life through the centuries
Open 10am–12pm and 2–6pm daily except Sundays and public holidays
☎ 04 95 38 12 83, www.adecec.net

Musée Pasquale Paoli
In Morosaglia in the hamlet of Stretta
Open 9am–12pm and 2.30–7.30pm, daily except Tuesday April to September and 9am–12pm and 1–5pm out of season. Closed in February. ☎ 04 95 61 04 97

Musée Départementale d'Aléria Jérôme Carcopino
Museum and site of Roman ruins, west of the main road, just south of the river
Open 8am–12pm and 2–5pm (until 7pm from mid-May to October), daily, all year. Closed Sundays out of season.
☎ 04 95 57 00 92

5. Porto Vecchio, Bonifacio and the far south

The central mountain range ends abruptly north-west of Porto Vecchio, and Corsica's far south is characterized by low-lying granite hills, topped by rocky outcrops. At the island's southern tip, the granite gives way to chalk and the iconic cliffs of Bonifacio. Groves of cork oak typify the surrounds of Porto Vecchio but elsewhere, buffeted by wind and scorched by fire, much of this exposed and dry region struggles to hold on to its parched scrub.

The rugged, indented coastline is blessed with a winning combination of the island's best beaches and gorgeous turquoise seas, and predictably gets more than its fair share of summer visitors. August is best avoided when the area becomes a hot-spot for Italian visitors. Development along the coast has been intense but it is almost entirely restricted to low-rise villa complexes, such as those of Santa Giulia, Cala Rossa and San Ciprianu, and discreet

Opposite: Palombaggia beach, near Porto-Vecchio

campgrounds. For visitors, the main challenge in high summer is getting around on the narrow, traffic-choked roads and finding a place to park when you get there. You can get avoid this in July and August by using the bus services linking Porto Vecchio and some of the outlying beaches.

Vying with the beaches for attention is the extraordinary town of Bonifacio, perched on a dramatic cliff top, facing Sardinia. It's easy to escape the beach scene by driving up one of the twisting roads into the mountainous interior, where swift-flowing streams drain off the highest summits, their rock pools perfect for a riverside picnic.

'The sun made love to the sea so many times that eventually they gave birth to Corsica'

Antoine de Saint Exupéry

Porto Vecchio Town

Porto Vecchio (population 8,000) is divided into two parts, a modern lower town with the marina, port and commercial district, and a historic, walled upper town on the hill behind.

In 1539, the Bank of St George, backed by the republic of Genoa, established a fortified base on a granite spur at the head of the Gulf of Porto Vecchio, to complete their coastal defences around the island. With its five towers, **the citadel** aimed at resisting the Barbary pirate attacks, especially those of the Turk Dragut, whose 27-

year campaign of sacking and abduction in the Mediterranean had begun the previous year. The defences were evidently less than successful as between 1546 and 1589 the fort was destroyed and rebuilt four times.

In the seventeenth century Genoa gave privileges to the noble families of Quenza, who for the next hundred years reserved the sole right to reside within the walls. Avoiding the malarial summer months, their shepherds came down from the mountains to graze their flocks on the surrounding plains in winter. As well as livestock rearing, the growing of cereals, grapes and olives and the harvesting of cork oak, timber and salt from the salt marshes ensured a steady growth and by 1848 the town had a population of 2,000 and a road connection was made to Bastia.

Today, the old citadel retains some of its original character, most evident

Corsica's south-west coast

in the narrow **Rue Borgo**, running alongside the east wall. Its higgledy-piggledy houses are built into the ramparts, and several are converted into restaurants, with panoramic terraces overlooking the port. **Le Roi Théodore** is the place to splash out but there are cheaper options. Here you'll also find the **La Taverne du Roi**, a popular nightspot with live Corsican music by the Genoese gate, once the home of the chief magistrate or *podestat* and, until the other two gates were added, the only entrance into the citadel. Protected by a solid gate and cannon, it gave access to the port, which is still reached by the same steep and narrow descent.

At the north end of rue Borgo is the recently restored **Bastion de France**, whose courtyard is used as a summer concert venue. A few doors down, another throbbing nightspot, **Le Bastion**, boasts a huge selection of beers. If ice cream's your thing, then don't miss out on your pick of 40 different types in the **Glacier de la Place**, opposite the church in the Place de la République. On Cours Napoléon, just off the square is another eatery, **Le Tourisme**. Don't be put off by the name; the food is good and the menu includes light meals if you can't face the full three-course affair. Towards the north end of the same street is another great place for a light bite, **A Cantina di l'Orriu**, a bar attached to a shop selling Corsican specialities.

Just north of the square is the Tourist Office, while the street west of it hosts the **Sunday summer market** of Corsican produce. Here you'll find every imaginable kind of *charcuterie*, and plenty of cheeses, honey and jams.

There are several small grocers in the citadel area but the main supermarkets are in the commercial district in the north of the town. Banks and post office are in Rue Général Leclerc in the upper town.

Unless you're travelling out of season, don't attempt to drive through the upper town. Either park by the marina or port, or in the car park at the south end of town, coming in from Bonifacio. There's a useful town bypass for through traffic.

Once you've explored the citadel, head through **Porte Genoise** and down to the marina. Boat trips leave from the north side, while at the south end there are a cluster of cafés, bars and a nice crêperie. Out beyond the ferry terminal, Gare Maritime, are the **salt pans** and at the end of the road a path takes off through pine and cork oak woods to the river estuary, where shags, gulls, kingfishers and egrets can be spotted.

Boat trips

A boat trip along the coast is a relaxing way to escape the summer heat, discover the less accessible beaches and coves and visit some of the offshore islands, including the stunning Lavezzi archipelago. The *Ruscana* departs Pinarellu and Porto Vecchio marina daily, sailing south to Bonifacio, via the nature reserve islands of Cerbicale and beaches of Palombaggia, Santa Giulia and Rondinara, with swim stops along the way. After lunch on board, there's time to explore the Îles Lavezzi. From Santa Giulia, the smaller *Djinn* cruises a similar route and includes the chance to go fishing. Advance booking is recommended and note that the commentary on board may only be in French.

Cork Oaks (*Quercus suber*)

Around Porto Vecchio you may see the stripped red trunks of cork oaks, whose bark has just been harvested. These trees occur naturally throughout the Mediterranean and can reach 20m (65ft) in height. They grow a thick, rugged bark that offers protection from fire damage and by the time it is 25 years old it is ready to be harvested as cork. Removing this outer bark from the lower trunk does not harm the tree and it will regenerate to be cut again every 10 to 12 years. This is a perfect, renewable resource and a tree can be harvested a dozen or more times in its life.

Exploring around Porto Vecchio

When you've had your fill of white, powdery sand and turquoise seas, there are a number of interesting things to see and do away from the beach and some very scenic mountain drives.

It's hard to beat the view at sunrise or sunset from the lovely historic lighthouse at **Punta di a Chiappa**, at the entrance to the Golfe de Porto Vecchio. To get there, turn left off the Palombaggia road, just before the hamlet of Picovaggia and follow the single-track road to the end. Park by the entrance to the nudist colony, from where it is a five-minute walk to one of Corsica's first five lighthouses, built around 1845. A path leads from the lighthouse down to the rocky shore, where you'll find a surprising variety of spring flowers.

The *Castellu* and *Torri* of the far south

They may not be as famous as the Alta Rocca sites, but the Castellu d'Araghju, Tappa and a cluster of other remains from the second millennium BC are worth a visit if you're interested in the island's early history. Typical of these sites are the cyclopean walled fortresses and enigmatic *Torri*, tower-like structures that have puzzled historians and given rise to conflicting theories about Corsica's early inhabitants. It was once believed that the *Torri* were built by invaders, whom historians named Torréens and whose superior bronze weapons allowed them to defeat and displace the original Stone Age settlers. In the 1980s, however, archaeologists unearthed evidence to suggest that such weapons had long been made at a site near Aléria and that the *Torri* could be a thousand or more years older. Whatever you decide to believe, there seems little doubt that many of these sites, placed on high ground or rocky outcrops, were chosen for defence.

About 5km (3 miles) down the D859 Porto Vecchio to Figari road, turn left to the hamlet of **Ceccia**. A steep path leads to a single cylindrical *Torre*, with inner chamber, sited on a rocky outcrop, overlooking the coastal plain. A little further along the D859, the larger walled complex of **Tappa** is a ten-minute walk across farmland to the left of the road. Here a single tower, one of two or possibly three original structures, may have been used for milling, as well as storing grain in its chambers. **Torre**, signposted to the right off the N198, 5km (3 miles) north of Porto

Left: Piscia di Gallo Falls Right: Bonifacio

Vecchio and shortly after the junction with the D759, has preserved some of its roofing slabs and, like other sites, is built around the surrounding granite. The most spectacular location has to be the **Castellu D'Araghju**, sited above the D759, which runs inland from the main N198. Use the car park at the south end of the village of Arraggio, then follow signs to the start of the path. It's a steep, 20-minute climb on a rough trail, but worth it for the panoramic view of the coast if nothing else. The impressive portal allows access to the fortress through the massive 2m (6ft) thick circular wall, which has numerous chambers built into it.

Mountain Drives

It's a short and very spectacular drive into the mountains and the fragrant, shady pines of the **Forêt de l'Ospédale**. In just 13km (8 miles) the D368 zig-zags up 900m (3,000ft) in hair-raising switchback turns to the village of **l'Ospédale**. Few live here year-round but the population swells in summer, as people escape the searing heat of the coastal plain. From the village café, you can sip a coffee and take in the panoramic view of Porto Vecchio's coast, before plunging into the shade of the forest, where there are plenty of easy walking and cycling trails. There's also the Xtrem Sud adventure park, offering a circuit of nerve-testing challenges – there's a minimum height requirement for children of 130cm (4ft 2in).

Just beyond the village the road skirts the reservoir which supplies Porto Vecchio – look out for colourful hoopoes feeding on the forest floor by the side of the road. Around 1km (half a mile) beyond the dam, draw into a

Thistle Thief

Goldfinch *Carduelis carduelis*
This bright little songbird, though protected by law, is often captured for aviaries. Look for it perched on thistles as it extracts the seeds for food, especially in autumn and winter. In fact its Latin name means 'thistle'. Because of this, the goldfinch has sometimes been associated with the Passion and Christ's crown of thorns in Christian symbolism.

Porto Vecchio, Bonifacio & the far south, Propriano, Alta Rocca & the Sartenais

Best of the beaches

Porto Vecchio itself has no sandy shore but within 24km (15 miles) of the town are a dozen of the most beautiful beaches in Corsica. Between June and September expect to pay to park near them. It makes sense to use the car parks for the shade they may offer and your car is less likely to get scraped than if you park on the verge of a narrow road, where you also run the risk of hindering the flow of traffic. Drive slowly on the approach tracks to the car parks, which can be very rutted. It's best to get there early and leave early, and in doing so avoid most of the traffic. In July and August buses run between Porto Vecchio and Santa Giulia, Palombaggia, Cala Rossa, San Ciprianu and Pinarellu.

East of Porto Vecchio

Palombaggia

Though Palombaggia is the best known, there are in fact a cluster of prize-winning beaches on the peninsula east of Porto Vecchio. Some years ago idyllic Palombaggia, with its clear blue sea and white sand, was deserted and you could camp wild in the shady pine forest behind its fragile dunes. No longer, it has to be said! This is one of Corsica's hedonist hotspots, though the gorgeous setting is unchanged – a narrow ribbon of sand, set among pink granite boulders. Approaching from the north, turn left 1.5km (1 mile) beyond the hamlet of Picovaggia, and continue to the end of the road, where there is a large shady car park at the northern end of the beach. At the southern end is the very pleasant beachside restaurant Le Tamaricciu, from where a short walk through the pines brings you to a second equally beautiful beach.

For those prepared to walk, another option is the sandy bay of Carataggio, north of Palombaggia. There is no road access but you can park by the side of the road at Foce Incesa, 500m (600 yards) south of Picovaggia, and take the rough path down to the coast, about a 20-minute walk. No refreshments are available there so take plenty of water.

Bus service: July and August, daily except Sundays
Departs Porto Vecchio, Agence Trinitours on Rue Pasteur,
at 10am, 2pm, 4pm
Departs Palombaggia Beach 10.30am, 2.55pm, 5.55pm

South of Porto Vecchio

Santa Giulia

The sheltered sandy bay of Santa Giulia, 7km (4 miles) south of Palombaggia, is perfect for children, but as it serves the vast, sprawling villa complex of the same name, it is far from quiet.

Bus Service: July and August, daily except Sundays
Departs Porto Vecchio port at 9.50am, 12.10pm, 3.05pm, 7pm
Departs Santa Giulia at 10.20am, 12.30pm, 3.45pm, 7.30pm

Rondinara

It takes a bit of effort to reach this gorgeous spot, but most agree it is worth it. About 14km (9 miles) south of Porto Vecchio turn off the D198 signed to Suartone. The single-track, pot-holed D158 winds uphill through scorched scrub to the hamlet, then descends to the Baie de Rondinara, a perfect semicircle of gently shelving white sand,

Best of the beaches

framing a shallow lagoon of turquoise sea. It's ideal for children and there is ample parking and a simple snack bar.

North of Porto Vecchio

To reach this string of good beaches, turn right on the D468, just north of the town. After 3.5km (2 miles), turn right again to reach the smallest of them, at **Cala Rossa**. Be careful not to detour into the private villa complex, where there is no public beach access. Back on the D468 continue for a further 1km (0.5 miles), then turn right again to **San Ciprianu**, another fine stretch of sand, but, like Cala Rossa, rather built up. The best of the bunch is **Pinarellu**, a further 7km (4 miles) north along the D468 and graced with a square Genoese tower on an offshore rocky islet. There is parking, a restaurant and a pizzeria.

Bus Service: July and August, daily except Sundays
Departs Porto Vecchio port 1.15pm, 7pm
Departs Pinarellu at 12.15pm and 6.30pm
Intermediate stops at Cala Rossa and San Ciprianu

Instead of taking the D468, head north from Porto Vecchio on the main road, the N198. After 14km (9 miles), reach the Genoese tower of **Fautea**, where you can park by the side of the road near a small beach. The 10-minute walk to the tower is worth it for the stunning views north and south along the coast. North of here are two other nice beaches at Tarco and Favone.

car park to the right and walk to the waterfall **Piscia di Gallu**, which correctly translates as 'Pine Falls' and not, as is often claimed, 'Cockerel's Pee'! The best time to see it is after rainfall – in high summer it often dwindles to a trickle. Descend by a dirt track to a small stream. Cross the stream and follow the path marked by cairns to the viewpoint, where the valley falls away sharply below you. The path continues left of the viewpoint, then bears right onto a rocky spur, from where the 70m (230ft) high waterfall can be seen plunging over the cliff in front of you. A sign warns that it is not wise to continue beyond here, and it isn't. In fact it's a tricky scramble, and can be dangerous too, especially in rain. The walk takes 1.5 hours there and back to the car park and proper footwear is needed.

This highly scenic drive continues through the forest to Zonza and the **Col de Bavella** (see the chapter on 'Exploring from Propriano').

Corsica's most scenic Mountain Drive – the D268 from Solenzara to Col de Bavella

You won't regret making a really early start for this drive, to catch the morning sun on the jagged teeth of the Aiguilles de Bavella and to miss the oncoming traffic on a route that is as narrow and twisting as it is dramatic. The road starts from the seaside resort of **Solenzara**, 41km (25 miles) north of Porto Vecchio. Winding along the banks of the boulder-strewn Solen-

Posidonia Oceanica

It's hard not to notice the heaps of rotting leaves on some of Corsica's loveliest beaches. Often mistaken for seaweed, *Posidonia oceanica* is an important aquatic plant that forms dense undersea meadows. One cubic metre of the stuff can contain over 7,000 leaves, which give off oxygen, making this plant a vital component of the ecosystem.

zara river on a hot day, you may be tempted to pull off and dip into one of the refreshing rock pools. Leaving the river, the heady scent of the *maquis* gives way to the more subtle fragrance of pine on the long haul up to the **Col de Larone**, an obligatory stop for the fine view of a horizon dominated by a chaos of pink granite peaks. It is hard to imagine the scene of devastation that followed the catastrophic fire of 1960, which decimated the Forêt de Bavella. It has been replanted with 120,000 maritime and Laricio pines, now achieving a credible height, but a few of the original giants remain. The road now dips down from the pass and the views are lost in a thickly forested basin before the final climb to the Col de Bavella, where at 1,218m (4,000ft) the air is noticeably fresher than on the coast. See the chapter on Propriano for walks from the Col de Bavella.

Unless you have a reason to return by the same route, it makes sense to continue the drive to Zonza and from there return to Porto Vecchio through the Forêt de l'Ospédale (see the previous 'Mountain Drive').

The D59 to Carbini & the Alta Rocca

This mountain road is an alternative route to the Alta Rocca, via the 809m (2,653ft) Col de Bacinu. It's definitely not as spectacular as the other routes, but neither does it get anything like the volume of traffic, which is as well because it is narrow and very winding. The D59 starts from the village of Sotta on the Figari to Portovecchio road. As it climbs out of the plain, there are great views back to the coast and in spring the cistus and lavender in bloom are especially vibrant. There's a place to pull off the road by a memorial to the resistance fighters of the Massif de Cagna during the liberation of Corsica in September 1943. Trees obscure the views at the Col, but the scenery opens out again on the approach to **Carbini**. Whichever way you come, it takes some effort to reach this unassuming and out of the way little village, sited on a rare spur of flat land high above the Fiumicicoli Valley. Its austere houses, with their defiant shutters, are in keeping with Dorothy Carrington's evocative description of her stay in the village in the 1950s (see 'Further Reading'). Apart from the bar, there would be nothing to detain you here, were it not for the almost perfect little Romanesque church, its absurdly tall campanile and the enigmatic tale of a persecuted fourteenth-century religious sect, the Giovannali.

It is unclear whether the sect took the name of one of its founders or that of Carbini's church, dedicated to St John the Baptist. Still standing today, the church and its campanile were built in the twelfth century, along with the

baptistry of San Quilico, now in ruins. The campanile, said to have once stood seven floors high, was built by Maestro Maternato. Those who had commissioned it were jealous of his success and plotted to kill him once the building was finished. Suspecting this might happen, Maternato sent for a special tool from his village as a pre-arranged warning signal to his family. Those who went to fetch it were then seized and held hostage until the builder returned safely home.

Punta di a Vacca Morta – a short hike to a marvellous viewpoint

Distance: 2.4km (1.5 miles) each way
Duration: 1 to 1.5 hours each way
Ascent & Descent: 300m (1,000ft)

Most people agree that the views from the 1,314m (4,300ft) summit of this unassuming and oddly named peak are worth every step of the climb. Brood-

ing hills and ridges fall away to the coast, as far as Bonifacio and, on a clear day, to Sardinia. The path up 'dead cow peak' starts from the car park of Le Refuge, a *gîte d'étape* and good restaurant, reached by a left turn down the dirt road between l'Ospédale and the reservoir, and signed to Cartalavonu. As you sweat your way up the rocky slope, follow the orange paint splashes for about 40 minutes to the grassy pass of Foce Alta, where the views are already pretty spectacular. Now ignore the orange marks, which descend to the right, and instead follow the small cairns straight ahead. Dipping back into the forest for a short while, the path then bears left, climbing among the rocks to reach the cluster of huge boulders atop the summit. Descend via the same route, but take care not to lose the main path as there are several side trails.

Bonifacio

Perilously positioned on the edge of a 60m (200ft) high precipice, **Bonifacio** looks set to topple at any moment. But this most intriguing of Corsica's towns is defiantly holding on to its cliff-top anchor almost 1,200 years after it was founded by Boniface, Marquis of Tuscany. Over a million visitors are drawn each year to marvel at the citadel's labyrinth of narrow, cobbled streets, flanked by impossibly tall houses, all crammed inside its forbidding walls.

The **citadel** faces the full force of the winds roaring across the Bouches de Bonifacio, the 14km (9-mile) wide strait that separates Corsica and nearby Sardinia. But nestled secretly behind the promontory on which it is built is a narrow, fjord-like inlet, providing a safe and hidden anchorage for boats. It is small wonder that this perfect little port took on immense strategic importance, becoming a pawn in the power struggles of southern Europe. Taking the town in 1195, the Genoese evicted the inhabitants, brought in their own people, and made sure its newly fortified walls would make it impenetrable. This was put to the test in 1420, when Alphonse V of Aragon finally retreated after laying siege to the city for months on end. But a town bursting at the seams was no match for the 1528 plague, which swept through, indiscriminately claiming 3,000 lives. Then in 1553, already weakened by the epidemic, Bonifacio was stormed and taken by the corsair Dragut, in league with the French. Rebuilt by France, it was once again ceded to Genoa in 1559

following a peace treaty.

Several famous names are associated with Bonifacio: **Ulysses**, some would believe, encountered the Laestrygonians, a race of oversized cannibals, below the cliffs of Bonifacio at the entrance to the port. Later, in 1215, **St Francis of Assisi** founded the Franciscan monastery of St Julien here, while in 1541 the **Emperor Charles V** resided in the town and his visit is still celebrated. A young and inexperienced **Napoleon Bonaparte** landed with his troops in 1793, aiming to invade the north of Sardinia. Defeated, apparently the 23-year-old soldier had yet to acquire his skills of conqueror.

Today, the town of around 4,000 inhabitants lives largely from tourism, whose revenue greatly exceeds that of the traditional industries of lobster fishing and the harvesting of coral, cork and olive oil. Be warned that the high season traffic can make getting in and out of town a very slow business. Aim to arrive by 8am to avoid the queues. The main road into town snakes through a ravine to emerge at the port and lower town, clustered around it. Public car parks are signposted to the left and it is best to leave your vehicle here, though by following signs to the upper town, **Haute Ville**, you will find limited parking there if you can't face the climb up the steps. Another choice for tired legs is the **Petit Train**, which departs from the car park nearest the port, taking you up and around the Haute Ville.

The most interesting part of the lower town surrounds the marina, where a promenade lined with hotels, cafes, restaurants and shops, among

A Tale of Revenge

Not far from the main Bonifacio to Propriano road, near Bocca di Testa, fugitive Jean-Camille Nicolai was killed by gendarmes on 19 April 1888. Some years earlier, his brother Napoléon had run off with Catherine Lanfranchi of Porto Vecchio. At the time, faced with parental disapproval, such couples' only recourse was to elope and hope that the 'fait accompli' would force the marriage. But Catherine's father took legal action instead and, unhappy with the light sentence, took the law into his own hands, killing the unfortunate young man and seizing back his daughter. When in turn he was acquitted by the court, Napoléon's brother Jean-Camille decided to avenge his brother's death, killing the father and hiding out in the *maquis*. Legend has it that this genteel young man was ill-suited to the life of fugitive. Disguised as a woman, he attended a wedding party, where his identity was discovered and he was shot dead as he tried to flee.

them a small supermarket, is lively both day and night. Quietly bobbing yachts and fishing boats add to the atmosphere, but it is the imposing bulk of the **Bastion de l'Étendard**, set high above the port, that draws the eye. To get there on foot you will need to run the gauntlet of enthusiastic boat trip operators, touting for business, along the quay. Past the **aquarium**, you will find a bank and the thirteenth-century **chapel of St Erasme**, patron saint of fishermen, built for those evicted when the Genoese erected the citadel. From here the broad steps of Rastello lead to **Col Saint Roch**, a stunning viewpoint of the citadel and the cliffs plunging abruptly to the sea below. The chapel here was erected on the spot where the last victim of the plague of 1528 died, a catastrophe which claimed the lives of three-quarters of the population. Steps lead down to the tiny **Plage de Sotta Rocca**, where bathing is possible when the sea is calm.

To the left of the Col St Roch, a footpath winds along the cliff top as far as the lighthouse of Pertusato, taking about an hour each way (see 'Walks from Bonifacio').

To enter the upper town, take the **Montée St Roch** to the **Porte de Gênes**, which was the only way into the citadel until the Porte de France was built in 1854. The huge gates, massively thick walls and drawbridge, which was added in 1598, suggest an impregnable fortress. The gate opens on to the **Place D'Armes**, where immediately to the right is the sixteenth-century **Bastion de l'Étendard**, which replaced earlier fortifications. The ticket includes access to the walls, a viewpoint towering over the marina and entry to the museum exhibits on the 'Dame de Bonifacio' and episodes from the area's history, including the visit of Charles V, the shipwreck of the *Semillante*, the Genoese guard and a market scene. Leading off the square is **Rue des deux Empereurs**, named in honour of Charles V and Napoléon I, who stayed in the town. The houses where they lodged, numbers four and seven, are marked by plaques.

The next street, Rue du Palais de Garde, leads to Bonifacio's oldest build-

The Giovannali

As religious and social changes swept through fourteenth-century Europe, the Third Order of St Francis emerged as a popular alternative to the established church. Though originating in the monasteries, its fraternities were open to both men and women, prepared to uphold a life of poverty, sharing and humility and to refuse allegiances and military service. Following decades of feudal domination, conflict, epidemics and famine, the once influential *pieve* of Carbini, set high in the mountains of the Alta Rocca, was isolated and its people destitute. A Corsican named Ristoro is said to have founded a fraternity there in 1352, with the backing of the Franciscan Giovanni Martini of Marseilles. Viewed as heretical, the sect was first excommunicated by the Bishop of Aléria and then rejected by the Pope and the Franciscan Order. Gaining popular support and taking on a political role, the Giovannali moved north to Alesani, where in 1354 they took over a monastery and, in the attack, two monks were killed. Over the next years, their doctrine spread over the island, but came to an abrupt end in 1362, when the Pope sent troops to eliminate them. The remnants of the sect took to the *maquis* and were systematically hunted down. Legend has it that the last of them were burned at Ghisoni.

ing, the twelfth-century **Église Sainte-Marie Majoure**, begun during Pisan times but added to at various stages. The square campanile's first floor is Romanesque but the upper three floors are Gothic, with elements of Aragonese decoration. Under lock and key in the sacristy is a precious relic of the True Cross, which legend has it was given to the town by a 'princess' who was saved from shipwreck. When violent storms threatened the town and its citizens, the relic was paraded about the town and believed to have a calming effect on the waves. To the left of the entrance is a third-century sarcophagus placed beneath a splendid fifteenth-century marble tabernacle. Outside the entrance, an arched loggia sheltered the town's notables, when they gathered to deliberate matters of importance. Under it was sited a huge cistern, which collected valuable rainwater via a network of aqueducts.

On the south side of the citadel is the **Place du Marché**, where the town's covered market once stood. Today, locals often gather here for a chat, but for visitors the attraction is the amazing view out to sea. The cliff west of here looks impossible to scale but, improbably, a flight of 187 steps was hand-carved out of it, legend has it, by the King of Aragon's troops, one night of the siege. Known as **L'Escalier du Roi d'Aragon**, the steps were more likely cut to access a spring of drinking water at the foot of the precipice. The steps, which are at the west end of the citadel, are open to the public, for a small entry fee. Also at this end of town is **Église Saint-Dominique**, one of only a handful of Gothic churches in Corsica, begun by the Templars in 1270 but completed by Dominicans in 1343. Its unusual tower is hexagonal in shape and adorned with ramparts. Only open in high summer, the church contains several statues carried by the brotherhoods, of which Bonifacio has five, during the Good Friday procession. Among them is a wooden statue of the martyr St Bartholomew, flayed at the hands of infidels, graphic in its detail and said to weigh 800kg (1750lb).

You can walk out past the town hall and the *Caserme*, the Genoese barracks which later housed the Foreign Legion, to the westernmost tip of the promontory and the neat baroque tombs of the sailors' cemetery. Facing west, this is a popular sunset spot, looking out over the **Phare de la Madonetta**, the lighthouse signalling the entrance to the port.

Finding a place to eat out of season, when many restaurants are closed, can be as challenging as in high summer, when most are frantically busy. As elsewhere, opt for the *menu du jour*. Look for *aubergines à la bonifacienne* – aubergines stuffed with *brocciu* cheese, a delicious vegetarian dish. In the upper town, the rustic **Cantina Doria** on rue Doria, which runs off Place du Marché, parallel to the cliff, serves genuine and unpretentious local menus at a reasonable price, but arrive early as it's always busy. At the other end of the same street, just off the Place de Montepagano, is **Stella D'Oro**, which is pricier but also good. Also in the upper town is the tiny **La Galiote**, in rue St Dominique, packed with locals, reasonably priced and serving good home-cooked fare.

Along the quai Jérôme Comparetti, waterfront restaurants, bars and cafes jostle for space and marina views. **L'Albatros** is good for fish, as is **Les Quatres Vents**, further along by the ferry terminal. For wine, local cheese, *charcuterie* and a limited menu try the **Kissing Pigs**, also on the quayside. On the opposite side of the marina, the **Centre Nautique**'s restaurant is open all year – it's fairly pricey but goes good pasta dishes.

Exploring around Bonifacio

There are plenty of things to see and do around Bonifacio, and you could easily spend several days in the area. The boat trip to Lavezzi Islands (see feature box) is a must, but if you can't find your sea legs there are lots of alternative land-based attractions.

West of Bonifacio

Head west of Bonifacio on the N196 in the direction of Sartène. About 3km (2 miles) from the roundabout, turn left on a narrow road to **Hermitage de la Trinité**, set among granite boulders at a superb viewpoint back towards Bonifacio. Built of white chalk and containing vows and offerings, the church attracts hordes of visitors on the annual 8 September pilgrimage procession on the Nativity of the Virgin Mary.

Back on the main road continue for about 500m (600yds) to **Bocca D'Arbia** where there is an easy walk on a dirt track to the lighthouse at Capo di Feno. Continue on the N196 for just over 2km (1.2 miles) to the D358, which bears left to **Tonnara** and its sandy beach.

About 20km (12 miles) from Bonifacio is the unassuming village of **Pianottoli**, with a useful small supermarket and a cluster of cafés and restaurants. The coast south of here is unspoiled and has several nice beaches, including that of **Chevano** (also spelled Kevano). Without a four-wheel drive, it may be difficult to get there – ask at the village before you set out. From the N196, take the D122 and then turn right down a track after 1km (half a mile). Reach the beach after about 3km (2 miles), shortly beyond Camping Kevano. Take food and water.

Just west of Pianottoli, the D150 takes off to the right to the peaceful village of **Monaccia D'Aullène**. Historically, the winter grazing rights in this area belonged to the shepherds of the Alta Rocca village of Aullène. This dead-end road continues for a further 8km (5 miles) to the hamlet of Giannuccio, at the foot of the prominent mountain, called **l'Uomo di Cagna**. An indistinct trail leads from the hamlet through *maquis* and pine forest to the 1,217m (3,990ft) summit, which is topped with a massive boulder that is technically impossible to scale without special equipment. It is easy to get lost in this sparsely inhabited mountain region, so be especially cautious and seek advice locally on the state of the trail and its markings.

Walk to Capo di Feno

Distance: 4km (2.5 miles) each way
Duration: 1 hour there and 1.5 hours back
Ascent & Descent: gentle descent and ascent of about 150m (500ft)

Park at Bocca D'Arbia on the N196 4km (2.5 miles) west of the roundabout outside Bonifacio and take the dirt track down towards the sea, through the *maquis*. As you approach the sea the huge wind- and wave-eroded granite boulders become more frequent and more impressive. The trail ends on a grassy plain (in Corsican *feno* meaning 'hay') from where the splendid square lighthouse dating from 1884 can be seen atop the rocky promontory of Capo di Feno. If you scramble over the rocks to the west on an indistinct trail, you will reach a small cove where you can bathe.

Figari and Surrounds

Southern Corsica's main airport is located 4km (2.5 miles) from the village of **Figari**, just off the D859. In July and August only, it runs a bus service four or five times a day to Bonifacio and Porto Vecchio.

France's southernmost wine-producing area, Figari has its own AOC. Cultivation of vines in this hot and arid region is said to date back to the sixth century and today, traditional local varieties, such as the *carcajolu neru* grape, producing full-bodied fruity reds, are still cultivated. There are five main vineyards – **Clos Canarelli**, at Tarrabucceta on the D22, 6km (4 miles) north of Figari, is highly rated.

Don't miss the delightful twelfth-century chapel of **San Quilico**, a right turn off the D859, 5km (3 miles) north of Figari.

East of Bonifacio

From the marina follow the one-way traffic system inland away from the port and head out of town on the D58. Almost immediately bear right and climb steeply on the road to Capo Pertusato. A turning right leads to the **Pertusato** lighthouse but continuing on the 'main' road brings you to the small beach of **Piantarella**, with its unbelievably turquoise sea. This is a paradise for windsurfers – gear can be rented on the spot. From the southern end of the beach you can access some Roman remains, which include fragments of mosaic. Nearby is the exclusive **Sperone Golf Course**, while lying offshore is the island of **Cavallo**, a private resort.

Now backtrack to Bonifacio and instead of turning left into town, bear right on the D58, passing the **Couvent de St Julien**, which became a Franciscan order following the visit of St Francis of Assisi in 1215. Shortly after, there is a turning right to the lovely **Plage de Calalonga**, 6km (4 miles) from Bonifacio and at the end of the road. Continue on the D58 to the **Golfe de Santa Manza**, popular with windsurfers, where the road follows the coast past several sandy coves. At the end of the road, you can walk a short way along the coast on a trail.

Walks from Bonifacio

The Pertusato Lighthouse

Distance: 4km (2.5 miles) each way
Duration: 1 to 1.5 hours each way
Ascent & Descent: mostly level

This is one of Corsica's most dramatic coastal paths and even if you walk just a part of it, you will get fantastic views of the town, the wave-lashed cliffs, and the Bouches de Bonifacio, with the misty silhouette of Sardinia beyond. You'll also find a whole new set of

Barraconi

Known in mainland Provence as *Bories*, these enigmatic, igloo-shaped dry stone huts are prevalent in the surrounds of Bonifacio. Their age is in most cases undetermined but their ingenious construction makes them very long-lasting and some may date back thousands of years.

flora that may be unfamiliar and not found elsewhere on the island, because only certain species can thrive in the alkaline soil.

The path departs from Col St Roch, just outside the upper town walls. It climbs gently following the cliff edge (be vigilant if you have young children) then joins a dirt road past some abandoned bunkers. Continue on or beside the road, which then splits to the right to reach the lighthouse.

Early morning is best for this walk. Avoid the middle of the day as there is no shade and take plenty of water.

Fazio and Paraguano Bays (west of Bonifacio)

Distance: about 5km (3 miles) each way
Duration: 1.5 hours each way
Ascent & Descent: several short ascents and descents totalling about 250m (800ft)

An easy walk through olive groves to two gorgeous secluded bays. The path starts from the main road out of town, about 200m (200 yards) from the marina, past the fuel station and just by the snack bar U Veni Qui. The trail climbs steadily through woodland

Top Left: Porto-Vecchio market, charcuterie stall
Top Right: Porto-Vecchio
Left: Cork oaks in the surrounds of Porto-Vecchio
Below: Place de la République in the heart of of old Porto-Vecchio

The Lavezzi Islands

This is one trip you won't want to miss. It's a great day out on a Robinson Crusoe island, but you should be prepared to share it with hundreds of others in season. Boats depart on demand from Bonifacio's marina and in 35 minutes you'll land on a tiny archipelago in the Straits of Bonifacio, a little closer to Corsica than Sardinia. The main island, just over 1km (half a mile) long and barely as wide, is surrounded by the clearest water imaginable and an abundance of marine life. There are several tiny coves of pure white sand, framed by granite boulders, some the size of houses, others shaped to fire the imagination. This is a diver's paradise, one of the most famous sites being **Mérouville**, where divers come to gape at the dozens of friendly brown grouper, which can reach over 1m (3ft) in length. Snorkellers can have as much fun, though you'll need to bring your own gear unless you take one of the snorkelling trips organized by the dive operators.

Unless you arrive on your own boat, the only way to get around the island is on foot and good shoes are needed as the paths are rough and rocky. On land look for some unusual flora, including the spectacular spring-flowering dragon arum, *Dracunculus muscivorus*, whose huge burgundy flowers smell of rotting flesh to attract pollinating flies. The islands are a protected nature reserve and there are no facilities or shade. Take plenty of water, even for a short visit, and food if you plan to stay the day. Peaceful they may be today, but these islands were the scene of the worst shipwreck in the Mediterranean, when on the night of 15 February 1855 the *Semillante* was blown aground in fog and high winds. The ship had set sail from Toulon the night before, bound for the Crimea with 773 servicemen and crew on board. Not one survived. Some of the victims are buried in the island's cemetery but most are remembered only by the pyramid-shaped memorial, erected on the rocky islet you pass as the boat approaches Lavezzi.

on a stepped path. At the crossroads continue straight over and then descend steeply. At the bottom, the trail divides. You can detour on the path to the left, which leads to a small cove. Back on the main trail, continue uphill to a plateau, where the woodland gives way to more open scrub and the remains of walled terraces and circular stone *barraconi* to either side of the path. About 1.5km (1 mile) from this trail junction, take the trail left (opposite a substantial stone wall) and descend through woodland and olive groves for 1km (half a mile) to a sheltered bay of turquoise sea, guarded by the Île de Fazio, whose striking chalk layers are stacked up like pancakes. Return to the main trail and stone wall, turning left and after 1km (half a mile) reach the Cala di Paraguano, another stunning sandy bay, marking the end of the limestone and the transition to granite. Take water and a swimsuit.

Sardinia

Just across the strait Sardinia's misty silhouette may beckon those with a day to spare. The pretty town of Santa Teresa di Gallura has nearby beaches and similar granite landscapes to southern Corsica. It takes around an hour by ferry from Bonifacio.

Places to Visit

Porto Vecchio

Porto Vecchio Tourist Office

Rue Camille de Rocca Serra, in the old town

Open 9am–8pm Monday to Saturday (Sunday 9am–1pm) May to September; Out of season 9am–12.30pm and 2–6.30pm Monday to Friday and Saturday 9am–12.30pm

☎ 04 95 7009 58

www.destination-sudcorse.com

Petit Train

Shuttle between the port and the church in the upper town every 15 minutes, 10am–12pm and 5–7pm

Xtrem Sud Adventure Park

Ospedale

Open daily May to September

Reservations essential

☎ 04 95 72 12 31

www.xtremsud.com

Horse Riding

Centre Equestre d'Arraggio

Near Castellu d'Araghju

☎ 04 95 70 52 06

Guided Botanical Walks

Discover the secrets of the *maquis* with Stephane Rogliano in the hinterland of Porto Vecchio

☎ 04 95 70 34 64

Diving Kalliste

Palombaggia Beach

☎ 04 95 70 44 59

www.corsicadiving.com

Diving Sud Corse Loisirs

Santa Giulia Beach

☎ 04 95 70 22 67

www.corsicasub.com

Helicopter flights: Hél'île de Beauté, Porto Vecchio

See Corsica from the air

☎ 04 95 72 18 63

www.helicorse.com

Boat trips

Ruscana, Porto Vecchio

An informative day out on board the *Ruscana*, passing the nature reserve of Îles Cerbicale and several of the region's best beaches en route to Bonifacio. Includes lunch and stops for bathing along the way as well as time on shore at the spectacular Lavezzi Islands.

Departs Porto Vecchio and Pinarello 9am daily,

☎ 04 95 71 41 50 & 04 95 70 33 67,

www.croisieres-ruscana.com

Djinn, Santa Giulia

Lavezzi Islands and fishing trips

☎ 04 95 70 56 61

http://ledjinn.free.fr

In and around Bonifacio

Boat Trips

Rocca Croisières

☎ 04 95 73 13 96

www.rocca-croisieres.com

Don't miss the dramatic views of Bonifacio and the cliffs from the sea. There is no shortage of companies offering cruises from Bonifacio, with regular departures all day long from the marina. Sensibly, they won't operate in windy conditions, but you should try and pick a calm day anyway. Some offer discounted or free parking and it's worth haggling if you are several people travelling together out of the high season. There are two basic itineraries:

The short one-hour cruise takes you along the base of the cliffs, with the town towering overhead, to the Grain de Sable, then loops back to the Sdragonato Cave and Bay of Fazio. The longer 90-minute cruise includes all the above, but then heads out to the Lavezzi Islands, taking in Île Cavallo, Sperone and Pertusato on the return journey. Most cruises allow you to stop off on Lavezzi and return with a later boat, so you can make a day of it. Children under 12 go free.

Golf

The 18-hole Sperone golf course is world-famous and has dazzling views out to sea from its stunning location at the end of a promontory, 6km (4 miles) east of Bonifacio
☎ 04 95 73 17 13
www.sperone.net

Windsurfing

At Piantarella Beach, 4km (2.5 miles) from Bonifacio, windsurfers and fun boards can be rented.
☎ 04 95 73 52 04
www.bonifacio-windsurf.com

Wine Tasting

Clos Canarelli vineyard, Tarabucetta, Figari
☎ 04 95 71 07 55

Diving

Atoll Diving

At Hotel A Cheda on the Porto Vecchio road and by the ferry terminal in the port.
☎ 04 95 73 02 83
www.atoll-diving.com

Trips to Sardinia

Moby Lines have four or more sailings a day from early April to late September between Bonifacio and Santa Teresa di Gallura, across the Bouches de Bonifacio. The journey takes around one hour
☎ 04 95 73 00 29
www.mobylines.it

Saremar sail the same route year round, but on a reduced service in winter
☎ 04 95 73 00 96
www.saremar.it
Santa Teresa di Gallura has its own website:
www.santateresagallura.com

Propriano (Pruprià)

Set at the head of the Golfe de Valinco, **Propriano** (population 3,200) is backed by the fertile Rizzanèse Valley and a framework of lush, forested hills. Traces of settlement in the area date back over two thousand years, but harassment by Barbary and Turkish pirates made it impossible to live here and little of architectural interest is evident in the town. Eventually the sheltered bay was chosen as the port for the inland fortified village of Fozzano, but Propriano as a town only developed after 1860 with the trade in coal, olive oil and timber from nearby Sartène. Today, the ferry terminal and new marina ensure a steady stream of visitor traffic. With beaches and a sprinkling of sandy coves within walking distance, Propriano is a resort in its own right, as well as a focal point for those staying in its outlying areas. Set back from the seafront, the main street is flanked by a terrace of eye-catching shops, bars, cafés and restaurants. Banks, post office and two small supermarkets are clustered here and in the side streets, leading to the

new town, which sprawls across the hill behind. With its narrow streets, Propriano's summer traffic can be chaotic and a one-way system is in place. The tourist office is by the marina, where some parking is available. Alternatively, look for space at the west end of town, past the ferry terminal. Propriano's theatre stages concerts and plays – ask at the tourist office for any Corsican music events during your stay.

If you get rained off the beach, try the **Thermes de Baracci**, the indoor thermal baths, 1km (half a mile) down the D257 and inland from Plage de Baracci, just outside Propriano. Recently renovated, the art deco-style building houses a swimming pool and hot tub at 38–40°C (100–104°F).

From Propriano's marina, **boat trips** depart morning and evening to explore the bay. Full-day cruises head north to the Scandola Reserve and Golfe de Porto and south to Roccapina and Bonifacio. The best cruise is the leisurely day trip along the protected Sartenais coast, which is only accessible by boat or on foot, taking in its strangely eroded granite rocks and deserted coves and beaches.

Exploring around Propriano

Propriano is well placed for exploring the back roads of the **Sartenais**, where menhirs and dolmens lie hidden among colossal, statuesque boulders and thickets of fragrant *maquis*, providing an intriguing backdrop to what is arguably

> ## Beaches at Propriano
>
> In town, head for Plage du Lido, west of the lighthouse. For the best beach, follow Chemin des Plages for a dusty 2km (1.2 miles) to Capu Laurosu and a long arc of sand, backed by dunes. The water is beautifully clear and the beach clean, though it shelves steeply. A cluster of granite rocks at the northern end is tempting for snorkellers, while bird watchers should head for the Rizzanèse estuary.

Corsica's least developed coastline. Lapped by limpid seas, many of the desert-island beaches along here are only accessible by boat or on foot. In the brooding hills of the Alta Rocca are the most enigmatic of megalithic sites and tiny, defiant villages perched on rocky buttresses overlooking great tracts of undisturbed forest, stretching as far as the iconic peaks of Bavella.

Sartène (Sarté)

The hillside town of **Sartène** was described by Prosper Merimée as 'La plus Corse des villes Corses' – 'the most Corsican of Corsican towns' – around 150 years ago. Confidently surveying the Rizzanèse and Golfe de Valinco, this town of forbidding granite houses was built on the instigation of the Genoese in the early sixteenth century, to ward off Saracen attacks. Clearly the defences were not up to scratch when in 1583 the Moors swept in, sacking the town and carrying off hundreds of its citizens into slavery. The surviving nobility responded by building ever higher and more impregnable houses, seven or eight floors tall and spread over the town's two quarters of **Borgo**, the upper town, and **Santa Anna**, the lower town. Rivalry between the *sgio* families flared up from time to time (see feature box) and they and their supporters would barricade themselves into their family fortresses and hold out until hostilities waned. But some of these 'vendettas' were long-term affairs and it was only in 1834 that the rival factions were made to sign a peace agreement in the church of Ste Marie, to bury once and for all their differences.

L'église Sainte-Marie faces the cheerful tree-lined **Place de la Libération**, and, typical of Corsican towns, the square is open on one side. On display inside the entrance to the church is the huge wooden cross, weighing 30kg (66lb), and 15kg (33lb) chain, which gives its name to the Good Friday evening procession, the *Catenacciu* (chained one). Each year, a different local citizen, whose identity is a closely guarded secret, is chosen as *Grand Penitent*, to re-enact the Passion of Christ. As this deeply troubling and symbolic procession sets out from the church, the robed, hooded and chained penitent hauls the cross through the streets, falling and rising three times at predetermined places along the route. He is aided by the *Penitent Blanc*, robed in white and representing Simon of Cyrene, while to the rear eight others dressed in black bear a statue of Christ, chanting repeatedly. Inevitably, today

it has become something of a tourist spectacle but one which is perfectly in keeping with the town's ambience.

Much of the old town is a gloomy labyrinth of arched and vaulted passageways and steps, where the presence of stone is sometimes overwhelming, though the shade gives welcome respite from the summer heat. Here, visitors will also find shops selling Corsican delicacies and a cluster of inviting little restaurants, whose tables spill out onto the streets. Sartène also boasts the new and enlarged museum **Centre de Préhistoire**, by the hospital above Place de la Libération, documenting the island's history and the way of life of its early inhabitants.

The Sartenais

South of Propriano, the main road runs inland, penetrating the low-lying ranges, cut through by valleys, which form the hinterland to the **Sartenais coast**. The hills are peppered with granite outcrops, protruding from the dense covering of *maquis*. In the valleys, herds of cattle graze and some surprisingly good wines are produced from the sun-baked vineyards. Lush and flower-strewn in spring but dry and dusty by midsummer, this is a sparsely populated area that some might be tempted to ignore.

In a day it is possible to visit the Cauria and Palaggiu megalithic sites and the Genoese tower of Campomoro, but to fit in a half or full-day walk along the coastal path, or enjoy a swim or snorkel from one of its glorious beaches, more time is needed.

Campomoro, 18km (11 miles) from Propriano, lies on the south shore of

A Vindetta

From the early days, Corsica was a difficult and troublesome colony to administer. The Romans quickly found out that the mountainous interior was best left to the Corsicans. While the Pisans attempted to bring peace and prosperity, from the outset the Genoese struggled with law and order, notably in the rugged south and west of the island, for centuries the stronghold of the *sgio*, the local nobility who ruled by their own laws. There was always trouble on the horizon, whether it was the Saracen raids or the interfering tactics of foreign powers, who usually had their and not the island's interests at heart. Not surprisingly, when allegiances were traded as willingly as wine, and when justice, if there was any at all, was rough, Corsicans learned to look after themselves, as families first and clans and communities second.

Affairs of honour between families often did not reach the courts and were settled by a bullet or a knife in the back. But it was seldom a matter of 'an eye for an eye'. A vendetta (Corsican *vindetta*) wiping out whole families and spanning several generations may have stemmed from a simple dispute about land boundaries. The punishment was often way out proportion to the 'crime' and in this way violence could escalate dramatically, involving whole communities.

The Corsican vendetta was not always sparked by passion and often had a more sinister side to it. It could be set in motion by an innocuous comment or casual reference to a small unresolved matter of honour, then dwelled upon and brooded over until the time was right to plot, ambush and cold-bloodedly and dispassionately murder. Pasquale Paoli was so shocked by the appalling waste of life – a thousand or more killings a year attributed to vendettas – that he made it a capital offence.

With the passage of time, feuds became veiled in legend and hearsay to be romanticised and popularised by writers such as Maupassant and Merimée. In spite of attempts to wipe it out, the vendetta was as enduring as the *maquis* to which its perpetrators fled to escape the bullet. The last known feud ended in the 1950s.

A Corsican saying

'Pane e pernice, affari di casa ùn si ne dice' – 'Bread and partridge, family affairs are not discussed'

the Golfe de Valinco at the end of the winding D121. From the Sartène road, turn right just after the river. Past the airfield, **Portigliolo beach** comes into view, a wide arc of beautiful soft sand, with a campsite at its western end. Here, the road climbs above the coast, offering several good viewpoints before drop- ping down to Campomoro, an idyllic village on a sheltered bay. Its gorgeous sandy beach is ideal for children. There isn't much to the place and the shop, bar and two hotels are only open in season, but because it's at the end of the road there's no through traffic. If you park by the church, you can walk along the

Acorn Addict

Eurasian Jay
Garrulus glandarius
Every year a single jay can squirrel away and bury 5,000–10,000 acorns, choosing only the biggest and best of them. As many as half will not be found again and can grow into healthy, new oak trees. You can recognise jays by their screeching call, but they are also very good mimics. Their Latin name means 'talkative acorn eater'!

beach to one of Corsica's largest and best-preserved Genoese towers. A path meanders through *maquis* to the highly unusual star-shaped wall surrounding the tower, from where you can climb to its ramparts and enjoy a dazzling view out to sea and across the bay to Propriano. It's well worth exploring the granite rocks below the tower, where children love clambering among their strange, twisted shapes, which are also a great subject for photography. Campomoro is the start of the coastal path south to Roccapina.

Shepherds used to descend to the coast from the plateau of Coscione in autumn with their flocks of sheep and goats. The land was not theirs, but belonged to a few rich families, the *sgio*. The shepherds sowed cereals and lived in small huts made from branches of *maquis* or took shelter in the eroded caves, known as *tafoni*. Arrowheads found in the caves indicate that some bays were inhabited by much earlier Paleolithic peoples. In winter and spring, charcoal makers based themselves along the coast, building their huge woodpiles, covered with earth, which, burning slowly over a week, would form charcoal.

From Campomoro, backtrack 4km (2.5 miles) to the village of Belvédère, where the D21 takes off inland through the hills and valleys to **Grossa**. Beyond this village, look down the valley to the right to a church in a field. **San Giovanni de Grossa** dates from the twelfth century but was extended in modern times – to increase its capacity for storing hay! There is a gate to the right with a sign '*Soyez prudent, il y a des bovins*" – meaning 'cattle, drive with care'. This is a 12km (7.5 miles) four-wheel-drive track that leads to **Cala de Conca**, a secluded sandy bay, from where a path leads south-west to the lighthouse and the Genoese tower of **Senetosa**.

The **Megalithic sites of the Sartenais** are one of the highlights of a visit to the area. From the turn off just south of Sartène, the D48 follows a valley. After 9km (5 miles), there is a signpost to the Caurio sites, which are at the three apexes of a triangle. The road deteriorates and after 4.5km (3 miles) you reach a parking area. Four-wheel-drive vehicles can continue 600m (660yds) down the track to the right to the first of the sites. The alignments of **Stantari** are an impressive row of statue menhirs in a fenced-off enclosure, of which two bear traces of facial features, whilst a third is engraved with a sword. Experts believe they may be older than the better-known menhirs of Filitosa.

Leaving the enclosure at the far end of the row of menhirs, follow the path for about 250m (270yds) to an area of woodland, to find a second cluster, the menhirs of **Rinaghju**. Looking back from here to Stantari, the **Dolmen of Fontanaccia** is located to the left but the trail is not obvious. Instead, return to the Stantari enclosure and leave it by

Giovanni della Grossa

Born in the village of Grossa in the Sartenais in 1388, this staunch supporter of Genoa wrote the island's most valuable medieval history, providing fascinating details about the social structure and administration of rural Corsica at the time. Much of what is known about the island at the time comes from his writings.

the side gate. Follow the path round to the right and then join the main broad trail, which starts from the cork oak and boundary fence by the access road. The dolmen is about 300m (330yds) away, commanding a view of the surrounding plateau and hills beyond. Composed of six vertical standing slabs of granite supporting two massive roof slabs, it

Filitosa is Corsica's best known megalithic site and includes well-preserved statue menhirs

is open at one end and was used as a burial chamber. Legend connects the place with the devil, which accounts for the local name *A Stazzona di u Diavuli* – 'the devil's forge'.

Returning to the main Sartène to Tizzano road, bear left for Tizzano and after 3km (2 miles), the **Alignements de Palaggiu** are signposted on the right. Park and follow the broad dirt track to a rise, from where the menhirs can be seen in the distance, a further 1km (half a mile) away. Consisting of a staggering 258 stones set in seven rows, it is the largest collection of menhirs in Corsica. Some standing, some fallen, this battalion of granite statues does not readily yield up its secrets but the place has a magical if eerie quality about it.

With its beautiful, though exposed beach, **Tizzano (Tizzá)**, on the rugged Sartenais coast, is rapidly developing with extensive villa construction and a holiday camp. The Hotel du Golfe and several bars and restaurants are only open in season, flanking the single road which ends at a fjord-like inlet, whose protected waters allow for mooring of boats. A ruined fort lies on the other side of the inlet. From here the coast path leads to Campomoro in six and a half hours.

The Sartenais Coastal Trail

Hikers should not miss one of the best low-level walks in Corsica. This stunning coastal trail winds through uninhabited terrain, for the most part inaccessible to vehicles. It is neither well marked nor well advertised, though things may change as the protected coastline gains recognition. Dazzling spring flowers and a natural gallery of wind and sea-sculpted granite offer plenty of distractions along the way and if the heat gets too much, you can dip into the sea from one of the many idyllic beaches and secluded coves.

If you are planning a 'there and back' day walk, start either from Roccapina or Campomoro, which are the more interesting sections. Unless you are planning to walk the whole path (2 days), avoid the section west of Tizzano which is a trudge along a dirt track, while east of the village the path is difficult, exposed and rocky. Accommodation and restaurants are available at Tizzano and Campomoro, but only open in season. At least 3 to 4 litres of water per person should be carried to avoid dehydration in summer.

Distances: Roccapina to Tizzano 17km (10.5 miles); Tizzano to Campomoro 16km (10 miles)

Duration: two fairly long days but each section can be done as a day walk

Ascent & Descent: negligible as the path follows the coast

What to take: boots or sturdy trainers, picnic, plenty of water, sunhat, sunscreen, swimwear, mask and snorkel. There is almost no shade on this walk, so avoid July and August

Highlights: sculpted granite rocks, flora, secluded coves and wonderful deserted beaches

Access: by car (and by bus on the Propriano to Bonifacio route) to Roccapina; by car only to Campomoro and Tizzano

Cala di Roccapina to Plage d'Erbaju (1 hour)

If you have four-wheel drive, take the dirt track to the lovely sheltered Plage de Roccapina from Bocca di Curali and the Auberge Coralli. If you have an ordinary car check the condition of the track before you start off down it as it can be very rutted. Or park at the auberge and walk 2.5km (1.5 miles) to the beach. The coastal trail starts at the back of the beach and takes off through trees to the right as you face the sea. Take the left-hand trail where the path divides shortly after and reach a sign for the tower ('*tour*') and warning of the danger of rock falls. The path now climbs steeply for 20 to 30 minutes to a further fork. Turn right here and climb the remaining 20m (65ft) to the tower, from where there are exceptional coastal views. Return to the last fork and turn right, and following the blue marks descend to Plage d'Erbaju, reached after 20 to 30 minutes. Backed by dunes, this is a gorgeous, though exposed 2km (1.2 miles) long beach, which shelves steeply.

Plage d'Erbaju to Plage d'Argent and Plage de Tralicetu (1.5 hours)

At the north end of Erbaju beach, cross the river and continue on the coast path to the boundary fence of the private and exclusive Murtoli estate. Follow the perimeter fence inland past the estate gate, crossing the track. Continue around the perimeter fence until you meet another track. Cross this track and continue on the path, striking inland to cross the rocky Punta di Murtoli. After walking 2km (1.2 miles) from Erbaju, arrive at the tiny, secluded Plage d'Argent, from where the path continues for 500m (550yds) to the splendid and isolated Plage de Tralicetu.

Plage de Tralicetu to Tizzano (3–3.5 hours each way)

This is the least rewarding and most difficult part of the coastal trail. The trail is indistinct in places and easy to lose. From Plage de Tralicetu follow the jeep track west along the coast to the end, ignoring all side turnings. The track turns to a path marked sporadically by orange paint and cairns. Take special care as it is easy to lose the trail over the next 1.5km (1 mile). Beyond the headland, Tizzano comes into view and the route becomes rocky and tiring, traversing a steep slope above the coast. Finally, it drops down to the south end of the beach at Tizzano.

Tizzano to Phare de Senetosa (2.5 hours)

Depending on the condition of the track, it may be possible for ordinary vehicles to reach Cala di Barcaju 3km (2 miles) from Tizzano. If not you will need to walk this hot and dusty section. Just before the end of the dirt road, the path takes off into *maquis* to the right. At the time of writing there was no sign here and the path was far from obvious. After 2km (1.5 miles) reach the narrow shaded inlet of Cala Longa and shortly after, another perfect little cove and sandy beach, Cala di Tivella, where the boat trip from Propriano moors up to let passengers ashore. After 1.5km (1 mile) and a short ascent, reach the lighthouse of Senetosa. Built under the auspices of Corsican Giovanni de Cauro in 1609, the *Tour de Senetosa* is strategically positioned atop a rocky ridge above the lighthouse. The path to the tower takes off from the dirt track just east of the lighthouse.

Sunset Drive to Fozzano

If you're staying in the Propriano area, this little drive offers an unforgettable sunset view over the Golfe de Valinco. Take the D19 from from the hypermarket on the outskirts of town. After 4.5km (3 miles) reach Viggianello and stop by the sharp bend just after the village for a view. Continue to Arbellara and join the D19 climbing sharply to Fozzano, a village of forbidding granite houses. Here romantics can dwell on the setting of the enduring tale of blood and vengeance in Prosper Mérimée's *Colomba* and view the stern fortified houses, dating from the fourteenth and sixteenth centuries, where the tragic events are said to have unravelled. Past the next village, the narrow road climbs to the Col de Siu and a rocky outcrop of granite that glows red at sunset.

Phare de Senetosa to Campomore (3.5–4 hours)

From below the lighthouse, the path continues for 3km (2 miles) to the beautiful beach and sheltered inlet of Cala di Conca. This is a great spot to bathe and snorkel in crystal-clear turquoise sea. After 2km (1.5 miles) the path cuts inland for a short way, crossing a rocky peninsula, then dropping back down to Cala D'Agulia, a sandy inlet. The next 6km (4 miles) follow the rock shore more or less continuously past some spectacular eroded granite formations to Campomoro, where the path ends on the dirt road by the tower. Bear left to reach the village.

Olmeto

Perched high above the Golfe de Valinco, 8km (5 miles) north of Propriano, **Olmeto** is the epitome of a Corsican village, its high-rise granite houses strung out along the flank of a forested hill. Though blighted by the main road running through it, Olmeto has the feel of a prosperous town and in the eighteenth century was second only to Ajaccio in population. In the town centre and marked by a plaque is the house where Colomba Carabelli-Bartoli lived her last years and died at the age of 96. Guarding the valley and perched on a rocky outcrop are the ruins of the Castello della Rocca, the fourteenth-century stronghold of Arrigo della Rocca, a powerful local noble who became known as Count of Corsica.

Filitosa, Porto Pollo and the lower Taravo

From the Ajaccio road, the D157 winds along the north shore of the Golfe de Valinco to the lower Taravo Valley. Before the bridge over the river Taravo, the D57 is signed to the right to Corsica's best known Megalithic site, **Filitosa** (see boxed text).

Porto Pollo is a tidy little resort, guarding the northern entrance to the Golfe de Valinco. Lying at the end of the D757, it is largely unspoiled, with a sandy beach suitable for children.

Prosper Mérimée and the real Colomba Bartoli

This nineteenth-century French writer is best known for his novel *Carmen*, which was the source of Bizet's opera. An earlier work, *Colomba*, was inspired by the writer's experiences in Corsica as Inspector General for Public Buildings, during which time he compiled an inventory of the island's architectural and archaeological heritage. An impressive number of restaurants and bars are named after Colomba, this most 'famous' of Corsican women, who in the novel is portrayed as a young woman of beauty, character and insistence. In vendetta tradition Colomba incites her brother to take revenge for their father's death and in doing so sets up a chain of tragic events. The real Colomba Bartoli had lost her only son in an armed skirmish and was left embittered by the lack of justice, though she was well into middle age when the author met her and her daughter, then living in Olmeto.

Zonza, Alta Rocca

The Statue Menhirs of Filitosa

Overlooked by Prosper Merimée during his survey of Corsican antiquities, the statue menhirs of Filitosa were first noted in 1946 by Charles-Antoine Cesari, on whose family land they had lain undisturbed for centuries. By 1954, excavations were in progress and under Roger Grosjean the finds were documented and interpreted. In recent years opinions have divided and while the importance of the site has not diminished, our knowledge of the people who lived there and their reasons for erecting the menhirs remains speculative. Corsica's statue menhirs are believed to date from the second millennium BC to around 700 BC. Some have distinct facial features, others bear weapons or appear to have holes on the head, which may have been used to fix animal horns or other decoration in place.

Start with a visit to the museum, where several menhirs are on display, alongside arrowheads, pottery fragments and tools that have provided valuable clues to the life of Filitosa's early inhabitants.

From the museum a track leads to the largest of the menhirs, the sword and dagger-bearing Filitosa V. Further down the track are the cave shelters, settlement and fort-like *Torre*, sited on a rocky outcrop, where a line of menhirs have been placed side by side. Among them is Filitosa IX, with its clearly defined facial features. These overlook the valley and stream, reached by a path leading to pasture, where the remaining five menhirs, three of them armed, are lined up by an olive tree. Behind is the quarry where it is believed some of the stone originated.

Villages of the Alta Rocca

Inland from Propriano, the Rizzanese and its tributaries cut through an enclave of foothills spilling off the flanks of 2,136m (7,000ft) Monte Incudine, the highest summit in southern Corsica. An indecipherable maze of twisting roads reflects the complex topography of this area, known as the **Alta Rocca**. Clinging to the upper valley slopes, and defiantly straddling rocky ridges, its villages are divided by deep, brooding valleys, densely clad in forests of holm oak. The terrain is as impenetrable at it looks and for centuries provided safety from pirate raids and a stronghold for

the della Rocca lords in their struggle against the Genoese.

To explore the Alta Rocca by car allow at least a day and prepare for interminably winding roads and breath-taking views. Charmed by its string of photogenic villages, you may need more time to fit in the Bronze Age settlement of Castellu de Cucuruzzu, a visit to the museum at Levie and a trip to the Col de Bavella. A solution would be to stop overnight at Zonza or the Col, with the added attraction of seeing the Aiguilles de Bavella at sunrise or sunset.

Leave Propriano in the direction of Sartène, then bear left on the D268/D69 signposted to the Alta Rocca. After about 3km (2 miles) make a stop at the remarkable **Spin a Cavallu**

(Horse's Back), a narrow, single-arched thirteenth-century bridge in almost mint condition and believed to be Pisan rather than Genoese. Leaving the Rizzanese, pass a sign to the right on the D148, leading to the **Bains de Caldane**, an outdoor geothermal pool, whose 38°C (100°F) waters are curative. Climbing steadily, the distinctive red-tiled roofs of **Sainte Lucie-de-Tallano (Santa Lucia di Tallà)** (population 434) come into view. Terraced olive groves surround the cluster of hamlets, producing a high-quality though expensive oil. During the annual 'Festa di l'Olio Novu', celebrating the new season's oil in mid-March, things get pretty hectic here. To visit the Olive Mill, park in the village square and follow the sign to 'U Fragnu'. The guided visit reveals the different stages in production at the mill, which dates from 1848.

Back in the square, take a look at the war memorial, incorporating a slab of rare orbicular diorite, formed of a mix of white feldspar and dark green amphibole, crystallised in concentric circles and known locally as *Petra Ucchjata*, 'eye rock'. Behind the church, look for an imposing fortified house, built in the sixteenth century. Its seven machicolations hint at troubled times – they were used to pour boiling oil or stones on would-be assailants. The village was the stronghold of the della Rocca family, until the assassination of Count Rinuccio by the Genoese in 1511. The village Gîte d'étape, U Fragnonu, is basic but clean and serves up a great set dinner to hungry walkers.

Cucuruzzu and Capula – Bronze Age village and fort

About 5km (3 miles) from St Lucie de Tallano on the road to Levie turn left and after a further 3.5km (2 miles) park by the entrance to one of Corsica's top archaeological sites. The site is open all year but is unmanned between late October and early April. The entrance fee includes use of a recorded commentary, which guides you round the circular 1 to 1.5 hour walk. Sturdy footwear is needed as the path descends through forest, weaving among giant moss-clad boulders to emerge on a rocky outcrop. Here, the *casteddu* (fort) of **Cucuruzzu** sits atop a cluster of boulders. Ingeniously incorporating natural features into its construction, the fort presides over the valleys and ridges beyond, to a horizon dominated by the Aiguilles de Bavella.

Excavated in the 1960s, the site is believed to have been occupied from the start of the second millennium BC, when a terraced village developed. Around 1500 BC a two-storey tower in the style of the Sardinian *nuraghi* was added, possibly used for flour milling and storage of grain. Later, the upper floor of the tower was demolished and as settlement in the area increased, numerous chambers were added to the site, each with a designated function: storing grain, milling flour, butchery, pottery and weaving. Sometime during the first millennium BC, the place was abandoned, a move possibly prompted by a change from an agro-pastoral to a trading society.

125

Sainte Lucie de Tallano, Alta Rocca village of red-tiled houses, surrounded by olive groves

Spin'a Cavallu bridge, near Propriano

The Alpine Circuit of the Aiguilles de Bavella

Distance: 15.5km (9.5 miles)
Duration: 6 hours
Ascent & Descent: about 700m (2,300ft)
Highlights of the walk: views

This ranks as one of Corsica's best one-day mountain walks. It's not for the faint-hearted, nor a walk for wet or icy weather, as sections of the path are rocky, with a tricky part involving a fixed chain over an awkward slab of granite. But the sheer excitement of being right in among the Bavella peaks with their unrivalled views makes it worth the effort. Start before sunrise, take 3–4 litres of water per person, picnic, sun hat and sunscreen.

From the statue on the col, take the GR 20 north, following the red and white splashes of paint. After about 10 minutes, watch for the yellow way-marks taking off uphill to the right, which signal the start of the *Variante* Alpine. Follow these carefully as there are many side trails on this section. Climb up a steep gully to the rocky pass of Bocca di u Travunu, then descend through pines and contour over bare rock at the head of a valley. Scramble up a gully at the foot of the second of the jagged peaks, Tour II, which leads to the main obstacle of the walk, a chain-assisted descent over a tilting slab. Once this is out of the way, you tackle the longest climb of the day, following the toothed ridge to Bocca di u Pargulu, at 1,662m (4,986ft) the highest point of the walk. Now leave the ridge and begin a rocky traverse and 400m (1,300ft) descent into juniper scrub, turning to a knee-crunching zigzag though birch and then pine forest. Meet the GR 20 path and bear left to contour in and out of the ravines below the Aiguilles but high above the Asinao valley, in due course returning to the Col.

Strange, eroded pinnacles in the Aiguilles de Bavella

127

Follow signs for **Capula** and in 20 minutes arrive at the second fort, also occupied in the Bronze Age, and until 1259, when the medieval castle built there by Count Bianco was destroyed. Standing below the fort, the small chapel of San Lorenzu was built in 1917 from the stones of the adjoining Romanesque church, which had fallen into ruin. To complete the circle, follow signs for '*Accueil*' and return to the car park in 10 minutes.

While you are in the area don't miss the chance to eat at the acclaimed **Ferme Auberge A Pignata**, on your right down a dirt track as you make your way back to the D268 – there's no sign for it. Reservations are essential for this place, which produces its own *charcuterie* and serves sumptuous dinners and Sunday lunches of local specialities.

Levie (Livia) has several shops, bars and restaurants but the main attraction here is the **Musée de L'Alta Rocca**, reopening in 2007 in new premises on the edge of town on the D59 to Carbini. On permanent display are artefacts unearthed at Cucuruzzu, Capula and other sites. Of particular interest are the oldest human relics found in Corsica, known as the **Dame de Bonifacio** and believed to be from the seventh millennium BC, the skeleton of an extinct rodent and a fifteenth-century ivory crucifix, said to have been given to the parish church by Félix Peretti, who became Pope Sixtus V in 1585 and whose parents came from Levie. Another famous Peretti from Levie was Marie de Peretti (1902–45) who became a doctor in Paris, joining the Resistance during the war. Betrayed and denounced, she was sent to Ravensbrück, where she died in the gas chamber just weeks before the liberation of the camp.

Beyond Levie, the road gradient eases, passing San Gavinu and the best-stocked grocery in the area. **Zonza**, at 784m (2,572ft) in altitude, is one of the highest and also liveliest of the Alta Rocca villages. Sited at an important crossroads and with several hotels it is recommended as a base to explore the region. Perched on an exposed mountain flank, it lies high above the Asinao Valley, which is wedged between the Aiguilles de Bavella and Monte Incudine.

Aiguilles de Bavella

This 4km (2.5-mile) long massif of granite towers, piercing the skyline of southern Corsica, is one of the island's most impressive sights. Rising to 1,855m (6,084ft), the *Aiguilles*, which translates as 'needles', draw climbers to scale an infinite variety of challenging rock faces, and walkers who can pace themselves for gentle strolls as well as full-day hikes. Mountain and climbing guides can be hired at the Col, but competent walkers will have no problem following the splashes of bright paint on rocks and trees that waymark the routes here. Access to the peaks is from the 1,218m (4,000ft) **Col de Bavella**, the high point on what many will justly claim to be Corsica's most spectacular drive, which links the east coast resort of Solenzara and the villages of the Alta Rocca.

You need to be there at dawn or sundown to see the peaks at their most stunning, a fiery orange, muted pink or mauve, depending on the light. The longer shadows of early or late in the day also give texture to the granite, adding to the spectacle, which is further enhanced by the many gnarled Laricio pines. This is also the time of day when mouflon are more likely to be observed so it makes sense to stay overnight in the area. For a comfortable bed, head for Zonza, but if you don't mind roughing it, the Auberge du Col offers basic dormitory rooms as well as a solid menu of Corsican dishes. A couple of other bars and restaurants, a sparsely stocked grocery and a cluster of tin-roofed stone huts make up the 'village' of Bavella, whose surrounding pastures were given to the inhabitants of Conca when their village was founded by Napoleon III in 1851.

The Col can be closed by snow between November and March but in summer it is very popular and swarming with picnickers and those leaving messages or offerings around the white statue of **Notre Dame de la Neige**. It takes little effort to escape the crowds by following one of the walking trails that start at the pass.

Forest walk to Tafonu d'u Cumpuleddu (Trou de la Bombe)

Distance: 6km (4 miles) partly circular walk

Duration: 2 to 2.5 hours

Ascent & Descent: about 100m (320ft), but more if you climb to the viewpoint at the end

This is Corsica's second-most-famous 'hole in the rock' (after Capo Tafonato). From the Auberge du Col, take the path south through the pine forest, marked with the red and white paint splashes of the GR 20. After 10 to 15 minutes, take the path to the right, marked with red paint, following it gently uphill to the crest of the wooded ridge, where it joins a path coming in from the right. Coal tits and great spotted woodpeckers may be seen in the forest here. The trail now bears left and after a further 30 minutes, the 8m (26ft) wide keyhole, topped by a natural stone arch, comes into view. Now follow the cairns to the base of the hole. It is just possible to scramble into the hole, but it is as rewarding to follow the cairned path steeply uphill to the left from where a stupendous view opens up over a gaping ravine, plunging 500m (1,640ft) to the east coast. Return by the same route but after about 1km (0.5 mile) bear left along a dirt track, which contours back to the car park, through open forest high above the road from Zonza, offering great views of the Aiguilles.

From **Zonza,** look back towards the Aiguilles en route to **Quenza**, a village of substantial granite houses, and traditionally the summer retreat for the coastal communities of Porto Vecchio, escaping the threat of malaria. Its wealthy landowning families employed shepherds to move the flocks between coast and mountains, where they spent the summer months in tiny hamlets above Quenza. Today, with fewer than a hundred permanent inhabitants, the village struggles to survive.

Though little more than a cluster of shepherds' huts and a riding stables, **Jallicu** deserves mention for its rustic eatery in a traditional stone *bergerie*.

Above: Plage d'Argent, Sartenais
Below: Roccapina beach Sartenais

Above: Sartene's narrow streets are flanked by austere, granite houses

Right: Olive mill, Serra di Scopamene, Alta Rocca

Below: Bizarre eroded granite forms line the shore at Campomoro

Guests are seated around a single table in front of a log fire, while Pierrot, the owner, keeps the wine and conversation flowing and cooks up genuine Corsican mountain food, which includes produce from his own garden. It is 5km (3 miles) up a dirt track, which takes off to the right leaving Quenza and heading south-east on the D420. Just beyond the turn-off, below the main road, is the Romanesque chapel of Sainte Marie. The foundation stone to the left of the side door dates it from the year 1000, suggesting it may be one of the oldest surviving churches in Corsica.

Leaving Quenza there are great views back to the Aiguilles de Bavella. After about 5km (3 miles) you reach the D20, an alternative route back to St Lucie. This minor but surfaced road winds around a mountain spur, then dips down through pristine holm oak forest into the wild depths of the Rizzanese. The river roars below sleepy, red-roofed **Zoza**, the only village actually sited in the valley. Facing north and overshadowed by Rocher du Tafunatu, it gets little sun in winter but is worth a glance for the variety of village architecture, from simple *caseddu* to solid family mansions and fortified tower dwellings.

Continuing instead on the D420, the road contours high above the valley past a string of settlements, competing with one another for the best view. **Aullène (Auddè)**, a village of sombre houses, spills over a ridge at an important crossroads. The inhabitants, today numbering just 138, used to take their flocks to the south coast, over-wintering at Monaccia D'Aullène, 40km (25 miles) away as the crow flies. The two villages, though far apart, continue to share grazing

rights. **Hotel de La Poste** is the place to eat in the area, but book ahead.

To return to Propriano, take the very scenic D69, which hangs above a gaping gorge as it plunges into the valley, passing **Cargiaca**, a peaceful village built into the side of the mountain. The bends on this stretch of road number hundreds but there is little traffic.

The Coscione Plateau & Col de la Vaccia

Wedged between the forested Alta Rocca and the bare summits of the dividing range, the Plateau de Coscione is an anomaly among Corsica's landscapes, its exposed grassy moorlands and rocky outcrops being reminiscent of Britain, especially when shrouded in mist and drizzle. Today the place is eerily empty and worked by only a handful of shepherds yet its lush, ancestral pastures were once grazed by hundreds of flocks of sheep and goats and herds of cattle. When enough snow falls, which is rarely, it becomes a popular cross-country skiing venue.

To get a feel of the place take the very spectacular drive on the D69 over 1,193m (3,913ft) Col de la Vaccia, which links Aullène with Zicavo to the north. From the pass, the views south over the Alta Rocca and north to the central mountains are breathtaking. The pigs, however, are a little over-friendly and you may find yourself enjoying the view from your car!

Places to Visit

Propriano Tourist Office
By the marina
Also sells tickets for concerts in the theatre
Open in season 8.30am–8pm (Sunday 9am–1pm and 4–8pm); rest of the year 9am–12pm and 2–6 pm, Monday to Friday only
☎ 04 95 76 01 49
www.propriano.net

Sartène Tourist Office
Cours Soeur Amélie
Open 9am–7pm daily, mid-June to mid-September; out of season 9am–12pm and 2–6pm, Monday to Friday
☎ 04 95 77 15 40

Thermes de Baracci
near Propriano
Thermal baths
On the D557, outside Propriano
Open 9am–12pm and 3pm–8pm daily, 1 June to 30 September; out of season by arrangement
☎ 04 95 76 30 40 or 04 95 74 60 73

Diving U Levante
Propriano
By the Tourist Office
Plenty of good dive spots in the Golfe de Valinco
Open April to October
☎ 04 95 76 23 83
www.plonger-en-corse.com

Filitosa
Major prehistoric site in the Taravo valley on the D57
Museum, menhirs, ancient fort
Open 8.30am to sunset, daily April to October and by arrangement out of season
☎ 04 95 74 00 91

Musée de L'Alta Rocca
Levie
On the Carbini road, at the exit to the village
New museum of historic and ethnographic interest, housing among other things the skeleton of the 'Dame de Bonifacio'
Expected to reopen fully in 2007
☎ 04 95 78 46 34

Centre de Préhistoire
Sartène
By the hospital
Expected to reopen in 2007
☎ 04 95 77 01 09

Moulin à Huile (Olive Mill), Ste Lucie de Tallano
Near the village square
Open 9am–12pm and 3–6pm, summer only. Closed Sundays

Col de Bavella Mountain guide Jean-Paul Quilici
Climbing, hiking and canyoning guided trips in the Bavella massif
☎ 04 95 78 64 33 or 06 16 41 18 53
www.jpquilicimontagne.com

Boat Trips

I Paesi di u Valinco Promenade en Mer
Propriano
Boat excursions from Propriano to the Golfe de Valinco, Scandola and Golfe de Porto, Bonifacio and the Sartenais coast. The last includes spectacular deserted beaches only accessible by sea or on foot
Daily, mid-May to late September, subject to demand
☎ 04 95 76 16 78
www.corsica.net/promenade

Locanautic boat rental
Propriano
At the marina, boat rental by the half day, day or longer, ideal for access to the Sartenais coast
Open all year
☎ 04 95 76 31 31
www.locanautic.com

7. Ajaccio and surrounds

Ajaccio (Aiacciu)

With around 60,000 inhabitants, Ajaccio is Corsica's largest town, the capital of Corse-du-Sud and seat of the regional government. Its sparkling, crescent-shaped bay, ringed by forested hills and distant peaks, attracted both Romans and Saracens but it was the warring *seigneurs* who ruled the '*Au delà des Monts*" until it came under the control of the Bank of St George and Genoa and Corsicans were banned from living there. Seized by Sampiero Corso, there followed a brief period of French domination from 1553–9, but once the Genoese regained control they held on to Ajaccio steadfastly until the rebellion of 1729. By coincidence, 1769, the year of Paoli's defeat at Ponte Nuovo, was also the year of Napoleon's birth in Ajaccio. After the collapse of the Anglo-Corsican Kingdom in 1796, the French returned and the town became capital of the newly formed *département* of Liamone, while Bastia remained capital of Golo. In 1811, under imperial decree, they merged into one, with Ajaccio as capital, to the annoyance of Bastia, a situation which remained unchanged until 1975, when the present divisions of Haute-Corse and Corse-du-Sud were agreed.

With its palm-shaded promenade and cafés, image-conscious Ajaccio could easily belong on the French

Riviera, but behind the chic façade this is a city that is struggling to cope with its own expansion. In 1801, when the population was just 5,000, it was widely considered the Mediterranean's prettiest town and one with a favourable winter climate; a fact noted by the British, who settled here in numbers. Today, ugly tower blocks are stacked up on the hills because of the shortage of land for building.

Visitors will find enough to keep them amused for half a day or so, once you get used to the paradox that Ajaccio's most venerated citizen, Napoleon, did nothing to further the cause of independence for his island of birth, yet he is the town's star tourist attraction. It's worth knowing that accommodation can be hard to find in Ajaccio, even out of season. For eating out, however, you'll have the best choice of restaurants anywhere on the island; but look further afield than those clustered around the port, which do not always offer the best food or value for money.

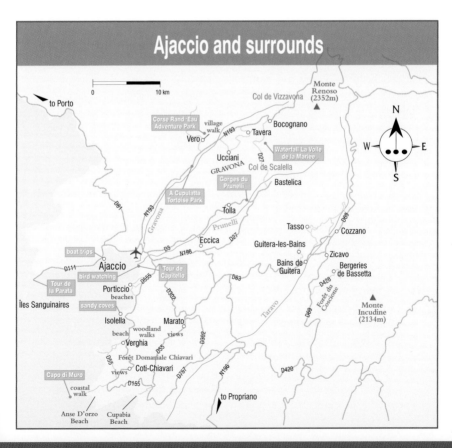

Ajaccio and surrounds

One place worthy of special mention is **A Casa**, where on Friday and Saturday nights a magician entertains the guests at dinner.

The main approach to the old town is along the seafront, where it is advisable to park if you are travelling by car, to avoid the traffic-clogged centre. **Cours Napoléon**, running parallel, is the principal commercial district, while the narrow streets between form the historic quarter, ending at the citadel, and are packed with bars, restaurants and boutiques. On **Rue Fesch**, flanked with ochre stuccoed houses, stands one of Ajaccio's surprises, the **Musée Fesch**. On display inside the nineteenth-century *Palais Fesch* is France's second most significant collection of Italian Renaissance art (after the Louvre). **Cardinal Fesch**, half-brother of Letizia, Napoleon's mother, had an illustrious career in the church before accompanying his nephew to Italy in 1796, as Commissioner of Supplies to the Army. Subsequent appointments as Archbishop of Lyon in 1802, Cardinal and ambassador to Rome, enabled the cleric to indulge in his passion for art in which he amassed an astonishing collection of canvasses. Among those on display are works by Titian, Botticelli, Veronese and Bellini, and, as is to be expected, there is a room in the basement dedicated to portraits of the Emperor. Adjoining the gallery is the nineteenth-century **Chapelle Impériale** and tomb of the Bonapartes, which was built on the orders of Cardinal Fesch, who wanted the family remains to be kept together in one place. There is one notable exception, Napoleon himself, who is interred in Paris. The left wing of Palais Fesch houses the **Municipal Library**, whose 70,000 volume wall-to-wall collection was instigated by Napoleon's brother Lucien in 1800 and includes a 1483 Bible and an atlas printed in 1657.

Square Campinchi, overlooking the port, hosts a lively local produce market but when it comes to local cheese and *charcuterie*, you should taste before buying. This leads to **Place Foch**, where a white marble statue of Napoleon as First Consul was added to the original granite fountain, embellished with four lions. The *Petit Train* departs from the lower end of the tree-lined square for a 45-minute circuit of the city and a longer trip out to Îles Sanguinaires. **Boat trips** with *Nave Va* to the islands and further afield to Scandola, Calvi and Bonifacio depart from the port facing the square.

Leading off the upper end of Place Foch, Cours Grandval skirts the **Place de Gaulle**, with another statue of Napoleon, this time on horseback with his four brothers. Just off the square in rue Levie is the **Musée A Bandera**, which portrays sensitively the many facets of Corsican history and culture, from medieval strongholds to the heroes of the *Résistance*, when the island was occupied by Nazi Germany. Entering the **Quartier des Étrangers**, built in the nineteenth century to accommodate the fashionable British visitors, who came for the mild winters, the street is bordered by fine mansions and the former Grand Hôtel, now the **Regional Assembly of Corsica**. On the right stands the one-time Anglican church, built at the instigation of Thomasina Campbell, who resided here and in writing *Notes on the Island of Corsica* encouraged others to do so. Now Cours Géneral Leclerc, the street ends at **Place D'Austerlitz** where another monument to the Emperor lists his victories and achievements and, on a more down-to-earth note, Napoleon is said to have played as a child in a small cave.

The oldest part of Ajaccio is the enclave of sunless passages and tall, red-tiled buildings adjacent to the **citadel**. Dating from 1492, the year the city was founded, the original citadel was added to by the French in 1553 but took on its present form after the Genoese returned to govern in 1559. The buildings are occupied by the military, but the Tourist Office arranges visits in the summer months. Opposite the citadel, the privately-owned **Musée du Capitello** provides further insight into the town's history. A plaque on the building's wall identifies it as the birthplace of Danielle Casanova, who died in Auschwitz in 1943. Another resistance hero, Fred Scamaroni, took his own life in the citadel, to avoid revealing vital secrets after he was captured by the occupying German forces. In his own blood he wrote on the wall of his cell: 'I did not talk, long live France, long live De Gaulle.'

Ajaccio's ochre-façaded sixteenth-century **cathedral** is in Venetian Renaissance style and attributed to Giacomo della Porta. On the right is the marble font where Napoleon was baptised at the age of almost two, while a pillar left of the nave bears a plaque indicating the Emperor's express wish to be buried alongside his family in their vault in the cathedral. Above the altar in the first chapel to the left is the *Vierge du Sacré Cœur* by Eugène Delacroix.

Îles Sanguinaires

This string of islands guards the entrance to the Golfe D'Ajaccio, 12km (7.5 miles) from the city, and is a popular spot for locals at weekends. Of ancient volcanic rock, the islands are composed of bands of darker diorite and lighter granite. At sunset they glow blood-red, and some people believe their name stems from this. Older maps show them as Îles Sagonares, a more probable, if less exciting answer – Sagone being the Golfe to the north. The road to the islands heads west out of the city along a shore of pretty sandy coves, somewhat spoiled by the extensive holiday developments creeping ever higher up the hillside. From the car park, a 30-minute stroll leads around La Parata, a rocky hillock crowned by a 12m (40ft) high, well-preserved sixteenth-century Genoese tower. The flora is of interest and includes salt-tolerant species such as *Limonium arcticulatum*, *Halimione portulacoides* and *Allium commutatum* in amongst a carpet of yellow-flowering *Senecio leucanthemifolius*. A lighthouse dating from 1865 stands on Mezzo Mare, the largest of the islands, together with the ruins of a sanatorium, where fishermen returning from Africa and suspected of leprosy were held in quarantine.

Boat trips to the islands run from Ajaccio, while La Parata is also served by Bus 5 from the city.

Coastal Drive South of Ajaccio

The region south of Ajaccio offers a beautiful but developed coastline contrasting with a wild and mountainous interior, criss-crossed by scenic and winding roads. Past the airport, the sprawling urbanisation of **Porticcio (Purtichju)** has plentiful restaurants and shops and a glorious golden arc of sand, the first of four fringing an azure sea. Dividing the beaches of Agosta and Ruppione is **Isolella**, a lizard-shaped peninsula whose coves offer sheltered bathing, even when the *mistral* blows. Next along is **Verghia** (Verchja), whose coarse sand is lapped by a turquoise sea, framed by offshore granite rocks, where shags haul themselves out to dry their wings.

These beautiful beaches are backed by the **forest of Chiavari**, named after a town in Liguria whose inhabitants were moved here by the Genoese in 1714. In 1855, the French set up a penal colony for 800 prisoners which closed in 1906, when the prisoners were moved to Cayenne. Behind the beach at Verghia, an interpretive board signals the start of a 2.5km (1.5 miles) circular walk through cork oak woodlands. Rich in wildlife, you may be lucky enough to spot a Hermann's tortoise in the woods, as well as many birds.

From Verghia, the D155 contours 250m (820ft) above the coast but access

Left: Ajaccio hosts many festivals throughout the year
Below: Ajaccio, Place Foch and statue of Napoleon

to the rocky headlands is difficult as most of the land is privately owned and peppered with luxury villas. It is possible to drive part of the way and then walk to **Capo di Muro**. To descend to the gorgeous secluded cove of Anse D'Orzo from the Capo di Muro road, the track is too rough for normal cars but it is about a 40-minute walk.

Once past the turning to Capo Nero, the *maquis* in all its glory takes over and the road turns to a patchwork quilt of short-lasting repairs. The road is slow but worth it for the views, which are spectacular. If by now you are longing for the sea, take the next turning right to **Plage de Cupabia**, which leads down to a broad sandy beach, backed by dunes. The *Mare e Monti Sud* trail takes off into the *maquis* from the approach road.

From Verghia an alternative high-level route, the D55, heads inland past the ruins of the penal camp, climbing tortuously through dense forest but clearing every so often to offer tantalising glimpses of the coast. Turn right to the village of **Coti Chiavari (Coti Chjavari)**, where a terrace reveals the view in all its splendour. A little further, Hotel Le Belvedere, deserving of its name, offers a mouth-watering panorama of the Golfe d'Ajaccio. Past the hotel, a sharp and winding scenic descent rejoins the lower D155.

Instead of descending via Coti Chiavari, the D55 offers a high-level route hugging the mountainous backbone. Emerging from the pine and cork oak forests, there is a fine view down to the fertile Taravo Valley from **Bocca di Chenova**. Beyond Marato (Maratu), which has a cluster of houses and an auberge, cross the D302, continuing past a granite outcrop. This stretch of road is rewarding for birdwatchers with possible sightings of red kite, buzzard, goldfinch, jay and crag martin. The D55 eventually joins the main N196 Ajaccio to Propriano road, just east of the Col de St Georges, with its mineral water springs and bottling plant.

Bastelica and the Gorges du Prunelli

A visit to the birthplace of Corsican hero Sampiero Corso combines with outstanding mountain scenery to make a worthwhile outing in the Ajaccio

---

Spreading Wings

Shag *Phalocrocorax aristotelis*
These members of the cormorant family were probably given their strange name by sailors because of their crest. Unlike other seabirds, their feathers have very little oil, which helps them dive for fish and eels. They are often seen perched on rocks, wings outstretched, as if drying them in the wind, but this may also be a signal to other shags.

Sampiero Corso

Bastelica has achieved almost legendary status because of its associations with Sampiero Corso (San Pieru Corsu). Born into a peasant family in 1498, Corsica's first freedom fighter's story has all the drama of a Shakespearean tragedy. Rising to military prominence in the service of Catherine de Medici, the distinguished soldier went on to save the life of the Dauphin Henri II of France in battle in 1543, for which he was rewarded with the rank of General of the Corsican infantry. Returning home, the now 50-year-old hero married Vanina D'Ornano, the teenage daughter of a Corsican aristocrat. Suspicious of his ambitions, the Genoese imprisoned Sampiero following his marriage, but intervention by the French King secured his release. With the support of the King, Sampiero set about ridding his homeland of the Genoese and in 1557, Corsica was declared part of France. Disappointingly, the island was handed back to Genoa just two years later, leaving Sampiero to fight on unsupported. As the web of political ambition and intrigue spread wider, Sampiero suspected his wife of collusion with the Genoese and murdered her. A reward of 2,000 ducats offered by the Genoese on his head, the hunt for Sampiero was taken up by his wife's family in traditional 'vendetta' style. On 17 January 1567, in an ambush orchestrated by Vanina's brothers, he met his death at the hands of Genoese troops in the village of Eccica, just off the Ajaccio to Propriano road

region. **Bastelica** lies near the head of the **Prunelli Valley**, whose trout-rich torrent is fed by melting snow from 2,352m (7,714ft) Monte Renoso, an imposing peak on the central range, which dominates the view. In summer, the Prunelli Valley is linked by the jaw-dropping D27 mountain route over **Col de Scalella** to the Gravona Valley to the north, making a very scenic circular route.

Bastelica is reached by a choice of route, snaking up either side of the Prunelli valley and meeting just short of the village to make a convenient circular loop. South of the river, the road is wider but marginally less scenic as it weaves through forest. The northern route gives dramatic views of the **Prunelli Gorge** as it hugs the precipice edge above the rapids. There are several worthwhile places to pull off the road, by the bridge over the river, in the gorge itself and at the pretty village of **Tolla**, perched on a spur high above the reservoir created by the Prunelli dam and hydroelectric project. Dominating the scenery here is a rugged ridge of tooth-like peaks, spilling off the central ranges.

Opposite Bastelica's church is a century-old bronze statue of the defiant Sampiero Corso, raised dagger in hand. Another, more recent bust of the hero adorns the upper road of the village. Though the Bastelica of Sampiero's era was torched and razed to the ground by Spanish and Genoese troops in 1564, the house where he was born has been rebuilt and is marked by a plaque. Today's village is graced by elegant fountains and many substantial houses from the seventeenth and eighteenth centuries, surrounded by apple orchards. Swelling to 1,500 in the summer months, the year-round population of 400 make a living from passing tourist traffic and the village's famous *charcuterie* industry, amply provided for by the many '*porcs coureurs*' who roam freely in its forested surrounds.

The Gravona Valley

The N193 Ajaccio to Corte road follows the broad and fertile Gravona Valley. Many visitors, relieved to be on a road in which fourth gear is finally an option, don't bother stopping at all. This is a pity, because there are a number of interesting places along the way and as varied and beautiful mountain scenery as you could wish for. Whether you chose to explore en route to Corte or treat the valley as a day trip in its own right, you will need the best part of a day to do it justice.

Do it by Train

The great thing about this area is that you can get there by train. Take the Ajaccio to Bastia morning train, leaving it at Bocognano. Explore this typical Corsican mountain town, with its traditional wood-fired bakery, then walk the '*Sentier des Bandits*' (3.45 hours) down to the village of Tavera. Catch the train here to return to Ajaccio, or continue the walk on the '*Sentier des Bergers*' (2.45 hours) to Ucciani, where the late afternoon train will take you back to Ajaccio.

Free-range Pigs

'*Porcs coureurs*' are domestic pigs allowed to roam freely by their owners. Amongst their favourite foods are chestnuts, which they feed on copiously and which give Corsican *charcuterie* its unique and rich taste. Some free-range pigs raid picnic spots, where they have been known to harass visitors. Don't feed them. You are unlikely to confuse these pigs with '*sangliers*' because wild boar are shy and seldom seen as they are the obsessive object of Corsican weekend hunting forays. You will probably see evidence of them, as they are efficient at ploughing up the ground where they browse for food.

Leaving Ajaccio, the broad floodplain of the Gravona has been exploited to the full as the city's light industrial quarter pushes inland, to the exclusion of the once important orchards and rich pasture. Eventually, the mountains draw nearer, and so too does the real Corsica. To the right of the road **A Cupulatta Tortoise Park** is one of the island's top family attractions. As well as the native Hermann's tortoise, there are 150 species from all over the world and a total of 3,000 animals in the park, which also serves as a research and breeding facility.

Vero Village Walk

Turn left on the D4 and in 3.5km (2 miles) reach the village of **Vero (Veru)**, where a short walking trail gives a flavour of rural life. Note the large wooden cross at the entrance to the village, and another erected further on. Wooden crosses, some huge in size, were erected to protect villages from evil or following the occurrence of a miracle.

At the second cross turn sharp left to reach the *Mairie* – easily recognisedby its clock face and yellow postbox. Park here and take a glance at the map of two marked walking trails that start further along the road by the water outlet.

The shorter of the two trails (35 minutes) shows a side to village life that is all but gone, as nobody farms here any ore and the terraced fields stand idle. The trail (marked by wooden posts with a brown rectangular plaque) climbs through walled fields, crosses a stream and follows a wall to the right, emerging into pine forest with an understorey of tree-heather. Spectacular views open to the valley below, while ahead stands an outcrop of crimson rock, known as the castle –'U Casteddu'. Following a right fork, the path contours briefly then joins a gravel track, descending past several stone buildings. Bear right into the village past one of its original wood-fired ovens.

If you're backtracking to the N193, stop for a drink at the picturesque Bar Luna Rossa before leaving the village. Alternatively, if you're feeling adventurous, stay on the winding D4 on its tortuous but scenic way north into the mountainous heart of the Cinarca region. Just above Vero the **Corse Rand'Eau Adventure Park** is a fantasy of ropes and aerial walkways that will thrill budding Tarzans of all ages.

The N193 continues to **Bocognano (Bucugná)**, an attractive town set among chestnut groves on a balcony overlooking the Gravona, roughly midway between Ajaccio and Corte. There are a traditional bakery and several good restaurants in the village, which was birthplace to two famous nineteenth-century bandits, Jacques and Antoine Bellacoscia. Their father was born a Bonelli but his reputation as a ladies' man, having fathered 18 children by three sisters, gave him the nickname of *'bellacoscia'* – beautiful thighs. After an attempted murder and kidnapping, the brothers took to the mountains where they thwarted and mocked the authorities for half a century, achieving almost cult status. Bocognano hosts one of the busiest country festivals in Corsica, *La foire à la Châtaigne*, a three-day celebration of chestnuts, in early December each year.

La Volle de la Mariée – Bridal Veil Falls

To reach the falls, take the D27 south, just past the *gendarmerie* at the western entrance to Bocognano. After 3km (2 miles), the falls come into view. Park near the bridge and cross the stile. Where the trail divides, take the left fork and reach the falls after 10 minutes' climb on a rough trail. The 70m (230ft) falls are best viewed in the afternoon sun and in spring when the meltwater makes them quite spectacular. In summer they may disappoint.

The legend goes that Grisalida, wife of the Count of Corsica, had injured her hand and only the sacred waters of the *Funtana Santa* would heal it. The place was cursed by an ogre, who could only be placated by a gift of her bridal veil. Dipping her hand in the water she was instantly cured, but the ogre had

Opening Hours of Museums

FESCH MUSEUM – AJACCIO MUSEUM OF FINE ARTS
From May to September : Monday 10.30 a.m. to 6 p.m.,
Wednesday 10.30 a.m. to 6 p.m.,Thursday noon to 6 p.m.,Friday
noon to 6 p.m. and 8.30 p.m. in July and August only for temporary
exhibition rooms, Saturday 10.30 a.m. to 6 p.m.,Sunday noon to 6
p.m. Closed on Tuesday
From October to April : Monday 10 a.m. to 5 p.m., Wednesday 10
a.m. to 5 p.m., Thursday noon to 5 p.m. Friday noon to 5 p.m.,
Saturday 10 a.m. to 5 p.m. and Sunday noon to 5 p.m. Closed on
Tuesday and Sunday (except on the 3rd week-end of each month)
Price : 8€ - Reduced fee : 5€ - Fidelity card : 30€

IMPERIAL CHAPEL
*Timetable identical to Palais Fesch. Subject to occasional changes
to the opening times
Price: 3€*

CITY LIBRARY – PATRIMONIAL READING ROOM
All year long: from Monday to Friday : 9 to 12am and from 2 to 5pm

BONAPARTE HOUSE NATIONAL MUSEUM
Last admission 30 minutes before closing hour.
From April 1st to September 30th. From 10.30 am to 12.30 and from
1.15 pm. to 6 p.m. Closed on Monday.
From October 1st to March 31st. From 10.30 a.m. to 12.30 and from
1.15 p.m. to 4.30 p.m. Closed on Monday
*Price : 7€ submitted to change. Under 26 years old : free. Audio-guided visit :
40 min. Downloadable, see the museum website.*

NAPOLEONIC MUSEUM – CITY HALL
From June 15th to September 15th : from 9 a.m. to 11.45 a.m. and
from 2 p.m. to 5.45 p.m. monday to friday
From September 16th to June 14th : from 9 a.m. to 11.45 a.m. and
from 2 p.m. to 4.45 p.m. monday to friday
Closed on Saturday, Sunday, public holidays and in case of official
reception. *Price : 2.50€. Free : under 15.*

LAZARET OLLANDINI – MARC-PETIT MUSEUM
From June to September, on Saturday from 4 p.m. to 7 p.m.
Free entrance

A BANDERA MUSEUM.
History of Corsica
Closed

Office Municipal de Tourisme d'Ajaccio
3 boulevard du Roi Jérôme - BP 21
20181 Ajaccio Cedex 01

Horaires des musées

Palais Fesch – Musée des beaux-arts d'Ajaccio
De mai à septembre : lundi 10h30-18h, mercredi 10h30-18h, jeudi
12h-18h, vendredi 12h-18h et 20h30 en juillet et août uniquement
pour les salles d'expositions temporaires, samedi 10h30-18h,
dimanche 12h-18h. Fermé le mardi
D'octobre à avril : lundi 10h-17h, mercredi 10h-17h, jeudi 12h-17h,
vendredi 12h-17h, samedi 10h-17h et le dimanche de 12h-17h.
Fermé le mardi et le dimanche (sauf le troisième week-end de chaque
mois)
Tarifs : plein tarif 8€, tarif réduit 5€, carte de fidélité 30€.

Chapelle impériale
Mêmes horaires que le Palais Fesch.Ouverture sous toutes
réserves. Contact : Palais Fesch : 04.95.26.26.26
Tarifs : 3€

Bibliothèque municipale, salle patrimoniale
Toute l'année : Du lundi au vendredi de 9h/12h et de 14h/17h

Musée national de la Maison Bonaparte
Dernière admission 1/2 heure avant l'heure de fermeture.
Du 1er avril au 30 septembre 10h30-12h30 / 13h15-18h fermé le
lundi
Du 1er octobre au 31 mars de 10h30-12h30 / 13h15-16h00 Fermé
lundi
Tarifs : 7 € sous réserve de modification. - de 26 ans : gratuit
Durée de la visite audio guidée : 40 minutes.
Téléchargeable sur le site du musée

Salon Napoléonien de l'Hôtel de Ville
Du 15 juin au 15 septembre de 9h à 11h45 et de 14h à 17h45
Du 16 septembre au 14 juin de 9h à 11h45 et de 14h à 16h45
Fermé samedi, dimanche, jours fériés et en cas de réception officielle
Tarifs : 2,50 € - gratuit -15 ans

Lazaret Ollandini – Musée Marc-Petit
De juin à septembre les samedis de 16h à 19h.
Entrée libre. Visite groupe selon demande
Musée ouvert aussi lors des différents évènements.

Musée A Bandera
Musée d'histoire Corse Méditerranée
Fermeture définitive depuis le 31/12/14

I ✳
AJACCIO

Office Municipal de Tourisme d'Ajaccio
3 boulevard du Roi Jérôme - BP 21
20181 Ajaccio Cedex 01
tél. 04 95 51 53 03 - fax 04 95 51 53 01
www.ajaccio-tourisme.com

A Cupulatta Tortoise Centre

Cascade du voile de la mariée in the Gravona Valley

spotted her from his cliff-top perch and pushed away the rocks that held back the water of the stream he had dammed, unleashing a torrential flood. In flight Grisalida lost her veil and as the ogre attempted to retrieve it he was swept away by the flood he had created. The ogre perished, the lady escaped and the waterfall is still there today.

The Upper Taravo Valley

The mountainous terrain east of Ajaccio remained for centuries a secret enclave and inland refuge from Saracen attack. Today, even in the height of summer it is seldom invaded, perhaps because its country roads are so narrow and twisting. For those keen to experience mountain Corsica, this forested valley, culminating in 2,136m (7,000 ft) Monte Incudine, is a credible alternative to the busier Corte area. You could spend days exploring its back roads and not cover the same route twice. Walkers will find plenty to get their teeth into with its well-marked trails that dip in and out of the chestnut forests but you may also be drawn to the high summits and the GR 20 mountain path, just a few hours' hike away. The Mare a Mare Centre coast to coast route also traverses the heart of this genuine Corsican backcountry and offers a splendid two-day circular walk for those who want a short and not overly demanding trek. The route takes in Zicavo, Guitera, Tasso and Cozzano, with *gîte* accommodation available at all places.

Zicavo is a solid granite village, wedged up a side valley, where its houses are strung out along the flank of the mountain. The village rose to fame in the Napoleonic era when Jean Charles Abbatucci, born there in 1770, shot through the ranks to become general at the age of 25. Today it's a sleepy little place, with a rather nice guesthouse, Le Paradis.

From Zicavo the D69 winds through chestnut and beech forest to Col de la Vaccia; 4.5km (3 miles) before the pass a turning left on the rutted D120 leads through the dense beech woods of the **Forêt de Coscione**, twisting tortuously to emerge above the tree line at the **Bergeries de Bassetta**, where goats' cheese is still made. A rustic guesthouse makes an early start possible for those intent on reaching the 2,136m (7,006ft) summit of **Monte Incudine**, a seven-hour round trip to southern Corsica's highest peak.

Down in the main valley, the **Bains de Guitera** has rather passed its glory as a spa but you can still enjoy the natural hot water by bathing in one of the rustic tubs, just off the main road in the village centre.

Places to Visit

Ajaccio Tourist Office

3, boulevard du Roi Jérôme
Open 8am–8pm daily (Sunday 9am–11pm & 3–7pm), July and August; 8am–12.30pm & 2–6pm, Monday to Friday (Saturday 8am–12pm & 2–5pm, closed Sundays and public holidays) November to March; at other times of year 8am–7pm daily (Saturday 9am–1pm, closed Sundays)
☎ 04 95 51 53 03
www.tourisme.fr/ajaccio

Parc Naturel Régional de la Corse

2, rue Sergent Casalonga
Information on the park, leaflets and guidebooks for Corsica's walking routes.
☎ 04 95 51 79 00
www.parc-naturel-corse.com

Ajaccio Museum Card

Valid for 7 days, the card allows entry to most museums, offering considerable savings. On sale at the museums and Tourist Office.

Musée Fesch

50, rue Fesch
Open 2–6pm Monday, 10.30am–6pm Tuesday to Thursday and weekends and Friday 2–9.30pm July and August; 9.30am–12pm & 2–6pm, Tuesday to Sunday April to June & September; 9.30am–12pm and 2–5.30pm Tuesday to Saturday only October to March.
☎ 04 95 21 48 17
www.musee-fesch.com

Maison Bonaparte

Rue St Charles
Open 9am–12pm and 2–6pm daily except Monday morning, April to September; 10am–12pm and 2–4.45pm daily except Monday morning, October to March
☎ 04 95 21 43 89

Musée A Bandera

1, rue Levie
Open 9am–7pm, Monday to Saturday (9am–12pm Sunday), 1 July to 15 September; 9am–12pm and 2–6pm Monday to Saturday (closed Sunday) 16 September to 30 June.
☎ 04 95 51 07 34

Musée du Capitello

18, Bd D. Casanova
Open 10am–12pm and 2–6pm daily (except Sunday afternoon), April to September.
☎ 04 95 21 50 57

A Cupulatta Tortoise Park, Gravona Valley

Gravona Valley, on the N193 just north of the D129 junction
Open 9am–7pm daily 1 June to 31 August and 10am–5.30pm daily 30 March to 31 May and 1 September to 17 November
☎ 04 95 52 82 34
www.acupulatta.com

Corse Rand'Eau Adventure Park

Gravona Valley
Just outside Vero on the D4 in the Gravona Valley
Open from Easter to mid-October, daily in high season, otherwise Wednesdays and weekends only
☎ 04 95 21 89 01
www.corse-rand-eau.ht.st

8. Porto and surrounds

Flanked by an impregnable jumble of granite pinnacles, nowhere epitomises the ruggedness of Corsica more starkly than **Porto**. Crammed behind a tight little bay in the innermost reaches of the Golfe de Porto, whose stunning scenery is now protected as a UNESCO World Heritage Site, for centuries this defiant settlement served as the port for Ota, which was prudently sited inland in case of Saracen attacks. Its solid square watchtower, erected in 1549 by the Genoese, guarded the landing stage and important mule route up the Gorges de Spelunca to Evisa.

Today Porto is a burgeoning resort and a base for hiking in the area, exploring the Calanche and the Gorges de Spelunca as well as for boat trips to the Scandola Nature Reserve, which leave from the marina by the river estuary. If you're driving, head for the shaded car park on the left bank, accessed by turning off the D81 south of the town, signed to 'Porto Rive Gauche'. The car park is also handy for Porto's **pebble beach**, but bathing is not recommended here if the sea is rough as there can be an undertow. A foot-

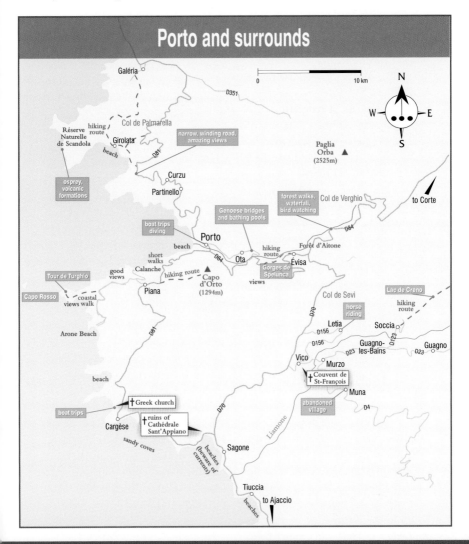

bridge over the river brings you to the quay where diving operators tout for business. With an exceptional clarity of water, **diving and snorkelling** can be very rewarding with precious red coral being the main attraction. Behind the quay is Porto's compact old quarter, which is almost entirely given over to hotels, shops and restaurants. A path leads to the rocky outcrop on which the **watchtower** is sited. There's a small entrance charge to visit the tower, but it's worth it for views of the town and its dramatic surrounds, as well as an interesting exhibit on Genoese towers in Corsica. The ticket includes a visit to the **Musée de la Bruyère**, a small exhibition about heather. Also worth a look is the **Aquarium**, housed in the old powder magazine on Place de la Marine, and showcasing Mediterranean fish like *loup de mer* (sea bass) and *daurade* (sea bream), that you may already have noticed on local menus, and others including rays, scorpion fish, moray eels, anemones and ornate wrasse. The rest of town, where the bank, supermarket and pharmacy are located, lies about 1.5km (1 mile) inland by the junction with the D81.

Exploring from Porto

All routes to and from Porto are narrow, twisting roads, bestowed with countless blind corners and views that will tempt you to stop where you should not. Allow plenty of time and in summer start at dawn to avoid the bottlenecks and enjoy the mountains lit up in the warm glow of the early morning sun. The Porto region is better known for scenery than beaches and it's becoming increasingly popular with walkers because of its hugely varied and spectacular mountain and coastal hikes, the most famous being the Mare e Monti.

Les Calanche

Arguably one of Corsica's top five scenic spots, the unearthly pinnacles of Les Calanche have been eroded by wind and water into a chaos of shapes to ignite the imagination. In 1880 writer Guy de Maupassant described them as 'monstrous figures and a nightmare menagerie turned to stone at the whim of some extravagant deity'. Composed of pink-tinged, alkaline granite, rather rare elsewhere in Europe, they plunge 400m (1300ft) to the deep-blue Golfe de Porto, affording one of the island's most iconic views. The tight and winding 3km (2-mile) stretch of road, built in 1850 and snaking through this jumble of natural sculptures, is an achievement in itself, but offers few obvious places to stop and admire the scenery. Besides, the prospect of encountering a 50-seater coach is enough to make most drivers not want to stop at all. The solution is to go on foot and there are several enjoyable short walks, as well as a challenging longer hike.

Some parking is available at Les Roches Bleues, the café east of Les Calanche, otherwise it's best to park in Piana and walk from there. The classic stroll is to the heart-shaped hole, 'Le Coeur', along a little path that starts from the Café Le Moulin, just below the road at the Piana end.

Les Calanche – 'Ancien chemin d'Ota a Piana', the old mule trail from Ota to Piana

Distance: 3km (2 miles) circular walk, part road and part trail
Duration: 1 hour
Ascent & Descent: about 100m (320ft)
What to take: walking shoes or boots, water, sun hat, sun screen
Highlights of the walk: Les Calanche without the traffic; wonderful views

Les Calanche start 1km (0.5mile) east of Piana and those who plan to walk should park by the football field, up a little access track to the right of the D81, coming from Piana – if you arrive at the bridge and Café Le Moulin, you have gone too far. Coming from Porto, drive through the Calanche, pass Café Le Moulin, cross the little bridge and the track is on your left. Now walk east along the D81 for about 1.5km (1 mile) until you come to Les Roches Bleues (toilets and refreshments). Just before Les Roches Bleues on your right-hand side, a shaded trail, marked with blue and white paint, takes off up steep stone steps among the trees. Don't be put off by the steep start as it will shortly level off and head west, contouring above the road. The views are wonderful but you must watch your step as the path, the main thoroughfare before the road was built, is rough in places. After about 30 minutes, join another trail coming in from the left and descend into woodland. Ignore the next turning left and cross the footbridge, which leads to the sports field. Cross it diagonally to reach the car park.

Les Calanche – Château Fort

Distance: 1km (0.5 miles) each way
Duration: 20 to 30 minutes each way
Ascent & Descent: mostly level
What to take: walking shoes or boots, water, sun hat, sun screen
Highlights of the walk: wonderful views of Les Calanche and the Golfe de Porto

The trail starts by the prominent rock 'Tête de Chien', shaped like a dog's head, on a sharp bend 0.5km (600 yds) from Les Roches Bleues in the direction of Porto, where cars park along the side of the road. The path, marked in blue and white paint, starts among rocks and trees just off the road but it is not obvious and several side trails make it confusing. It's a fairly easy trail, leading along and then to one side of the crest of a ridge, reaching a rocky platform, known as Le Château Fort. The views of the Golfe de Porto are unsurpassed, especially at sunset.

Capo D'Orto (Capu D'Ortu)

Distance: about 6km (4 miles) each way
Duration: 3 to 4 hours up, 2 hours down
Ascent & Descent: 843m (2,765ft) each way
What to take: walking boots, picnic, at least 2–3 litres (5–8 pints) of water per person, sun hat, sun screen
Highlights of the walk: views of Golfe de Porto, Spelunca Gorge and central range; abundant flora in spring
Note: start at dawn for the best views and to beat the heat. It is not advisable to do this walk in July and August because of the heat

Capo D'Orto is the monstrous 1,294 m (4,244 ft) granite outcrop towering over Porto. It looks impossible to climb but, from just outside Piana, a path winds up a valley to its gentler south face. Few will dispute that this is one of the best viewpoints in all of Corsica.

Park by the football field, up a little access track to the right of the D81, 1km (0.5 mile) east of Piana – if you arrive at the bridge and Café Le Moulin, you have gone too far. Coming from Porto, drive through the Calanche, pass Café Le Moulin, cross the little bridge and the track is on your left.

Walk diagonally across the sports field, cross the wooden bridge and follow the signs for Capu D'Ortu and Foce d'Ortu. The trail, marked in green and orange paint, climbs through shady pine forest, gently to start with, then on a series of switchbacks. Ignore the fork to Roches Rouges and descend briefly. The path then divides again and you should bear left to Capu D'Ortu.

Now follow the small cairns steeply uphill, through a jumble of rocks which require a little gentle scrambling. There are two peaks at the summit and you should head for the right-hand one, where mouth-watering views are in store.

Return by the same route and don't be tempted by the alternative route indicated on the map to descend to Foce D'Ortu unless you're a seasoned rock climber.

Piana

This neat little town of 430 inhabitants hangs on a plateau 438m (1,436ft) above the Golfe de Porto, overlooking the famous Calanche. Piana was the stronghold of the de Leca nobles, who held out against the Genoese until 1489, when their fort on the slopes of Capu di u Vitullu was razed and its defenders massacred. Following their defeat, all the local communities were

Piana

expelled and for 200 years the region was uninhabited.

There's a good choice of accommodation, including the excellent **Gîte d'Étape Giargalo**, serving a popular home-cooked set menu, and the characterful **Hôtel des Roches Rouges**, whose panoramic terrace is the place to go for a drink at sunset. In the village centre, **Le Casanova** does a decent set menu and wood-fired pizzas. There's a tourist office in the village and a small supermarket on the main road, but the nearest bank and ATM are in Porto. Once you've explored the eighteenth-century church of Sainte-Marie and cluster of old stone houses in the centre, you should focus on the surrounds of the village, which have some of Corsica's most beautiful scenery and walks. The nearest beach to Piana is the tiny **Anse de Ficajola**, reached by the winding D624 that plunges to the coast below the village.

Capo Rosso and Plage D'Arone

Plage D'Arone, south-west of Piana, is reached via a suberb 12km (8-mile) drive along the D824. The first part is especially scenic as it contours vertiginously above the coast. There are plenty of spots to draw off and enjoy the panorama of the Calanche, Golfe de Porto, Scandola Peninsula and the central ranges, topped by shapely Paglia D'Orba. For scenic picnic spots, you are spoiled for choice. After 6km, the road bears sharply to the left at a shepherd's hut, where a footpath sign points to Capo Rosso, a prominent headland crowned by a well-preserved

Genoese tower, which comes into view as the road descends to the coast. After a further 6km (4 miles), a campsite and small but tasteful holiday complex herald the end of the road and the gorgeous sandy beach of **Arone**. The beach shelves steeply so is not ideal for children and you should watch the undertow when the waves are big. In season, a bar and restaurant are open.

Capo Rosso Walk

Distance: about 4km (2.5 miles) each way
Duration: 1.5 hours each way
Ascent & Descent about 400m (1,300ft) with a steep climb to reach the tower at the end
What to take: plenty of water, walking boots, sun hat, sunscreen

This is possibly the most rewarding short walk in Corsica, with mouth-watering coastal scenery and superb views. If you don't have a car, you'll need to make a day of it and hike the 6km (4 miles) from Piana to the start of the walk and back, albeit a very scenic addition. Take the D824 from Piana, signed to Plage D'Arone, and after about 6km (4 miles) park by the shepherd's hut and footpath signposted to Capo Rosso. The trail, which is rough underfoot, descends steadily almost to sea level, then climbs the less steep south slope of the prominent red rock headland. The Genoese **Tour de Turghio** is well-preserved and a stunning vantage point.

Exploring inland from Porto – Ota, Gorges de Spelunca, Evisa and Col de Verghio

If you thought the scenery couldn't get any more inspiring than Porto, prepare to be surprised. Once you leave the coast, things get ever more dramatic on the long haul up to the mountain village of Evisa. The road then dips into pine forest but emerges above the tree line at the Col de Verghio, Corsica's highest road pass, from where you have access to some of the island's best alpine walking routes. You could easily spend several days exploring Porto's back-country and, the roads being what they are, it's best not to rush things.

Leaving Porto, take the D124 to **Ota**, a traditional red-roofed village, strung out along the flank of the valley in full view of the terrifying north face of Capo D'Orto. But it is Capo D'Ota, towering above the village, that the locals feared more. Believing it would collapse onto the village, they got monks to secure it in place with a chain, or so the legend goes. Ota has a tiny shop and two *gîtes d'étapes*, each with its own panoramic terrace and restaurant of Corsican specialities. For walkers who want a quiet base for a few days with good food and reasonably priced accommodation, Ota is ideal. The Mare e Monti hiking route passes through the village allowing day hikes in either direction. To the north, the hike up 914m (3,000ft) Capu San Petru is a tough but rewarding climb

and descent, while in the other direction the orange paint splashes lead you into the depths of the shady Spelunca Gorge, with its Genoese bridges and bathing pools.

From Ota the road drops to the river and perfectly preserved Genoese bridge of **Ponte Vecchiu**, a popular bathing spot. Just beyond here, a double bridge marks the start of the rugged **Gorges de Spelunca**, which are only accessible on foot. The trail through this rocky and impregnable terrain was first forged by the Romans, later becoming a trade route linking the chestnut-growing village of Evisa to the coast. After winding along the river, with its huge rounded granite boulders, the route climbs a little to give impressive views of the 300m (1,000ft) high gorge walls, before reaching the confluence of the Tavulella after 35 minutes. Here, jostling for space with the moss-clad holm oaks, is **Pont de Zaglia**, which dates from around 1769. Beyond the bridge is a grueling 500m (1,648ft) climb to Evisa, which is rather unrewarding as it is almost entirely through forest.

A better option is to return on foot by the same route and drive the hugely scenic D84, which you reach as you climb up out of the valley on the D124. This is a 'balcony' drive, looping high above the Gorges de Spelunca, whose cathedral-like red spires are rivalled only by those of Les Calanche. There are so many bends and sheer drops on this vertigo-inducing drive you'll be relieved to reach **Evisa**, situated on a plateau overlooking the gorge with views to the coast. Chestnut groves surround this prosperous village of solid square houses, which hosts a September chestnut festival and is situated at 876m (2,873ft), where the air is noticeably fresher than at sea level. The Mare e Monti and Mare a Mare Nord trails run through the village. For a taste of these famous routes, there's a beautiful forest walk, departing opposite Bar de la Poste and marked by the characteristic orange paint splashes, heading east towards Col de Verghio.

Beyond Evisa the red granite gives way to grey and the views are obscured as you enter the **Forêt d'Aïtone**, where some of Corsica's finest Laricio pines can be found. About 4km (2.5 miles) from Evisa the Mare a Mare Nord trail comes in from the left to meet the D84 and cars are often strung out along the side of the road. There's an easy 15-minute descent on a broad forest trail to the **Cascades d'Aïtone** and **Piscine Naturelle**, a series of idyllic bathing pools, shaded by pines, with a restored chestnut mill nearby.

About 3km (2 miles) further on the D84 a parking area marks the start of the **Sentier de la Sitelle**, which may tempt birdwatchers to walk a circular woodland trail where the endemic **Corsican nuthatch** can be seen, darting up and down branches and tree trunks in its search for insects in the bark. Part of the two-hour trail is known as 'Route des Condamnés' because it was built by convicts brought in to extract timber in the nineteenth century. The Genoese, however, had earlier felled most of the finest trees and taken them by road to Sagone, from where they were exported for building ships.

From here it's a short drive to reach the **Col de Verghio (Verghju)**, at 1,477m (4,845ft) the highest road pass

---

Laricio Pine (*Pinus nigra ssp. Laricio*)

These lofty giants can grow to 50m (164ft) in height, live for 800 years and are typically found in the sub-Alpine zone. Their tall, straight trunks made them ideal for ships' masts and the Genoese built broad mule trails into Corsica's wild forests for the extraction of the valuable timber. Dye, used to colour fishing nets, was extracted from the bark, while the resinous heart of the trunk was used for torches to light houses.

---

in Corsica. It's a bare and wind-lashed place, with a sweeping view of the Niolo region to the east. See the chapter on Corte and the Central Mountains for mountain hikes in the area.

The Road from Porto to Galeria

A drive along this section of the D81 is one of Corsica's great adventures. It's hair-raising, eternally twisting and in places badly potholed, but worth it for the incredible scenery and views of the coast. The tiny isolated villages of Osani, Curzo and Partinello are perched along the road, while far below Girolata can be seen at the head of its own perfect little bay. Allow two hours for the 45km (28-mile) drive and pick a day when the visibility is good.

Girolata

This little gem of a village has no road access and can be only reached on foot, or by boat. In its heyday, there were 100 inhabitants and 30 children at the

Scandola Reserve

Shaped like a dog's head, the rugged features of the Scandola Peninsula and its red volcanic rhyolite rocks are a landmark for miles around. However, this protected nature reserve can only be appreciated from the sea as all access on land is prohibited. There's a good reason for keeping visitors at arm's length because from March to November the reserve is the breeding ground for 32 pairs of osprey *Pandion haliaetus*, who build their massive one-metre (3ft) diameter nests on prominent pillars and rocky outcrops along the coast. These impressive, fish-eating birds of prey are on the road to recovery after hitting an all-time low of just six pairs in 1977. Mating for life, ospreys are migratory but sadly not protected throughout their North African wintering grounds, where they may fall prey to hunters. Cory's shearwaters *Calonectris diomedea* and shags *Phalocrocorax aristotelis* are also found in the area.

Formed in 1975, Scandola Reserve is now part of the National Park and also protects an astonishing variety of marine life, including 125 species of fish and crustaceans, and underwater meadows of *Posidonia* which can photosynthesise at a depth of 50m (190ft) in this exceptionally clear water. Monk seals were once found in the area but were hunted out by local fishermen and the last known sighting was in 1970. There are also some rare plants on land, among them *Armeria soleiroli*, *Seseli praecox* and *Vitex agnus castus*.

The easiest way to visit the reserve is on a boat excursion from Porto, Galeria, Calvi and even Ajaccio, which run daily, weather permitting, from April to October. When the sea is calm the boats come in close to view the amazing volcanic basalt columns, pillow lavas and traces of a vast caldera, which hint at a complex geology. The impressive cliffs of the dominant red rhyolite have been eroded by sea and wind into fantastic shapes and are peppered with caves and arches. Most trips pass the little offshore island of Giargalo, now a research station where the scientists lodge in the restored Genoese tower, and also include a stop at Girolata.

village school but today only seven people live there year round. Shepherds from the mountainous interior grazed their flocks here in winter and the occasional wild goat or sheep can still be spotted. The impressive tower, erected by the Genoese around 1530 but with a later addition of outer wall and bastions, overlooks a gorgeous sandy bay. To avoid the hordes of day-trippers on the tour boats, it really is worth staying overnight and the modest Gîte d'Étape Le Cormoran is the place to go – book well in advance as its dormitories are always full. The tour boats can drop you off here, but it's a shame to miss the wonderful hike in.

Girolata Hike

Distance: about 4km (2.5 miles) each way
Duration: 1.5 hours each way
Ascent & Descent about 300m (1,000ft)
What to take: plenty of water, walking boots, sun hat, sunscreen, swimsuit
Highlights of the walk: fantastic coastal views, colourful *maquis* and pretty seaside village and beach

Shy Acrobat

Corsican nuthatch *Sitella whiteheadi*
Look for these tiny, shy birds scuttling around, often head down, looking for insects on the trunks of pine trees in mountain forest between 800 and 1800m (2,000 and 6,000 ft). On sunny winter days, Laricio pine cones open and drop their seeds. The nuthatch cleverly collects them and stores them in the bark of the tree so it will have food on days when the sun is not out. Back in 1883, Englishman John Whitehead recognised this bird as different from other nuthatches. Along with the Corsican finch, it is today acknowledged as one of the island's two endemic species.

Penthouse Dweller

Osprey *Pandion haliaetus*
With its huge high-rise nest atop a rocky perch above the sea, this is a bird that likes a room with a view. Corsica has about one quarter of the Mediterranean population of these fish-eating raptors, who use smash and grab tactics to get their prey, their nostrils closing when they hit the water. Osprey talons are equipped with rough scales to lock prey in place so they do not lose it in flight, but they must judge the size carefully, otherwise both may sink and perish. Look for them on the Scandola Peninsula and rocky coast from Cargèse to Calvi between March and November.

Leave your vehicle at Col de la Croix (Bocca a Croce) 21km (13 miles) north of Porto at an altitude of 269m (882ft). From here a trail descends to the small cove of Cala di Tuara. On the far side of the beach the path splits but both trails lead to Girolata. The coastal route is more scenic, while the other climbs above the bay to meet the Mare e Monti trail, where you should bear left to descend to Girolata.

An alternative to consider is to leave your vehicle in Galéria and take the afternoon bus from the junction by the bridge over the Fango to the Mare e Monti route, where it crosses the D81 just beyond Col de Palmarella. From here it's a 1.5- to 2-hour descent to Girolata. Stay the night here and then in the morning hike the Mare e Monti route back to Galéria, a stiff climb and ridge walk to 750m (2,460ft) and a steep descent to sea level but with some memorable views. It's a demanding six- to seven-hour hike, to be avoided in the heat of July and August.

A Circular Coastal and Mountain Drive from Porto

Allow a whole day for this 100km (62-mile) circular drive as there is plenty to see along the way and the roads are slow. It takes in Les Calanche, Piana, Cargèse, Sagone, Vico, Evisa and the Gorges de Spelunca. There's also the option to add on an extra loop into the hidden valleys of Deux Sorru, set among the forested foothills of the Central Range, west of Monte Ritondo.

From Porto take the D81 west. It's worth getting up for sunrise on the Calanche and then stopping in Piana for breakfast. Beyond Piana the road heads over Bocca di San Martino, from where it's a long descent down to the Chiuni Valley. A road goes off to the right to **Plage de Chiuni**, the pick of the area's beaches though somewhat marred by an extensive resort development. Ruins of a tower stand sentinel west of the bay.

About 8km (5 miles) further on the D81, **Cargèse (Carghjese)**, sited atop a rocky promontory, has an interesting history. You may already have realised it is something of an anomaly for a coastal town in Corsica not to be protected by a citadel, and this is because Cargèse is a relatively new town. In 1663, some 800 Greeks from the southern Peloponnese abandoned their homes in the wake of the Ottoman conquest. Appealing to the Genoese for a new homeland, in 1676 they were given permission to settle at Paomia, in the hills just inland from where Cargèse now stands. In the Corsican uprising against the Genoese

Dragut Reis – Corsair Extraordinaire

Born in Anatolia, Turkey between 1514 and 1518, Dragut Reis became one of the Mediterranean's most notorious pirates. He took to the seas in 1538, beginning a long-standing campaign of harassment of the Naples, Sicilian and Corsican coasts, in which over 7,000 men were abducted into slavery. In 1540, he was captured by the Genoan Andrea Doria near Girolata, and taken to Genoa, where he became galley slave to the Admiral's nephew. Ransomed in 1544, he went on to gain control of Tunisia, Gozo and Tripoli and may well have succeeded in taking Malta in 1565, had he not been otruok in the head by a splinter of rock, dislodged by a cannonball during the siege.

in 1729, the Greeks sided with Genoa. The shepherds of Vico and the Niolo, now excluded from their traditional grazing lands, were quick to react and evicted the Greeks, burning their homes to the ground. For a time they settled in Ajaccio but then on the advent of French rule returned to establish a permanent community at Cargèse, whose inhabitants now number a thousand. Today more Corsican than Greek, it is only the descendants' Orthodox church and a number of surnames ending in -acci, a corruption of the Greek -akis, that gives a clue to their origins. The gleaming white church, built in 1852 by the villagers, replaced the original one, and contains some valuable seventeenth-century icons, brought over from Greece, among them a portrait of St John the Baptist. Facing the Greek church is the Baroque one, erected in the early nineteenth century by the increasing numbers of non-Greek citizens. The highlight of the year in this quiet little town is the Easter Monday procession, in which both faiths take part.

There's a helpful Tourist Office in the centre of town above the churches and several hotels of which the Continental, on the left arriving from Piana, offers simple but reasonably priced rooms and good local food. Le Saint-Jean by the crossroads in the town centre is more recent and has several types of room. Just north of the town is the Plage de Pero, while boat trips to Capo Rosso, Scandola and Girolata leave from the marina.

From Cargèse to Sagone, the road hugs the coast and a couple of small beaches may tempt you to halt. **Sagone**'s beaches are not the best for children because of a strong undertow and are somewhat blighted by unsightly buildings. This ancient settlement was founded by the Romans and by the sixth century had become an important bishopric. Enjoying prosperity under Pisa, by the sixteenth century it was all but in ruins and the seat was moved to Vico and later Calvi. Past the well-preserved Genoese tower at the west end of the beach turn left immediately before the river to visit what remains of the twelfth-century **cathedral of Sant'Appiano** and two ancient menhirs.

At the east end of the beach take the D70 in the direction of Vico. It's a steady climb to the Col de St Antoine, where

Vico (Vicu) comes into view, set in a natural amphitheatre overlooking the forested Liamone Valley. With a population of just under a thousand inhabitants, this quiet little town of narrow streets flanked by austere granite houses has plenty of charm. It's also the only place in this mountain enclave where you will find any shops. Just outside town is the monumental **Couvent Saint-François**, founded in 1481. The present buildings are from the seventeenth and eighteenth centuries and are occupied by oblates of Marie. Visitors are welcome in the afternoons and you can even stay there overnight. The church contains an ornate chest of carved chestnut in the sacristy and probably the oldest wooden cross in Corsica, which may have been brought from Italy by the founders.

From Vico, the D70 climbs to a forested plateau, where pigs roam freely. Just beyond the Col de Sevi, the road descends gently to join the D84 (see section on Ota, Gorges de Spelunca and Evisa for details of this part of the route).

The Hidden Valleys

If you have time, there are some tempting side trips into the shady forested foothills of the central range. From Vico the D23 drops to **Murzo**, famous for its honey festival, celebrated over the last weekend in September. The village's Auberge U Fragnu, housed in a converted olive mill, does a tasty Corsican menu. Passing through the spa village of Guagno Les Bains, cross the river again. On the north side of the bridge a path takes off downstream through beautiful woodland, then

Above: Girolata, a coastal village only accessible by boat or on foot

Right: Les Calanche, iconic red rock formations near Piana

Below: Ota, a beautiful village of red-tiled granite houses set among towering peaks

Above: Golfe de Porto
Below left: Capo d'Orto hike, near Porto
Below right: Sunset over Golfe de Porto

Corsica's most hair-raising road?

There are many roads that deserve the title but a short section of the D4 from Murzo to Muna is a strong contender. The D4 is a narrow and largely single-track road that twists through the hills and valleys inland from the Golfe de Sagone. From Murzo, near Vico, it winds above the Liamone valley where in sections it is cut into the cliff face. Though not a trip for the faint-hearted, it is worth it for the chance to visit the tiny and all but abandoned village of **Muna**, 8km (5 miles) from Murzo. Stacked up on the hillside above the road, Muna has only two permanent residents but enjoys a stunning location below the crags of Punta di a Spusata.

climbs to reach the hillside village of Letia after two hours. From the bridge at Guagno Les Bains, the D323 and then D123 wind up the north side of the valley to **Soccia**, an attractive village, with a busy little restaurant, A Merendella, which has a good reputation. Beyond Soccia, the single-track road continues for a further 4km (2.5 miles) to a car park and pizzeria, the start of the trail to **Lac de Creno**.

It is also possible to continue the drive up the main valley on the D23 to **Guagno**, located on a spur dividing two valleys. This sizeable village was once surrounded by 80,000 chestnut trees and had a population of a thousand. Today, there are fewer than a hundred inhabitants, a small snack bar and shop and a *Gîte d'Étape*. Plans were once drawn up to build a road across

the mountains to Vivario, but they never came to anything, ensuring that the village remains in splendid isolation. From here walkers can hike up the valley to join the GR 20 route.

Lac de Creno hike

Distance: about 3km (2 miles) each way
Duration: about 1 hour each way
Ascent & Descent about 300m (1,000ft)
What to take: plenty of water, walking boots, sun hat, sunscreen
Highlights of the walk: mountain views; a pretty lake shaded by pines

From the car park above Soccia follow the path marked by yellow paint splashes up the right flank of the valley. There is little shade to begin with but after about 40 minutes' gentle climb the trail dips into pine forest, passing a drinking fountain and heralding your arrival at Lac de Creno. Just 6m (20ft) deep, legend has it this little glacial lake was formed by a stroke of the devil's hammer. There are plenty of shady picnic spots here, but for the view of Monte D'Oro walk to the end of the lake then bear left, climbing with care to a breathtaking viewpoint.

Places to Visit

Porto

Porto Tourist Information
On Place de la Marine
☎ 04 95 26 10 55
www.porto-tourisme.com

The Genoese Tower
Open 9am–9pm daily, April to October

Aquarium de la Poudrière
Place de la Marina
Open 10am–7pm (9pm in July and August), daily, all year
☎ 04 95 26 19 24

Boat trips to Scandola & Girolata

Nave Va
Large, stable and comfortable boats. Choice of several itineraries, departing from Porto Marina
April to October, weather permitting
☎ 04 95 26 15 16 or 04 95 21 83 97
www.naveva.com

Porto Linea
Book at Hotel Monte Rosso
Small 12-person boat allows for a closer approach to the rock formations but a rougher ride unless the sea is calm
☎ 04 95 26 11 50 or
06 08 16 89 71
www.portolinea.com

Diving

Centre de Plongée du Golfe de Porto
Diving and snorkelling in the Golfe de Porto
Ultra-clear water and some superb spots make for memorable encounters with the undersea world
☎ 04 95 26 10 29
www.plongeeporto.com

Around Porto

Cargèse Tourist Office
Rue Docteur Dragacci
Open 9am–7pm daily, June to September; 9am–12.30pm and 2.30–6pm rest of the year
☎ 04 95 26 41 31
www.cargese.net

Boat trips from Cargèse with Grand Bleu
Trips to Scandola depart daily in high season
☎ 04 95 26 40 24

Couvent Saint-François
Vico
Open to visitors 2–6pm daily, all year
☎ 04 95 26 83 83

Centre Équestre Deux Sorru
Letia (near Vico)
Horse riding trips from an hour to a full day
Open all year but reservations essential
☎ 04 95 26 69 94

9. The Central Mountains

Those who can tear themselves away from the coast and venture inland will discover a different and often surprising side to this Mediterranean island. Tumultuous peaks, still snowbound well into summer, tower over the forested valleys, where clear-running torrents carve precipitous gorges. It is often overwhelmingly scenic, but also fragile. Protecting this natural heritage from the ravages of fire and the pressure of visitor numbers are two of the problems facing the Parc Naturel Régional de la Corse, whose boundaries embrace most of the central mountains. An equally important issue is depopulation and the loss of traditional lifestyle for the clusters of mountain villages clinging to the lower slopes of what was once the larder of Corsica. Today small-scale producers maintain the traditions of cheese-making, *charcuterie* production, milling of chestnut flour and making honey and jam but, even more than on the coast, tourism here is a seasonal activity.

*Opposite: Sunrise on the GR 20,
Corsica's famous mountain treck*

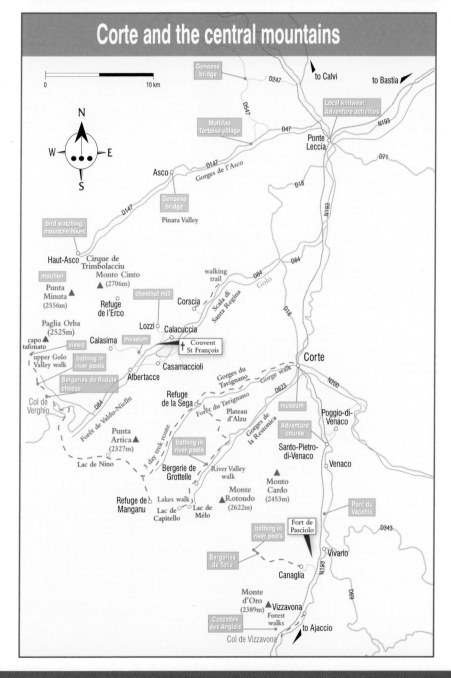

Corte and the central mountains

0   10 km

N
W   E
S

Genoese bridge

to Calvi

to Bastia

D247

D547

Local knitwear, Adventure activities

Moltifao Tortoise village

D47

N193

Ponte Leccia

D147

Gorges de l'Asco

D71

Asco

D18

Genoese bridge

Pinara Valley

D147

bird watching, mountain hikes

Haut-Asco

Cirque de Trimbolacciu

walking trail

D84

D84

Golo

mouflon

Monto Cinto

▲ (2706m)

D18

Punta Minuta (2556m) ▲

chestnut mill

Corscia

Scala di Santa Regina

Refuge de l'Erco

Lozzi

Calacuccia

Paglia Orba (2525m)

capo tafonato ▲

views

Calasima

museum

✝ Couvent St François

Corte

N200

upper Golo Valley walk

bathing in river pools

Albertacce

Casamaccioli

Gorges du Tavignano

Gorge walk

D623

museum

Bergeries de Radule cheese

Refuge de la Sega

Forêt du Tavignano

Poggio-di-Venaco

Col de Verghio

D84

Forêt de Valdu-Niellu

Plateau d'Alzu

Gorges de la Restonica

Adventure course

Santo-Pietro-di-Venaco

Punta Artica ▲ (2327m)

3 day trek route

bathing in river pools

Venaco

Lac de Nino

Bergerie de Grottelle

River Valley walk

Monto Cardo (2453m) ▲

Pont du Vecchio

Refuge de Manganu

Lakes walk

Monte Rotondo ▲ (2622m)

D343

Lac de Capitello

Lac de Mélo

Fort de Pasciolo

bathing in river pools

Vivario

Bergeries de Tolla

Canaglia

N193

D69

Monte d'Oro (2389m) ▲

Vizzavona

Cascades des Anglais

Forest walks

to Ajaccio

Col de Vizzavona

Corte (Corti)

With 6,700 inhabitants and 3,500 students, **Corte** is a busy university town ringed by soaring peaks at the confluence of the Restonica and Tavignano rivers. From its earliest days as a fortress, the settlement's fortunes swung back and forth as Moors, Vincentello D'Istria for the King of Aragon, the Bank of St George for Genoa and Sampiero Corso for France in turn occupied this strategic site in the geographic heart of the island.

Dominated by its landmark citadel, perched on a rocky crag overlooking the town, the island's only true inland town became the symbol of Corsica's short-lived independence from 1755 to 1769, when Pasquale Paoli made it the capital, drew up its avant-garde constitution and established the university.

Corte is compact enough to explore on foot but prepare for plenty of steps and steep alleys. Those with a car are advised to park in the Tufelli car park at the end of Cours Paoli or near the railway station and supermarket. After half a day you will probably have soaked up most of the sights. There are a few eateries of note in Corte. Along rampe Ribanelle outside the citadel walls is **U Museu**, popular among visitors for its good-value Corsican food, served on a shaded terrace, but only open in season. Locals frequent **A Scudella**, on Place Paoli, whose menu is based on what is seasonally available. **U Paglia Orba**, with a reputation for solid Corsican fare, is on rue Xavier Luciani, just off the top end of Cours Paoli.

Hotels, shops, bars and cafés line the main thoroughfare of **Cours Paoli**, which leads to **Place Paoli**, fittingly adorned by a bronze statue of the independence hero. From here it's a short climb up cobbled steps to **Place Gaffori**, where cafés spill out onto a broad square, dominated by a statue of the local doctor, later **General Jean-Pierre Gaffori**, who spearheaded the 1745 revolt against France. Opposite **L'Église de l'Annonciation**, Corte's oldest church dating from 1450, is the Gaffori family mansion, which was besieged by the Genoese in 1750 and remains pock-marked by bullet holes. Gaffori was absent at the time but his wife Faustina held out against the attackers until his return – an event depicted on the bas-relief of the statue. Assassinated by his own brother in the pay of the Genoese in 1753, Gaffori did not live to see the independence he fought for.

From Place Gaffori a stairway leads past the **Palazzu Nazionale**, where Paoli installed his government and established Corsica's university. For a time, this grand old building was also Paoli's home but today it serves as a university research centre for Corsican Studies. The ground floor is open to the public and hosts exhibitions.

It was Vincentello D'Istria who built the castle at the southern end of the **Citadel** around 1420, adding to fortifications that had already been erected before the Genoese took over. Its bastions are crowned by a watchtower, known as the **Nid d'Aigle** (eagle's nest), where there is a sheer drop to the Tavignano river and a superb viewpoint from which to admire the rugged mountains encircling the town. Access to this part of the citadel is through the museum, but for another equally dramatic viewpoint you can head for the **Belvédère**, reached by a walkway outside the walls at the southern end of the citadel.

Occupied by the French Foreign Legion from 1960 to 1983, the austere red-roofed **Caserne Padoue** was once a prison but it now forms part of the university and also houses the **Tourist Information Office** and the *Fond Régional d'Art Contemporain*, an exhibition space. Opposite is another former barracks, the **Caserne Serrurier**, home to the **Musée de la Corse**, which is a must for anyone even vaguely interested in Corsican history and culture. The exhibitions are thematic and take in the discovery of Corsica, recognition of its heritage, crafts and skills, the shepherd's way of life, the development of industry and the role of the brotherhoods.

The Asco Valley

The most northerly of Corsica's high alpine valleys, the 30km (18-mile) long **Vallée de l'Asco** is also one of its wildest and richest in wildlife.

From its junction with the N197 just north of Ponte Leccia, the D47 crosses the flat and arid lower valley. Just past the second turning to Moltifao, the village scattered over the hillside to the north, the now D147 arrives at the **Village des Tortues de Moltifao**, which is worth a stop if you're interested in Corsica's largest reptile, the endangered Hermann's tortoise. There's a self-guided walk through a holm oak forest past several enclosures of these animals, which are threatened by forest fires, road traffic and illegal collecting, or you can join a guided

tour of the site.

The road now enters the rugged **Gorges de l'Asco**, where for the next 4km (2.5 miles) it is hemmed in by splendid crags. Beyond the gorge, high above the valley, lies the village of **Asco**, which until the road was completed in 1937 had been one of the remotest settlements in Corsica. The road through Asco is for residents only but you can take the bypass above the village to continue up the valley. At the west exit from the village a very steep and narrow road descends to a perfect little Genoese bridge. Turning and parking are tricky here so it makes sense to leave your car at the top and walk. Across the bridge a path leads into the wild and beautiful **Pinara Valley**, which once linked Asco to the Niolo region.

The road drops and crosses the river (now confusingly called the Stranciacone), then winds through the Forêt de Carrozzica before the final haul up to the former ski station of **Haut-Asco** at 1,361m (4,464 ft). Now that there seems little likelihood of enough snow to ski, the unsightly lift apparatus is slowly being dismantled and the Hôtel Le Chalêt, which serves good food, and adjacent Refuge cater to walkers. The reason why you have come all this way is immediately apparent when you look across the valley to the massive north face of Monte Cinto. Few other places in Corsica have such a concentration of rugged peaks and challenging walks, which Austrian climber and explorer Felix von Cube discovered during his visits here in the early 1900s.

If you are a seasoned mountain walker you could happily base yourself here for a few days, but this is also one of the few places where the GR 20 route meets the road so there is a lot of passing foot traffic. The ascent of **Cinto** is an 8- or 9-hour round trip hike and scramble on rock and scree and should not be attempted unless the forecast is for clear weather. It is all too easy to lose the path amid the jumble of crags on this huge summit. The advice is to go with a guide or at least a party of other experienced walkers.

The Asco Valley is one of the top places to observe the **Corsican mouflon**. Your best chance is to depart at dawn along the GR 20 south, where you may see and hear them crashing among the rocks and alder bushes on the ridge to the north. With luck you may also catch a glimpse of **lammergeier**, a carrion feeder also known as the bearded vulture, and the delightful **wallcreeper**, which flits along rock faces searching out insects in the crevices.

Walk to the Cirque de Trimbolacciu

Distance: about 4 km (2.5 miles) round trip on a rocky trail
Duration: 1.5 hours
Ascent & Descent: negligible: the trail is mostly level
What to take: boots, polar fleece or sweater, water, sun hat, sun screen

The Corsican Mouflon (Ovis ammon musimon)

'Muvra', as it is known in Corsican, is considered an endemic sub-species, also found in Sardinia and probably descended from feral domesticated sheep, introduced during the Neolithic period. Their pelage (coat) is light brown in summer but darker at other times of year and they bear white patches on the face, backside and legs. On the female's face they give clues to her age – the more white, the older she is. About half of females have horns. Male horns are thicker and become longer and more curved with age.

Generally shy, they are most easily observed at dusk and dawn, when they are most active. They have a good sense of smell and may sound the alarm and flee long before they see an intruder.  Protected since 1955, Corsica's mouflon number between 400 and 600 but this is a fraction of the original population. Hunted as game and in stiff competition with domestic livestock, they found refuge in the highest and most inaccessible mountain regions, where they can be observed clattering among the rocks or browsing on alder thickets. Today, small flocks survive in the Bonifato–Asco–Lonca ranges in the north and around Bavella in the south.

Highlights of the walk: high mountain scenery and a spectacular rocky valley

This is a walk that takes you into a beautiful and wild valley at the foot of Monte Cinto. The head of the valley is framed by a ridge of pointed crags, known as the Cirque de Trimbolacciu. The trail leaves from behind a hut in the woods by the car park opposite Le Chalêt and it is the same trail as for the ascent of Monte Cinto. It winds through pine forest to start with, but the terrain becomes rockier down in the valley. From the bridge over the stream, which you will reach after 30 to 40 minutes, there is an impressive view of the cirque and gloomy north face

Bone Breaker

Lammergeier *Gypaetus barbatus*
Also known as bearded vulture, this magnificent high-mountain raptor typically has a wingspan of 2.5m (8ft). Feeding on sheep and goat carcasses, its decline is linked to changes in animal husbandry in Corsica. Its numbers are down from 15 pairs in 1981 to probably fewer than 10 pairs today. By dropping and shattering large bones on rocks, it feeds on the nutritious marrow, which explains its other name 'ossifrage' (bone breaker).

Seedy Character

Corsican Finch *Carduelis corsicanus*
One of Corsica's two endemic species, these busy little birds are often seen flitting through the forest searching for pine seeds and in large flocks on more open ground in the sub-alpine zone. This bird was formerly believed to be a subspecies of Citril Finch but is now recogniSed as a separate species.

Flashy Feathers

Wallcreeper *Tichodroma muraria*
In summer you'll have to hunt high for this beautiful but rare bird. It is sometimes spotted by walkers and climbers as it creeps along sheer rock faces and mountain ravines, flashing its bright wing feathers. Its long, slender bill is used for poking into crevices to extract insects and spiders.

Bergeries of Restonica and Tavignano

Possibly as many as a hundred shepherds once grazed their flocks in and around these two valleys but today just a handful still make a living from traditional cheese production. Many of their stone-built summer dwellings, known as bergeries, are abandoned, but the plateau d'Alzo, which divides the two valleys, is still actively grazed in summer by several thousand sheep and goats. From the Bergeries de Cappellaccia on 26 and 27 June the sun sets behind the natural arch below the rocky summit of Capo Tafonato to the west. Unexpectedly but briefly the sun reappears, its rays piercing the hole and illuminating it like a golden eye.

falls. Lower down and shaded by pines the granite has been scoured by pebbles into smooth, rounded basins, which provide many idyllic bathing spots.

Predictably, this beautiful valley is no well-guarded secret and in the height of the summer its single-track access road is choked with cars. To ease the problem in recent years there have been traffic restrictions on the upper section of the 15km (9.5-mile) road, with a free shuttle bus operating several times a day. The road ends at **Bergeries de Grottelle (E Gruttelle)**, a collection of stone shepherds' huts surrounded by statuesque Laricio pines, where a hiking trail snakes up to lakes Melo and Capitello. Here there is a café but the only accommodation is at two hotels near the valley entrance, and the nice shaded campsite at Tuani. There are restaurants at the Pont de Tragone and by the hotels at the entrance to the valley.

of Cinto. The route up the mountain starts beyond the bridge and becomes immediately more challenging.

The Restonica Valley

Massive granite buttresses guard the lower reaches of this superbly scenic alpine valley. Penetrating the heart of the Corsican mountain wilderness, the glaciated upper valley is a broad cirque, sided by sheer cliffs and soaring pinnacles. Wedged among giant boulders and moraines are a cluster of gorgeous little lakes, surrounded by alder thickets. From here the River Restonica begins its rough and tumble course, leaping over the rocks in a series of small water-

Hiking to Lac de Melo and Lac de Capitello

Distance: about 8km (5 miles) round trip on a rocky trail

Duration: 3 to 4 hours

Ascent & Descent: about 350m (1,148 ft) to Lake Melo and a further 200m (656ft) to Lake Capitello

What to take: boots, polar fleece or sweater, picnic, water, sun hat, sun screen

Highlights of the walk: high mountain scenery and beautiful lakes

This hike brings Corsica's high mountain scenery within reach of day walkers, prepared for a rocky and in places steep path. Park at the Bergeries de Grottelle at 1,370m (4,493ft), where there is a café, and follow the trail, which is marked in yellow paint. After about 30 minutes the trail divides. The left branch crosses the river and heads up its east side, while the steeper right-hand trail, which includes a short ladder and chain ascent, follows the west bank. Both meet again as the terrain levels out at the Lac de Melo at an altitude of 1,711m (5,612ft). Frozen for five or six months of the year, this beautiful lake is backed by alder scrub and the occasional lone mountain ash. There are plenty of good picnic spots but be careful not to damage the fragile *pozzines*, the spongy, matted turf surrounding the lake. If you have binoculars you can pass the time picking out the hikers on the GR 20 mountain route as they make their way precariously over what look like sheer rock slabs, just below the jagged ridge of Capitello, far above you to the west.

To reach the second lake, take the rocky trail behind the warden's stone hut, which ascends to the right of the stream. Then cross the stream and continue climbing until Lake Capitello comes into view to your right, locked in its glacier-scoured basin. Corsica's deepest lake is slightly smaller than Lake Melo, plunging 42m (138ft) from the sheer rock face behind, which gives a rather gloomy, even spooky feel to it.

Those who are undeterred by an even steeper path can continue on the trail, which climbs up a rocky corridor to meet the GR 20 on the ridge above. Following the GR 20 east along the ridge to Bocca a Soglia at 2,042m (6,700ft) a side path, still marked in yellow, then drops north off the ridge back down to Lac de Melo, making a splendid full-day hike for properly equipped and fit mountain walkers. A map is essential and snow may make this route unadvisable before midsummer.

The Tavignano Valley

Unlike the Restonica Valley, the Tavignano has no road access and consequently retains its wilderness appeal. Interestingly, this valley was the original trade route across the mountains and in places the paving slabs of the old mule trail are still visible, making for easy hiking. Later, valuable timber was extracted along the same route but thankfully the beautiful pine forests of its surrounds were never over-exploited. Halfway up the valley, **Refuge a Sega** owes its name to the saws that once felled timber here. Today, the conveniently sited mountain hut lies on the Mare a Mare Nord trail, a five-hour hike from Corte. The trail, which can be done in a longish day there and back, is an easy gradual ascent through a spectacular gorge, walled in granite.

The Niolo (Niolu)

Locked in by the formidable ravine of Scala di Santa Regina to the east and Corsica's highest mountain pass, the Col de Verghio, to the west, the secluded mountain enclave of the **Niolo** was barely known to the outside world until a hundred years ago, when the first tracks were forged. For centuries, its shepherd communities had lived here safe from Saracen raids, oblivious to the squabbles of local gentry and defiant against the Genoese and French. France's response to the supposed hotbed of dissent was harsh – on 23 June 1774, eleven suspected local insurgents, including a boy of 17, were rounded up and massacred. More recently dissent has focused on the creation, in 1968, of the island's largest artificial lake to feed a hydroelectric power station.

Corsica's national anthem, *Dio vi salve Regina*, was first sung in a humble Niolo chapel in 1730. Today the inhabitants' prowess at singing is still put to the test each year at one of the island's most authentic local festivals, **Santa di u Niolu**, a three-day event hosted by the village of **Casamaccioli** around 8 September each year. Some believe that Corsican polyphonic singing in its purest form can be heard in the traditional chants, sung during the Mass, but it is the *chjam' e rispondi* singing dialogues that arouse most excitement. The festival has its origins in a fifteenth-century legend which relates how the captain of a ship in distress off the coast near Galéria prayed for deliverance. A bright star appeared landward, in the direction of the monastery of Selva, and guided the ship to safety. The grateful captain promised a statue to the monastery, which was named Santa Maria di a Stella. During the Saracen raids the monastery was sacked and the monks fled to the Niolo with their precious statue on the back of a mule. It came to rest in Casamaccioli, where a chapel was erected to house the statue, today paraded around the village by the lay brotherhood of St Anthony during the festival. Over the years, this most Corsican of festivals became the focal point for shepherds before they rounded up their flocks

and embarked on their descent to the coast for the winter. Today, there are cheese and *charcuterie* stalls, handicrafts and religious souvenirs.

The broad, oval valley is sheltered by two of Corsica's highest mountains, the **Massif du Cinto**, which rises to 2,706m (8,875ft) and nearby **Paglia Orba**, the island's most distinctively shaped peak. Towards the head of the valley, the tributaries of Corsica's longest river, the Golo, run through the 4,638-hectare (11,460-acre) **Forêt de Valdu Niellu**, whose Laricio pines were once coveted by shipbuilders for their long straight trunks. The giant of all pines, which stood just off the D84 below the hairpin bend known as '*fer à cheval*', had a 36m (118ft) tall trunk with a circumference of six metres (20 ft) and was thought to be at least 800 years old.

Often described as the heart of Corsica and its people considered the

Pozzines

Many of Corsica's shallow glacial lakes are surrounded by **pozzines** (from the Corsican *pozzi* meaning wells), tiny freshwater pools and rivulets set in what looks like a well-manicured lawn. The water-logged peaty soil beneath this grassy carpet overlies a layer of impermeable glacial sediments. These curious features might be more at home on the moors of Great Britain than among the crags of Corsica, but they are very fragile and should not be disturbed. Here you will find several carnivorous plants: *Drosera rotundifolia*, *Drosera corsica* and the endemic *Pinguicula corsica*.

most Corsican of Corsicans, the Niolo comprises a cluster of mountain villages, today living mostly from tourism, with just a handful of people keeping up the pastoral way of life. **Calacuccia**, the largest of them, is strung out along the D84 and has a helpful tourist office, several hotels, shops and restaurants. Further up the road, **Albertacce** is quieter and has rather more character. There's a small archaeological museum on the main street, whose exhibits include a carved menhir head, found in the local area. Between the two villages is the seventeenth-century **Couvent de Saint François**, now a *Gîte d'Étape*, shaded by chestnut trees, with a memorial to the victims of the 1744 massacre. Opposite is the **Auberge Casa Balduina**, an intimate little hotel with a reputation for good food for its overnight guests. Gourmets should also

head for the **Restaurant du Lac**, down a pretty lane bordering the lake in the hamlet of Sidossi. Open from May to September, it serves Niolo specialities in a huge dining room, but sadly without lake views. **Restaurant Le Corsica**, on the left leaving Calacuccia by the Porto road, is open from April to October. As the name suggests, this is a place to try out Corsican fare.

Accessed by the D318, **Calasima**, at 1,100m (3,600ft) the highest village in Corsica, has a spectacular setting as it is backed by the daunting south-east face of Paglia Orba. A forestry trail continues beyond the village into a lovely wooded valley overlooked by the serrated peaks of the **Cinque Frati** (the Five Monks) and linking up with the GR 20 mountain path.

On the lower slopes of Monte Cinto, just above the hamlet of **Lozzi**, you can

Left: The clear mountain streams of the Niolo are perfect for bathing
Right: Vivario, central mountains

visit a working **Chestnut Mill**, learn how to make chestnut flour and take a stroll around a chestnut grove, and in doing so support an important traditional local industry. A twenty-minute walk downhill from the mill along an old mule track is a secret little Genoese bridge, nestled in a valley, with a beautiful view of Monte Cinto. Lozzi is also the departure point for the hike up the south face of **Monte Cinto**. A 4WD dirt track leads to the Bergeries de Petra Pinzuta from where it's a thirty-minute walk to the Refuge D'Erco at 1,667m (5,467ft). It's still a scramble of 1,100m (3,860ft) over rock and scree on an indistinct path, marked intermittently by small cairns, to reach the summit. Allow at least ten hours there and back from Lozzi and be prepared to descend at the first sign of cloud on the summit. Unless you're very experienced, it's best to go with a guide as the mountain has claimed many lives.

Walking in the Niolo

With the Mare a Mare Nord and GR 20 routes traversing the valley there is no shortage of trails and the Niolo is a choice spot for a few days of mountain walking.

The Upper Golo Valley Walk

Distance: about 16km (10 miles) round trip

Duration: 6 to 7 hours return trip

Ascent & Descent: 650m (2,132ft)

What to take: boots, picnic lunch, water, sun hat, sun screen (plus a fleece and a swimsuit)

Highlights of the walk: the upper Golo Valley, its river and bathing pools, working bergerie and fresh cheese, and jaw-dropping views of Paglia Orba and Capo Tafonato

The trail starts at the *'fer a cheval'*, a hairpin bend on the D84 about 5km (3 miles) east of the Col de Vergio, and is signposted to **'Bergeries de Radule'**. The trail plunges into beech forest and climbs gently to meet the GR 20 path, marked by red and white paint, after 10 minutes. Bear right here and in 15 minutes emerge onto the rocky surrounds of the shepherd's huts, where in high summer you can buy *brocciu* cheese. Keep on the GR 20 and descend to the river above the **Cascade de Radule**, a small waterfall. Cross the river by the bridge and bear left on the GR 20 up a rocky V-shaped valley dotted with giant Laricio pines. Above the tree line, the valley takes on a classic glaciated U-shape, and the limpid waters of the Golo tumble over polished granite, forming a chain of inviting little bathing pools. The massive bulk of Paglia Orba looms on the horizon but the path now hauls 200m (650ft) up the left flank of the

Lac du Cinto

This is a tiny glacial lake nestled below the summit of Monte Cinto. Legend has it that the King of Calasima decided to look for water on the mountain to give to his livestock to drink. Climbing the mountain he found no sign of water and was about to give up when a fairy showed him a cave full of diamonds. When the sun reached its zenith they turned into fountains and the lake was created.

valley to a ridge. Follow the ridge, gaining stunning views as well as height. Contour around the head of the valley for a further 30 minutes to the **Refuge Ciottulu di i Mori**, whose panoramic terrace is a great place to stop for a drink and at an altitude of almost 2,000m (6,500ft) it is the highest on the GR 20. Just above the hut is the source of the River Golo.

If you still have plenty of energy, a path leads from the hut up a valley strewn with boulders, whose pink granite is spattered with yellow-green lichen. In among the rocks you may spot the papery white flowers of *Helichrysum frigidum*, an endemic Corsican flower that thrives in crevices. After 30 minutes the path reaches the Col des Maures, whose skyline is guarded by a row of intimidating stone giants. A trail marked by cairns veers right before the Col, heading off to the 2,525m (8,282ft) summit of Paglia Orba, a rough scramble with some tricky sections and definitely not one for the faint-hearted. Most mountain walkers should be able to manage the first part, which brings views of the pierced summit of Capo Tafonato.

Capo Tafonato (Capu Tafunatu)

Yet another creation of the devil, this 2,335m (7,650ft) high rocky ridge is pierced by a natural hole. According to popular belief, the devil was working his field with a team of black oxen when St Martin appeared and began to taunt him. Enraged, the devil picked up the ploughshare and hurled it at the mountain, piercing it through.

From the refuge, continue on the GR 20 for about 25 minutes, to the next saddle which offers amazing views of Paglia Orba's sheer face. The GR 20 now drops east but you should bear west back down into the Golo Valley, which you follow until the rejoin the route you came in on earlier. You must now retrace your steps back to your vehicle.

Scala di Santa Regina

The Niolo region was cut off by this impenetrable rocky ravine, formed by tectonic forces combined with the relentless erosion of the Golo river on its journey eastwards. The D84 narrows to a single track as it winds through the red-walled gorge, where signs remind you that bathing is forbidden because of the danger of flooding from the dam above. This should be one of Corsica's most scenic spots but it is somewhat spoiled by a line of rusting pylons. To really appreciate the atmosphere of the place, draw off the road by the tiny shrine and fountain on your right as you travel up the gorge. This marks the start of a walking trail that follows the original mule route through the ravine that was known as '*a Scala*', the staircase. In about 2 hours you will reach the village of Corscia but even just a short way up the trail you will get the feel of just how wild the place can be.

Vizzavona, Vivario and Venaco

Lying between Corte and the Col de Vizzavona, this trio of mountain settlements is on the main N193 route from Ajaccio to Bastia. It would be all too easy to rush through but there is much to see and enjoy in the forested mountain enclave that divides Corsica geologically, a division reflected by that of the two *départments* of Haute-Corse and Corse-du-Sud. If you don't have your own transport, this is one area of Corsica where you can reasonably get around, hopping on and off the Ajaccio to Bastia train.

Leaving Corte, the road climbs steadily to a cluster of typical hill villages. Straddling a spur above the Tavignano Valley, **Poggio** has dramatic views and a friendly welcome from the Hotel Casa Mathea and local *Gîte d'Étape*, both of which are open all year round. Nearby **Santo-Pietro-di-Venaco** is the start of the August pilgrimage to the **chapel of St Eliseo**, the patron saint of shepherds, which sits on the flank of Monte Cardo. The five-hour circular hike takes off 30 minutes' walk up the zig-zag forestry track behind the village, and is marked sporadically in orange. Beyond the chapel the path swings around the head of a valley past a cluster of *bergeries*, before dropping down a scenic ridge to return to the village.

The larger sprawling village of **Venaco (Venacu)** has several shops and cafés and hosts an annual cheese festival, '*A Fiera di u Casgiu*', in early May. Outside the baroque church of St Michel, a poignant First World War memorial testifies to the huge loss of life – 77 of the Venacais men did not return. South of here the old road and railway line cross a 220m (720ft) wide ravine by the splendid **Pont du Vecchio**, dating from 1825 and designed by Gustave Eiffel (of Eiffel Tower fame).

Shepherds, the vagabond and a stolen saint

The shepherds of Corte honoured St Eliseo and their flocks gave abundant, creamy milk. The shepherds of Venaco were not so lucky and struggled in poverty. One day they met a vagabond who told them that only a saint could help them – '*un santu solu vi po salva*'. So the Venachesi stole the statue of St Eliseo. Since then their flocks have prospered, as more recently has their cheese industry.

At **Vivario (Vivariu)** the road swings back and forth in a series of sharp bends, climbing steadily. The sombre houses of this attractive mountain town are stacked up against the hillside and divided by tiny alleys. Perched above the village overlooking the Gorge du Vecchiu and accessed by a path off the Ajaccio road is the ruined **Fort de Pasciolo**, built in 1770 by the French and later used as a prison. The 30-minute walk is worth it for the extensive mountain and valley views. Sadly the fire-scorched hills to the east are a grim reminder of the ongoing hazard of forest fires. About 5km (3 miles) south of Vivario, the D23 drops into the valley to the hamlet of **Canaglia**. From here a trail leads 4km (2.5 miles) along the **Manganello River**, through pine forest. Cross the river by the bridge where the trail meets the red and white markings of the GR 20 and continue a short way to the **Bergeries de Tolla**, where refreshments as well as cheese can be bought. Further up this gorgeous valley, the river drops in

Top: Corte's Citadel commands a panoramic view of the surrounding countryside

Above: The Musée de la Corse in Corte portrays the island and its people through the centuries

Left: Ghisoni

175

a series of waterfalls, each with its own idyllic pool.

Vizzavona is the last station before the railway plunges into the 5km (3-mile) long tunnel through the mountain. Situated off the main road, the **Gare de Vizzavona** has a restaurant and bar with a pleasant outside terrace and good, reasonably priced food. Vizzavona once appealed to the English community of Ajaccio, who flocked here to escape the summer heat.

Lodging at the grand Hotel Monte D'Oro, on the 1,163m (3,800ft) **Col de Vizzavona**, 3km (2 miles) further along the Ajaccio road, they picnicked in the cool of the luxuriant beech and pine forests along the banks of the Agnone, which tumbles over smooth granite forming a series of small waterfalls, aptly named the **Cascades des Anglais**. It takes 20 minutes to walk down through the beech forest on a path starting on the north side of the N193, just east of

Places to Visit

The Asco Valley

Le Village des Tortues de Moltifao (Tortoise Village)
Children will love the chance to see tortoises in their natural surrounding
Open Monday to Friday, April to September and also weekends July and August
☎ 04 95 47 85 03

In Terra Corsa
Ponte Leccia railway station
Adventure sports operator offering canyoning, trekking, rock climbing and via ferrata in the Asco Valley
☎ 04 95 47 69 48, www.interracorsa.fr

Lana Corsa
(Natural wool knitwear)
Ponte Leccia (on the main road)
Beautiful rustic knitwear, made locally of Corsican wool
Open 9am–7pm, Monday to Saturday, May to October; out of season phone for opening hours
☎ 04 95 48 43 79, www.lana-corsa.com

The Niolo

Tourist Information
In Calacuccia, on the main road in the village centre. Useful advice on walking routes and information on guided walks
☎ 04 95 47 12 62 or 04 95 48 05 22

Musée Archéologique, Albertacce
Small collection of Megalithic to Roman artefacts
In theory, open daily in summer 10am–12.30pm

U Mulinu Chestnut Mill
Lozzi
Above the village of Lozzi on the road to Monte Cinto, by Camping Arimone
Visit a working chestnut flour mill and take a walk around a chestnut grove, where interpretive panels explain it all (in French). This is well worth a visit and you will be supporting an important local cottage industry
Open daily May, June & September 3–7 pm and July and August 9am–1 pm and 4–8 pm, ☎ 04 95 48 09 08

the Hotel Monte D'Oro and nearby café. A slightly longer trail to the falls, marked in the red and white of the GR 20, starts near the station.

The path continues above the falls following the valley until it hauls up the west flank of the **Monte D'Oro**. But this is not the recommended route up this imposing pinnacled *massif*, which is best approached from the east via a path that winds up from the forestry trail, off the GR 20 on the east bank of the

Agnone opposite the village. Even this trail to the 2,389m (7,835ft) summit is no Sunday stroll, demanding stamina and concentration. The last part of the climb is a scramble, there is no water along the way and if cloud descends on the summit it is not advisable to continue. That said, it is worth it for the view, which stretches both east and west to the coast and beyond.

Mountain Guides
Guided ascent of Monte Cinto and other circuits, ☎ 04 95 48 10 43

Corte and the Restonica Valley

Tourist Information
In the citadel
Open July and August, daily 9am–8pm; June and September, daily except Sunday, 9am–12pm and 2–6pm; October to May, Monday to Friday 9am–12pm and 2–6pm
☎ 04 95 46 26 70
www.corte-tourisme.com

Musée de la Corse and Citadel
In the citadel
Open 22 June to 20 September daily 10am–8pm; 1 April to 21 June and 21 September to 31 October, daily except Monday 10am–6pm; November to March daily except Sunday and Monday 10am–5pm; closed 1 May, 14 December, 31 December to 14 January and public

holidays in winter
Audio guide available in English. Entry to the museum also includes access to the citadel
☎ 04 95 45 26 06, www.sitec.fr/museu

U Trenu
Miniature train which does a 30-minute guided tour (in English and French) of the citadel and old town. Out of season it departs from near the railway station but from the Tufelli car park in July and August.

Vizzavona, Vivario and the Venaco

Accro-Branche, Saint Pierre de Venaco
Family adventure course for budding Tarzans, using nets and ropes from tree to tree and a botanical trail
Open mid-June to mid-September
☎ 06 03 83 68 36
www.grandeurnature-corse.com

Palombaggia is famous for its red rocks

Getting to Corsica

Direct Flights From the UK

UK tour operator Holiday Options (see under 'Package Holidays') offer charter flights from several UK airports to Bastia, Calvi and Figari Airports. These flights operate on Sundays between May and September as does British Airways' scheduled service from London Gatwick to Bastia.

Flying from North America

There are no direct flights from North America to Corsica, but by flying to Paris (France), London or Manchester (UK), you can connect with direct services from these countries.

Flying from France

Whilst there are no internal flights within Corsica, there are many flights from mainland France to the island. Air France (www.airfrance.fr) fly from Paris Orly to Bastia, Calvi and Ajaccio, while Nice, Marseille and Lyon connect with Bastia and Ajaccio. Compagnie Corse Méditerranée (www. ccm-airlines.com) link Nice and Marseille with Ajaccio, Bastia and Calvi. French tour operator Nouvelles Frontières (www.nouvelles-frontieres.fr) run their own flights to Corsica.

Flight plus Ferry

Budget airlines including easyJet (www.easyjet.com) and Ryanair (www.ryanair.com) serve French and Italian ports with direct ferry links to Corsica. It can be a juggling act to find connecting flights and ferries which do not involve overnight stops, but it can be done. Nice (France) and Livorno (Italy, via Pisa Airport) are popular routings.

Ferry Travel to Corsica from France and Italy

Corsica Ferries: sail year round between Nice and Toulon (France), Savona and Livorno (Italy) and Calvi, Ajaccio, Île Rousse and Bastia (Corsica). www.corsicaferries.fr

SNCM: sail from Nice and Marseille (France) to Bastia, Ajaccio, Calvi, Île Rousse, Propriano and Porto Vecchio (Corsica). www.sncm.fr

Euromer: sail from Marseille, Toulon, Nice (France) and Savona, Genoa, Livorno, La Spezia and Naples (Italy) to Ajaccio, Bastia, Calvi and Porto Vecchio. www.euromer.net

Moby Lines: sail from Genoa and Livorno (Italy) and Bastia (Corsica) and also between Santa Teresa (Sardinia) and Bonifacio (Corsica). www.mobylines.fr

CMN: sail from Marseille to Ajaccio, Bastia and Propriano. www.cmn.fr

Escorted Tours & Package Holidays

Corsica is generally considered a mid-range to upmarket destination, with prices reflecting this. However, bargains can often be found if you are prepared to book late and travel out of high season. A number of reputable tour operators arrange packages, including flight, accommodation and car hire, which is the most popular holiday formula for British visitors. Most of these companies use the services of the charter flights arranged by Holiday Options or the British Airways service to Bastia.

In the UK:
Corsican Places: www.corsica.co.uk ☎ 0845 330 2059
Direct Corsica: www.directcorsica.com
Corsican Affair: www.corsicanaffair.co.uk ☎ 0207 385 8438
Holiday Options: www.holidayoptions.co.uk ☎ 0870 420 8386
Simply Travel: www.simplytravel.co.uk ☎ 0870 116 4979
Simpson Travel: www.simpsontravel.com ☎ 0845 811 6501
Voyages Ilena: www.voyagesilena.co.uk ☎ 0207 924 4440
VFB Holidays: www.vfbholidays.co.uk ☎ 01242 240331
Exodus Holidays: www.exodus.co.uk ☎ 0208 675 5550
Explore: www.explore.co.uk ☎ 01252 760000

In the USA & Canada:
Kalliste Tours: www.kallistetours.com ☎ 831 438 0907

World Expeditions: www.worldexpeditions.com ☎ 1 800 567 2216
Adventure Center: www.adventurecenter.com ☎ 1 800 228 8747

In France:
Nouvelles Frontières: www.nouvelles-frontieres.fr

In Corsica:
Ollandini Voyages: www.ollandini-voyages.fr

Getting Around Corsica

By Car

Bringing your own car

Bringing your own vehicle to Corsica from the UK involves two ferry crossings and a long drive through mainland France. It's really only recommended if you are planning a long stay or wish to bring a lot of luggage or camping gear. When calculating the costs, don't forget to include a hefty sum for motorway tolls and fuel as you travel through mainland France. You will need to adjust your headlamp beams by attaching a deflector for driving on the right, so as not to blind oncoming traffic. By law you must carry a reflective warning triangle, to be used in the event of a breakdown, and your vehicle must bear a sticker indicating its country of origin – GB for Great Britain, for example.

Hiring a car

Car hire is a little more expensive than in mainland France but, by shopping around, good deals can be found. The best prices are usually found by booking in advance, while on-the-spot rentals are often more expensive. Most visitors opt to pick up and drop off at the main airports of Bastia, Calvi, Ajaccio and Figari, but car hire companies often have offices in major towns as well.

Budget: ☎ 04 95 30 05 05 www.budget-en-corse.com
Hertz: ☎ 04 95 30 05 00 www.hertz-en-corse.com
Ada: ☎ 04 95 54 55 44 www.ada-en-corse.com

Make sure that any prices quoted include pick-up or drop-off fees and taxes. Prices quoted normally only include basic insurance cover and full insurance is at a supplement.

When collecting your rental car, be sure to check very carefully and report any signs of damage to the lights, bodywork and interior upholstery, even minor scratches. Make sure these are recorded on your rental agreement otherwise you may be liable for someone else's damage to your vehicle.

Be wary of driving ordinary cars on dirt roads, which are often only for four-wheel-drive vehicles. The roads can be very rutted and you may be liable to pay for any damage you cause to the underside or bodywork of the car.

Note that nearly all rental vehicles are manual shift. If you require automatic, you must specify this at the time of booking.

Driving in Corsica, as in the rest of France, is on the right side of the road and cars are left-hand drive. Visitors from EU countries, the USA, Canada and many other countries can drive using the driver's licence issued by their home country. Note that you should be in possession of a full driver's licence for a minimum of a year and in most cases the minimum rental age is 21 (occasionally 25) to hire a vehicle. A credit card is usually required.

Road Safety

Most of Corsica's roads are very narrow and winding and you must drive carefully and slowly. It can be helpful to sound your horn on blind corners on narrow roads. Apart from on the main 'N' roads, you should allow for an average speed of 40–50km/h (25–30mph). Pigs, cows, sheep and goats often use the roads too and it is essential to slow down or stop to let them pass.

Unless otherwise specified, speed limits in built-up areas are 50km/h (31mph) and 90 km/h (56mph) on open roads but 80km/h (50mph) when it is raining. Fines for drink- driving (blood-alcohol concentration in excess of 0.05%) are severe and random breathalyser testing is done.

On roads and intersections marked at regular intervals by signs with a yellow diamond with black diamond in the middle, you have priority. Where a diagonal line goes through the diamond sign, priority shifts to those joining the road from the right, even if they are entering a major road from a minor one. This is known as *priorité à droite* (give way to traffic from the right). Sometimes, notably at roundabouts, this is suspended and will be indicated by the sign *cédez le passage* (give way) or *vous n'avez pas la priorité* (you do not have priority).

Place Names

On road signs, place names are given in both French and Corsican, unless they are the same. On maps, they are usually in one language or the other.

Bus Transport

Corsica's bus services are notoriously irregular and run by many different operators. Some also function as school bus services. Most routes do not operate on Sundays and public holidays. Brief details of the services are given here but it is advisable to phone for up-to-date information and times. A convenient website has full details of the routes and timetables in English: **www.corsicabus.org**

For town and airport services in and around Bastia see **www.bastiabus.com** and for town and airport services in and around Ajaccio see **www.bys-tca.fr**

Ajaccio–Corte–Bastia: Eurocorse Voyages, twice daily except Sunday and public holidays, all year. Northbound, departs Ajaccio at 7.45am and 3pm, Corte at 9.30am and 4.40pm and arrives Bastia at 10.45am and 6pm. Southbound, departs Bastia at 7.45am and 3pm, Corte at 9am and 4.15pm, arriving Ajaccio at 10.45am and 6pm. ☎ 04 95 21 06 30 www.eurocorse.net

Bastia–St Florent: Transports Santini, twice daily except Sunday and public holidays, all year. Departs St Florent 6.45am and 2 pm, arrives Bastia 7.30am and 2.45pm and departs Bastia 11am (12pm Wednesday and Saturday in school term time) and 6pm, arriving St Florent 11.45am and 6.45pm. ☎ 04 95 37 02 98

St Florent–Île Rousse: Transport Santini, twice daily except Sunday and public holidays, July and August only. Departs St Florent 9am and 4 pm, arriving Île Rousse 10am and 5.30pm and departs Île Rousse 11am and 6.30pm arriving St Florent 12pm and 7.30pm. ☎ 04 95 37 02 98

Bastia–PortoVecchio: Les Rapides Bleus, twice daily late June to mid-September and twice daily except Sundays and public holidays rest of the year. Departs Bastia 8.30am and 4pm, arriving Porto Vecchio 11.30am and 6.45pm and departs Porto Vecchio 8am and 1pm, arriving Bastia 10.45am and 4.30pm. ☎ 04 95 70 96 52 and 04 95 31 62 37.

Ponte Leccia–Calvi (connects with Ajaccio and Corte): Les Beaux Voyages, July and August Monday to Saturday, rest of the year Monday to Friday, departs Ponte Leccia 5.15pm, arrives Calvi 6.30pm, departs Calvi 6.45am, arrives Ponte Leccia 8.35am. ☎ 04 95 65 11 35

Corte–Porto: Autocars Mordiconi, daily except Sunday and public holidays, 1 July to 20 September; departs Corte at 8am and Porto at 2pm. ☎ 04 95 48 00 04

Corte–Restonica Valley: Autocars Cortenais, daily 15 July to 15 August, hourly from 7.30am to early afternoon, from Point Info at Chjarasgiolu near the start of the valleys to Bergeries E Grutelle. Returns hourly until late afternoon. ☎ 04 95 46 02 12

Corte–Aléria–Ghisonaccia: Autocars Cortenais, three to five services weekly, all year. ☎ 04 95 46 02 12

Ponte Leccia–Asco Valley: Grisoni Voyages, twice daily except Sundays and public holidays, May to October, departs Ponte Leccia at 10.30am and 3pm, arriving Haut Asco at 11.30am and 4pm and departs Haut Asco 11.40am and 4.40pm, arriving Ponte Leccia 12.40pm and 5.40pm. ☎ 04 95 38 20 74

Bastia–La Porta (Castagniccia): Transport Ampugnani, once daily Tuesday and Friday, July and August (rest of the year once daily except Sunday and public holidays. Departs La Porta 7am, arrives Bastia 8.30am and departs Bastia 3.45pm, arriving La Porta 5.30pm. ☎ 04 95 36 98 26

Bastia–Cap Corse:
Bastia–Barretali: Transports Saoletti, Wednesdays only, all year. Departs Barretali on Cap Corse at 7am, arrives Bastia at 8am, departs Bastia at 4pm arrives Barretali at 5pm. ☎ 04 95 37 84 05

Bastia–Canari: Transports Saoletti, Wednesdays only, all year. Departs Canari 7am, arrives Bastia 8am, departs Bastia 4pm, arrives Canari 5pm.

Calvi–Calenzana: Les Beaux Voyages, twice daily except Sundays and public holidays, 1 July to 15 September. Departs Calvi 2.30pm and 7pm, arriving Calenzana 3pm and 7.30pm and departs Calenzana at 3pm and 7.30pm, arriving Calvi at 3.30pm and 8pm. Rest of the year school bus service only. ☎ 04 95 65 15 02 www.lesbeauxvoyages.com

Calvi–Galéria: Les Beaux Voyages, daily except Sundays and public holidays, 1 July to 1 September. Departs Calvi 3.30pm, arrives Galéria 4.10pm and departs Galéria 4.30pm, arriving Calvi 5.15pm. ☎ 04 95 65 15 02 www.lesbeauxvoyages.com

Calvi–Porto: Autocars SAS AIB, daily except Sunday and public holidays 15 May to 30 June and daily 1 July to 16 September. Departs Porto at 9.45am, arriving Calvi at 12.30pm and departs Calvi at 3.30pm, arriving Porto at 6pm. ☎ 04 95 22 41 99

Calvi–Porto Vecchio–Bonifacio: Les Beaux Voyages, daily except Sundays and public holidays, all year. Departs Calvi 6.45am, arrives Porto Vecchio 11.30am and Bonifacio 12.30pm and departs Bonifacio 7am, arriving Porto Vecchio at 7.30am and Calvi at 6.30pm. ☎ 04 95 65 15 02 www.lesbeauxvoyages.com

Porto Vecchio–Bonifacio: Eurocorse Voyages, daily except Sunday and public holidays, 1 July to 15 September. Departs Portovecchio at 8am, 1pm, 3pm and 7pm and Bonifacio at 7.30am, 12.30pm, 4.15pm and 7pm, arriving 30 minutes later. Sundays and public holidays departs Porto Vecchio at 8am and 12pm and Bonifacio at 2pm and 7pm. Rest of the year departs Porto Vecchio at 12pm and Bonifacio at 7.30am and 2pm. ☎ 04 95 70 13 83 www.eurocorse.net

Bonifacio/Porto Vecchio–Sartène–Propriano–Ajaccio: Eurocorse Voyages, 1 July to 15 September, daily except Sunday and public holidays. Departs Bonifacio/Porto Vecchio at 6.30am, 8.30am and 2.15pm, Sartène at 7.55am, 9.40am, 3.25pm and 4pm, Propriano at 8.10am, 9.55am, 3.45pm and 4.15pm, arriving Ajaccio at 10am, 11.45am and 6pm. Departs Ajaccio at 8am, 8.30am, 3pm and 4pm, Propriano at 9.50am, 10am, 4.30pm and 5.30pm, Sartène at 10.15am, 10.20am, 4.45pm and 5.4pm, arriving Porto Vecchio at 11.45am and 6pm and Bonifacio at 11.45am and 7pm. Rest of the year, daily except Sunday and public holidays. Departs Bonifacio at 6.30am and 2pm, Porto Vecchio at 6.30am and 2.30pm, Sartène at 7.55am and 4pm, Propriano at 8.10am and 4.15pm, arriving Ajaccio at 10am and 6pm. Departs Ajaccio at 8.30am and 4pm, Propriano at 10.15am and 5.30pm, Sartène at 10.35am and 5.50pm, arriving Porto Vecchio at 12pm and 7pm and Bonifacio at 12.30pm and 7pm. ☎ 04 95 70 13 83 www.eurocorse.net

Porto Vecchio–Bavella–Zonza–Aullène–Ajaccio: Balesi Evasion, 1 July to 31 August, daily except Sunday (rest of the year Monday and Friday only). Departs Porto Vecchio at 6.45am, Bavella at 8.15am, Zonza at 8.20am, Aullène at 8.40am, arriving Ajaccio at 10.15am. Departs Ajaccio at 4pm, Aullène at 5.25pm, Bavella at 6.05pm, Zonza at 6.15pm, arriving at Porto Vecchio at 7.15pm. ☎ 04 95 70 12 31

Ajaccio–Cargèse–Porto–Ota: Autocars SAS AIB, year round, daily, but Sundays and public holidays only 1 July to 16 September. Monday to Saturday departs Ajaccio at 7.30am and 3.30pm, Cargèse at 8.25am and 4.25pm, Porto at 9.25am and 5.25pm arriving Ota at 9.40am and 5.40pm (Saturday departures from October to April from Ajaccio at 7.30am and 12.30pm). Departs Ota at 7.45am and 11.45pm, Porto at 8.15am and 2.15pm, Cargèse at 9.15am and 3.15pm, arriving Ajaccio at 10.20am and 4.20pm (Saturday departures from October to April from Ota at 7.45am and 10.15am). ☎ 04 95 22 41 99

Ajaccio–Bastelica: Transports Bernardi, July and August daily except Sundays and public holidays (rest of the year Monday, Wednesday and Friday only. Departs Bastelica 6.45am, arriving Ajaccio at 8am. Departs Ajaccio at 4.45pm, arriving Bastelica at 6.15pm. ☎ 04 95 20 06 00

Ajaccio–Zicavo: Autocars Santoni, Monday to Saturday except public holidays, year round. Departs Zicavo at 6.50am, arriving Ajaccio at 8.30am and departs Ajaccio at 4pm, arriving Zicavo at 6pm. ☎ 04 95 22 64 44 www.autocars-santoni.com

Ajaccio–Sartène–Zonza: Eurocorse Voyages, Monday to Saturday except public holidays year round. Departs Zonza at 5am, Sartène 6am, arriving Ajaccio 8am. Departs Ajaccio 4pm, Sartène 6pm, arriving Zonza at 7pm. ☎ 04 95 70 13 83 www.eurocorse.net

Ajaccio–Sartène–Zonza–Bavella: Alta Rocca Voyages Ricci, daily, 1 July to 15 September. Departs Bavella 7.45am, Zonza 8am, Sartène 9am, arriving Ajaccio 10.50am and departs Ajaccio 3pm, Sartène 4.45pm, Zonza 5.45pm, arriving Bavella 6pm. Rest of the year departs Zonza at 6am, arriving Ajaccio at 8.50am and departs Ajaccio at 4pm, arriving Bavella at 7pm. ☎ 04 95 78 86 30

Train Services

The delightful **Trinighellu** is a relaxing and enjoyable way to travel and it's worth taking a ride for the scenery alone. Opening in 1888, around 230km (140 miles) of track were laid, including 11km (9 miles) of tunnel, snaking along the coast and through the mountainous interior, with jaw-dropping mountain vistas. The section between Vizzavona and Corte offers the best views and crosses the famous Pont de Vecchio, built by Gustave Eiffel (of tower fame) to bridge a rocky ravine between Venaco and Vivario.

There are two main routes: Ajaccio–Corte–Ponte Leccia–Bastia and Calvi–Île Rousse–Ponte Leccia. New engines and carriages and upgrading of the track, starting in 2007, will improve the service. In the Gravona valley and between Vizzavona and Corte, walkers can use the train to return to the start of a walk, but remember that many of the minor stops are on request, 'Arrêt Facultatif', and must be arranged in advance. There are 4 to 6 services each way per day. Reservations are not needed but in high summer it's advisable to arrive early for a window seat. The best mountain views are from the right-hand side, travelling south, and the left side travelling north between Ajaccio and Ponte Leccia.

The **Balagne Tramway** runs a service from April to October between Calvi and Île Rousse, stopping off at villages and beaches along the way.

For timetables: www.train-corse.com (in French) or www.corsicabus.org ☎ 04 95 32 80 60

Taxis

Taxis are expensive but sometimes the only option, especially for hikers getting to the start of a trail. Major towns have taxi ranks but elsewhere you will need to phone. Check prices in advance and note that in the evenings and on Sundays and public holidays, prices may be higher. Tipping is not required.

Airport buses

Ajaccio and Bastia Airports are served by public buses all year. Figari Airport has a limited bus service in summer only, while for Calvi Airport the only option is a taxi.

Hitch-hiking

While this cannot be considered an entirely safe way to travel, hitching may be an option where public transport is not available. In view of the dearth of public transport, both locals and visitors may be generous with their lifts, especially if you look like a hiker and carry a rucksack. It is best to travel in pairs and do not hesitate to refuse a lift if you are unsure.

Accommodation

See 'Introduction' chapter for full details of the accommodation options in Corsica.

Hotels

Broadly speaking you can expect to pay the following prices for accommodation in mid-season, i.e. June or September:

    Budget Hotel : 40–60 euros (per room)
    Mid-range Hotel : 70–80 euros (per room)
    Top of the range: 120 euros and more (per room)

In July and August prices can easily be double what they are at other times of year. Prices are room only.

The following websites have details of many hotels, but it is often better to contact the establishment directly.

    www.destination-corse.com
    www.locationcorse.net

Self-catering accommodation:

This includes villas, mini-villas, studio flats, country houses and campsite cabins. It can be arranged directly with the owners, or as part of a package through a tour operator. If you're booking for the peak months or July and August, tour operator packages may offer better value for money than going direct.

In June or September, prices for a studio flat start at around 250 euros per week. For a two-bedroomed mini villa, allow 600–700 euros while for a villa with pool, weekly rentals start at around 1,000 euros. High season prices may be double these rates but bargains can be had out of season.

    www.directcorsica.com
    www.corsevilla.com
    www.locationcorse.com
    www.villas-du-sud.com
    www.location-france.com

Gîtes de France is a central booking agency for country and village properties, often with special character: www.gites-de-france.com (also in English) or www.gites-corsica.com (in French only).

Refuges, Hostels and *Gîtes d'étape*

Mountain refuges cost around 10 euros per person per night, are sited mostly on the GR 20 hiking route and cannot be booked in advance. There are currently no youth hostels in Corsica. The nearest equivalent are *gîtes d'étape*, which are usually sited on or near other long-distance walking routes and for which advance reservations are essential. Dormitory accommodation costs around 13–16 euros per person per night and with half board around 30–34 euros per person per night. A full list of when they are open, their contact telephone numbers and addresses is on www.gites-refuges.com

Fermes Auberges and Chambres d'hôtes

These country bed and breakfast and farm guest houses are often a great way to meet the locals. Prices for a twin room in June and September start at around 60 euros, room only. Details of the properties can be viewed on www.gites-de-france.com and www.hebergement-corse.com.

Camping

Wild camping is not allowed in Corsica and you must use designated campsites even if you have your own camping van. Details of campgrounds can be found on:

www.visitcorse.com
www.corsicacamping.com
www.corsecampings.com
www.gites-de-france.com
www.campingfrance.com

Most sites are only open between May and September. There are almost no campgrounds open out of season. The following sites may appeal if you're looking for a beach holiday.

La Rondinara
Open 15 May to 30 September
300m from one of Southern Corsica's best beaches, a 3* site with plenty of facilities
www.rondinara.fr
☎ 04 95 70 43 15

Arutoli
Open April to October
Lovely 3* shaded site, inland from Porto Vecchio. Minibus transfer to the beaches
www.arutoli.com
☎ 04 95 70 12 73

U Pirellu
Open April to September
3* site, 3km from Palombaggia Beach. Plenty of facilities
www.u-pirellu.com

Eating Out in Corsica

If you are prepared to be a little adventurous in your tastes, eating out in Corsica will bring many surprises, and most of them pleasant. Wherever possible opt for the 'Menu' or 'Menu du Jour', the set menu of the day, which will be freshly cooked and good value for money. There's often a choice of set menu at different prices – note that in French menu means the set meal of the day but carte is the full menu which details all the dishes on offer.

Restaurants

Corsican towns generally have a good choice of places to dine but in the villages many establishments are only open in high season. In seaside resorts, those clustered around the marina may have nice views, but not always the best food or service. Dogs are often admitted into restaurants. If you are travelling with children, it is worth asking if the establishment offers a child menu (Menu Enfant). Many restaurants do not accept credit or debit cards so make sure you always have cash with you, just in case. Reservations are advisable for popular places, especially in the summer season. Service is normally included and the addition (bill) should indicate this with the letters 'SC' (service compris). If not, add the 10–15% on to the bill yourself.

Hotel Restaurants

In July and August, many hotels will insist that you take their half board supplement. This can represent good value for money, but can also be irritating if you wish to eat out elsewhere, so be sure to check when you make your reservation.

Fermes Auberges

These are family-run, country establishments usually offering a set menu, which may include local or regional delicacies or home-produced *charcuterie*. The menu is often copious and you may be expected to last out four or five courses.

Cheap Eats and Snacks

Paillote: a beach-side establishment, offering anything from a simple range of drinks and sandwiches to a full restaurant service.
Pizzeria: many restaurants serve pizzas in addition to their normal menu. Look for those with a wood-fired oven.
Crêperie: café-style eatery featuring sweet and savoury filled pancakes, cooked to order.
Glacier: bar or café, specialising in ice creams.
Pâtisserie: shop, often with limited seating, serving cakes and sweet and savoury pastries

Vegetarian & Vegan food

Vegetarians fare better in Corsica than in mainland France and will usually find meat and fish-free pasta or pizza items on the menu. It is always worth checking when you phone for a reservation, especially if you are planning to eat at a *Ferme Auberge* or *Gîte d'Étape*, where a set menu may be all that is offered. Vegans will struggle as most meat and fish-free dishes contain cheese. (See introductory chapter for further information.)

Where to stay and eat

Calvi and surrounds

Hôtel du Centre

Rue Alsace-Lorraine by Ste Marie Majeure church
Centrally located budget option with simple rooms, open April to October
☎ 04 95 65 02 01

Hôtel Casa Vecchia

Ten minutes' walk from town off the main Île Rousse road
Mid-range hotel in quiet garden setting, a short walk from the beach. Open all year
☎ 04 95 65 37 93
www.hotel-casa-vecchia.com

Hôtel le Belvédère

Opposite the citadel, a mid-range hotel in a top location, open all year.
☎ 04 95 65 26 95
www.calvi-location.fr

Hostellerie de l'Abbaye

Route de Santore, just outside the town centre, close to the beach
Converted monastery, now a 3* hotel of character. Open April to October
☎ 04 95 65 04 27
www.hostellerie-abbaye.com

Restaurant Le Tire Bouchon

At the citadel end of rue Clemenceau, with an elevated terrace overlooking the bustling street
Traditional food with a Corsican bent. Open April to October
☎ 04 95 65 25 41

Restaurant A Candella

At 9 rue St Antoine in the citadel off Place d'Armes
Corsican specialities in a peaceful setting
☎ 04 95 65 42 13

U Fanale

On the Galéria road, on the outskirts of town
Fine dining in the courtyard under a huge pine tree or inside with stunning views of the Revellata lighthouse
Open mid-March to December, but weekends only October to December. Popular with locals as well as visitors. Reservations essential
☎ 04 95 65 18 82

Chez Tao

Famous restaurant, bar and club with panoramic views from its citadel terrace. Expensive but atmospheric. Reservations essential.
☎ 04 95 65 00 73

Around Calvi

Gîte d'Étape Municipal

Calenzana
Budget dormitory accommodation in four-bedded rooms with bathroom
Open April to October
☎ 04 95 62 77 13

Restaurant chez Michel

Calenzana
On the main road, opposite the church
Closed January to mid-February. Corsican food and pizzas. Reservations essential
☎ 04 95 62 70 25

Auberge de la Forêt

Bonifatu
Country inn with a few nice rooms and hostel-style dormitory. Great place to stop for a drink or meal at the end of a hike
Open April to Ocober. Reservations advisable in season
☎ 04 95 65 09 98

In the Balagne Villages

Casa Musicale

Pigna
Guesthouse and restaurant with a musical theme and great views
Closed mid-January to mid-February.
Reservations essential. Annual music festival during first half of July
☎ 04 95 61 74 28
www.casa-musicale.org
www.festivoce.casa-musicale.org

Restaurant le Bellevue

Sant'Antonino
Simple menu of home grown produce in a gorgeous village setting
Open Easter to September. Reservations essential
☎ 04 95 61 73 91

Hotel Mare e Monti

Feliceto
In an old family mansion of character, owned by the Renucci family, of vineyard fame
Open April to October
☎ 04 95 63 02 00

Restaurant U Mulino

Feliceto
Outside the village on the road to Nessa, in an old olive mill
Open March to October, daily except Tuesdays, but only at weekends out of season. Corsican food with flair! Reservations essential
☎ 04 95 61 73 23

Auberge chez Edgard

Lavatoggio
In the heart of the village, a place to enjoy Corsican country cooking. Copious set menu guaranteed to satisfy meat eaters
Open May to September, evenings only.
Reservations essential
☎ 04 95 61 70 75

Hôtel A Spelunca

Speloncato
Formerly a cardinal's summer residence, now a hotel of character in the heart of the Balagne
Open April to November
☎ 04 95 61 50 38
Email: hotel.a.spelunca@wanadoo.fr

Hôtel Restaurant Le Grillon

Île Rousse

Av. Paul Doumer
Cheap and cheerful budget hotel in the heart of the town
Open March to October
☎ 04 95 60 00 49
Email: hr-le-grillon@wanadoo.fr

Restaurant A Siesta

Île Rousse
Reputable beachside fish restaurant
Open April to December, closed Mondays out of season
☎ 04 95 60 28 74

The Giunssani and Ostriconi

Auberge l'Aghjola Pioggiola

Giunssani
Country Inn at Pioggiola, above the village, with rooms and restaurant
Open April to October for copious, mouth-watering Corsican food
☎ 04 95 61 90 48

Pizzeria Chez Jul's

Lama
Village pizza place just up from the church.
Cheap and cheerful
Only open in summer
☎ 04 95 48 23 97

Domaine de l'Ostriconi

Just off the main N1197, a short drive from the
Ostriconi beach and Agriates trail
Restaurant serving innovative cuisine using
home-grown produce with four stylish B & B
rooms in an adjoining restored mansion
Open March to October. Restaurant
reservations advisable out of season
☎ 04 95 60 53 29
www.domaine-ostriconi.com

St Florent

Hôtel La Roya

Well-appointed but expensive hotel on La Roya
beach, west of the town
Open April to mid-November
☎ 04 95 37 00 40
www.hoteldelaroya.com

Hôtel Maxime

Modern mid-range hotel, in the centre of town
on the road to the cathedral, overlooking the
Poggio river
Open all year
☎ 04 95 37 05 30

Villa Bleu Azur

Family-run guesthouse with gardens, by
the beach just outside town. Six rooms with
private facilities
Open all year
☎ 04 95 37 20 05
www.villableuazur-corse.com

Hôtel de L'Europe

Modest hotel and restaurant in the old town
overlooking the port
Open March to October
Tel 04 95 37 00 03
www.hotel-europe2.com

Cap Corse

Auberge I Fundali

Piazza, Luri
Unusual country guesthouse, with its own
medieval tower, on the D 532 near Piazza in
the Luri Valley.
Open mid March to mid November.
Reservations essential
☎ 04 95 35 06 15

Osteria di U Portu

Macinaggio
On the waterfront in Macinaggio, this popular
seafood restaurant also has a few simple
rooms
Closed January and Wednesdays from
November to March
☎ 04 95 35 40 49

Hôtel U'Sant Agnellu

Rogliano
This eye-catching pink mansion with blue
shutters has been sympathetically converted
to a hotel with panoramic coastal views from
its terrace and sea-facing rooms
Open April to September
☎ 04 95 35 40 59
www.hotel-usantagnellu.com

Hôtel Le Vieux Moulin

Centuri
Restored nineteenth-century *Maison
d'Americains* (with annex) furnished in period
style with its own restaurant and terrace
overlooking the port
Open March to October
☎ 04 95 35 60 15
www.le-vieux-moulin.net

Résidence I Fioretti

Canari
On the west coast of the Cap
This former sixteenth-century monastery has
been converted to comfortable hotel and *gîte*
accommodation, with superb coastal views
Open all year
☎ 04 95 37 13 90
www.ifioretti.com

Les Gîtes du Cap Corse

Marine de Negru
This cluster of tasteful self-catering units, in the
maquis behind a sheltered bay with its own
Genoese tower, is run by a knowledgeable
local couple, who also offer bed and breakfast
in their home
Open April to October
☎ 04 95 37 27 50
www.cap-corse.com

Bastia

Hôtel Central

3, rue Miot
Centrally located, reasonably priced, family-run 2* hotel, 10 minutes' walk from port, bus and train stations. Open all year.
☎ 04 95 31 71 12
www.centralhotel.fr

Hotel Posta Vecchia

Quai des Martyrs
Good location by the old port and convenient for the citadel. 2* hotel with budget and more expensive sea-view rooms.
☎ 04 95 32 32 38
www.hotel-postavecchia.com

Hôtel Les Voyageurs

9, Ave Maréchal Sebastiani
Centrally located and recently renovated stylish 3* hotel, convenient for the port, bus and train stations. Open all year.
☎ 04 95 34 90 80
www.hotel-lesvoyageurs.com

Les Zephyrs

One of the many eateries spilling onto quai des Martyrs. Good value crêpes, pizzas, pasta and Corsican menus are served out of the tiniest kitchen. Only open in season.

Le Colomba

Pizzeria and à la carte menu on the north side of Vieux Port. Closed in January and February.
☎ 04 95 32 79 14

A Casarella

At the north end of rue Sainte-Croix, in the citadel by the Palais des Gouverneurs. Mid-price-range restaurant with excellent traditional Corsican fare. Closed during November, Sundays and Saturdays at lunchtime.
☎ 04 95 32 02 32

Le Caveau du Marin

quai des Martyrs
Closed January and Sunday and Monday lunchtime. Popular mid-price-range fish restaurant, also offering a Corsican menu.
☎ 04 95 31 62 31

The East Coast

Hôtel and Restaurant Le Refuge

Piedicroce, Castagniccia
Ask for a room with valley view. Restaurant open all year except mid-October to end November. Hotel open April to mid-October
☎ 04 95 35 82 65
hotellerefuge@wanadoo.fr

Chambres d'hôtes La Diligence, Verdèse

near Piedicroce in Castagniccia
Family run B & B in a beautiful eighteenth-century mansion
Open April to October
☎ 04 95 34 26 33

Auberge du Corsigliese

Casaperta, near Aléria
At Casaperta 10km (6 miles) down the Aléria to Corte road. Modest, reasonably priced hotel and restaurant. Open all year.
☎ 04 95 57 04 87

Le Kyrié Eleison

Ghisoni
Mountain restaurant and hotel in the village centre. ☎ 04 95 57 60 33

Gîte d'Étape de Catastaghju

San Gavino di Fium'Orbo
Hostel-style accommodation and home-cooked meals
Open April to October
☎ 04 95 56 70 14
paoli.colette@wanadoo.fr

Les Deux Magots

Ghisonaccia
Modest fish restaurant and pizzeria on the beach at Ghisonaccia
Open April to November
☎ 04 95 56 15 61

L'Ortu

Vescovato
Corsica's only organic restaurant, situated on the D237 between Vescovato and Venzolasca in the Casinca
Open all year (but reservations essential out of season) Wednesday to Sunday
☎ 04 95 36 64 69

Porto Vecchio and surrounds

Grand Hotel de Cala Rossa

Boutique 4* hotel on the beach, just north of Porto Vecchio
Open April to December
☎ 04 95 71 61 51
www.cala-rossa.com

Hotel Le Pinarello

Boutique 4* hotel on one of Corsica's loveliest beaches, north of Porto Vecchio
Open 11 April to 28 October
☎ 04 95 71 44 39
www.lepinarello.com

Hotel Alcyon

Rue Général Leclerc
3* hotel in the town centre. Good value low-season rates
Open all year
☎ 04 95 70 50 50
www.hotel-alcyon.com

Le Goeland

Ave Georges Pompidou
Seaside location, north of the marina. Family-run 2* hotel with small private beach and gardens
Open April to October
☎ 04 95 70 14 15
www.hotel-le-goeland.com

Le Mistral

Rue Jean Nicoli
Small 2* hotel in town centre, with reasonable low-season rates
Open March to October
☎ 04 95 70 08 53

Modern'Hotel

10, cours Napoléon
Simple, clean and bright rooms, in the town centre
Open April to September
☎ 04 95 70 06 36

Restaurant Le Roi Théodore

By Porte Génoise
Upmarket restaurant with prices to match. Reservations essential
☎ 04 95 70 47 98

Restaurant Le Tourisme

12, cours Napoléon, in the upper town
Regional cuisine with flair
Closed Sunday lunchtime. Reservations essential
☎ 04 95 70 06 45

Cantina de l'Orriu

5, cours Napoléon, in the upper town
Wine bar and shop serving simple but tasty local charcuterie and cheese
Open May to September
☎ 04 95 70 26 21

Auberge Le Refuge

Cartalavonu, near Ospedale
Mountain inn, 4 km (2.5 miles) off the Zonza road, patronised by walkers
Offers dormitory beds, double rooms and a decent à la carte menu
Open all year but weekends only from November to March
☎ 04 95 70 00 39

Le Tamaricciu

Palombaggia Beach
Beachside eatery with beautiful views, down a lane at the south end of the beach. Well-prepared but fairly expensive fresh fish, pasta and salads
Open May to October. Reservations essential
☎ 04 95 70 49 89

Bonifacio

There are no bargains to be had in high season so prepare for high prices

Hotel des Étrangers

Avenue Sylvère-Bohn
On the main road into town, 200m (200yds) from the port. Parking. The only budget hotel in town. Simple rooms but a warm welcome
Open mid-March to mid-November
☎ 04 95 73 16 97

Hôtel Royal

Place Bonaparte
Small hotel in the heart of the citadel, with reasonable low-season rates, but pricey in high season. Pleasant, modern rooms. Café and restaurant
Open all year
☎ 04 95 73 00 51
Email: leroyal4@wanadoo.fr

Le Roi D'Aragon

13 quai J. Comparetti
Modern 3* hotel facing the marina. Good low and shoulder season rates
Open all year
☎ 04 95 73 03 99

Hotel & Restaurant Centre Nautique

Intimate and tasteful hotel on the north side of the marina, with spacious rooms sleeping 3–4. Parking and an excellent restaurant
Open all year
☎ 04 95 73 02 11
www.centre-nautique.com

A Trama

Located 1.5km (1 mile) outside Bonifacio, this tasteful, modern 3* hotel is set in lovely grounds, with swimming pool and a good restaurant. Each room has its own private terrace
Closed January
☎ 04 95 73 17 17
www.a-trama.com

A Cheda

Intimate and charming hotel, with highly individual rooms, a swimming pool and beautiful gardens, located just outside Bonifacio, on the road to Porto Vecchio. Atoll Dive Centre located here
Open all year
☎ 04 95 73 02 83
www.acheda-ho☎com

Hôtel Genovese

Luxury hotel with swimming pool by the old city ramparts, overlooking the port. Pricey, but full of charm
Open all year
☎ 04 95 73 12 34
www.hotel-genovese.com

Cantina Doria

Rue Doria, in the citadel
Best to arrive early for this modest but popular place as it's often busy
Open March to late October. Closed Tuesdays out of season
☎ 04 95 73 50 49

Stella D'Oro

Rue Doria, in the citadel, just off Place de Montepagano
Fine dining with ambience

Open from Easter to September
☎ 04 95 73 03 63

La Galiote

Rue St Dominique, in the citadel
Cheap, cheerful and popular with locals at lunch

Les Quatres Vents

Quai Banda del Ferro, by the ferry quay
Popular fish restaurant
Open all year
☎ 0495 73 07 50

Propriano, Alta Rocca and the Sartenais

Hôtel Le Bellevue

Propriano
Av. Napoléon
Slightly dated rooms, but good location with views of the port
Open all year
☎ 04 95 76 01 86
www.hotel-bellevue-propriano.com

Hôtel Le Lido

Propriano
Av. Napoléon, past the port and on its own little beach
Charming little 3* newly renovated property
Open May to September
☎ 04 95 76 06 37
www.le-lido.com

Restaurant U Pescadori

Propriano
Av. Napoléon
Reputable fish restaurant overlooking the port
Closed December to March. Reservations essential
☎ 04 95 76 42 95

Restaurant Terra Cotta

Propriano
Av. Napoléon
Fine dining overlooking the port
Closed mid December to mid March. Reservations essential.
☎ 04 95 74 23 80

Hôtel Les Roches

Sartène
Av. Jean Jaurès
Solid but slightly dated 2* town hotel, with

panoramic views
Open all year
☎ 04 95 77 07 61
www.sarteneho☎fr

Hôtel Fior di Ribba

Sartène
On the Propriano road, just outside the town
Small 2* hotel with pool
Open mid-March to end October
☎ 04 95 77 01 80
www.hotelfiordiribba.com

Hôtel le Ressac

Campomoro
Family-run small hotel and restaurant set back
from Campomoro's lovely beach
Open April to October
☎ 04 95 74 22 25
www.hotel-ressac.fr

Chez Antoine

Tizzano
Taste the catch of the day on a lovely terrace
overlooking the sea
Open late May to September
☎ 04 95 77 07 25

Auberge Coralli

Roccapina
Hotel and restaurant on the main Propriano
to Bonifacio road 2.5km (1.5 miles) from the
beach
Open April to October, closed Wednesdays
out of high season
☎ 04 95 77 05 94

Gîte d'Étape U Fragnunu

Ste Lucie de Tallano, by the olive mill on the
road to Zoza
Hostel accommodation and excellent meals
Open April to October
☎ 04 95 78 82 56

Ferme Auberge A Pignata

Between Levie and Ste Lucie, on the road to
Cucuruzzu
B & B and splendid feast of Corsican
delicacies, including home-made *charcuterie,*
in the restaurant. Horse riding excursions also
offered.
Open all year. Restaurant closed Sunday
evenings. Reservations essential
☎ 04 95 78 41 90
www.apignata.com

Auberge Sole e Monti

Quenza
2* family hotel in the village with log fire and
gardens
Open May to September. Restaurant closed
Mondays
☎ 04 95 78 62 53
www.solemonti.com

Gîte d'Étape chez Pierrot

Jallicu, near Quenza
Rustic hostel accommodation, horse riding
excursions and genuine unpretentious
mountain food
Open all year. Reservations essential
☎ 04 95 78 63 21

Hotel de la Poste

Aullène
In the village
Basic hotel accommodation and excellent
restaurant
Open May to September
☎ 04 95 78 61 21

Hotel Clair de Lune

Zonza
Comfortable, new hotel of character in the
village
Canyoning, climbing and hiking excursions
Open all year
☎ 04 95 78 56 79
www.hotelclairdelune.com

Auberge du Col de Bavella

Hostel, with dormitory accommodation, and
restaurant
Open April to October
☎ 04 95 72 09 87
www.auberge-bavella.com

Ajaccio

Hôtel Marengo

2, rue Marengo
In a quiet location near the sea, a 20-minute
walk from the city centre. Reasonably priced
rooms with and without private facilities. Open
April to mid-November.
☎ 04 95 21 43 66
www.hotel-marengo.com

Hôtel du Palais

5, av. Bévérini-Vico (off Cours Napoléon)
A centrally located 2*, convenient for the
station. Open all year except November and

February.
☎ 04 95 22 73 68
www.hoteldupalaisajaccio.com

Hôtel Fesch

7, rue Fesch
A comfortable, classic 3* hotel in the heart of
the city. Open all year except 20 December
to 20 January.
☎ 04 95 51 62 62
www.hotel-fesch.com

Hôtel du Golfe

5, bd. Roi Jérôme
A 3* centrally located hotel. Most rooms with
balcony and sea view.
☎ 04 95 21 47 64
www.hoteldugolfe.com

Auberge Colomba

3, rue des Trois Marie, between rue Fesch and
rue Napoléon
Classic French cuisine and Corsican
specialities. Good value lunch menu.
☎ 04 95 51 30 55

Le 20123

2, rue Roi de Rôme
Corsican village décor in this popular eatery,
which focuses on typical mountain cuisine.
Open Monday to Saturday, evenings only.
Closed mid-January to mid-February.
Reservations essential.
☎ 04 95 21 50 05

Le Roi de Rôme

In the street of the same name, this restaurant
and wine bar is known for its range of Corsican
wines.
☎ 04 95 21 32 88

A Casa

21 av. Noël Franchini (a turning off the main
road around the bay, 3km (2 miles) from the
centre of town).
Closed Sundays. On Friday and Saturday
nights set menu and magic show. Special price
for children. Reservations essential.
☎ 04 95 22 34 78

In the surrounds
of Ajaccio

Le Maquis

Porticcio
On its own private beach at Porticcio

Luxury 4* small hotel with gourmet
restaurant.
Open all year.
☎ 04 95 25 05 55
www.lemaquis.com

Hôtel Le Belvédère

Coti Chiavari
On the D55A, west of Coti Chiavari
Family-run hotel and restaurant with a
panoramic terrace overlooking the Golfe
d'Ajaccio. Reservations essential. Open mid-
February to early November.
☎ 04 95 27 10 32

Chez Paul

Bastelica
In the hamlet of Stazzone, in the upper village
of Bastelica. Reasonably priced restaurant with
great mountain views.
☎ 04 95 28 71 59

Restaurant U Castagnu

Bocognano
At Bocognano in the centre of the village.
Traditional Corsican food, with flair. Open
all year, except January and Mondays and
Sunday evenings out of season.
☎ 04 95 27 44 75

Bergeries de Bassetta

Coscione, Upper Taravo Valley
On the route de St Pierre, a turning off the
Zicavo to Aullène road. Rustic guest house,
hostel and restaurant with genuine Corsican
mountain cuisine. Open May to September.
☎ 04 95 25 74 20
www.gitecorse.net

Le Paradis

Zicavo
Friendly family guesthouse, with home cooking
and charcuterie. Double rooms and dormitory
accommodation. Open all year.
☎ 04 95 24 41 20

Porto

Hotel le Colombo

On the Calvi road by the junction with the
D124
A small hotel of character with many thoughtful
and personal touches. Décor themed in blue,
featuring driftwood
Open April to October
☎ 04 95 26 10 14
www.hotellecolombo.com

Hotel le Maquis

On the Calvi road
Simple, well-priced rooms and an excellent restaurant
Open mid-February to mid-November
☎ 04 95 26 12 19
www.hotel-lemaquis.com

Around Porto

Gîte d'Étape Giargalo

Piana
Situated up a country lane, which takes off from the main road by the tourist office and opposite the square, this friendly guesthouse has rooms with private facilities on one floor and dormitories on the other. The set menu is copious, tasty and good value
Open all year. ☎ 04 95 27 82 05
www.gite-giargalo.fr.fm

Hôtel les Roches Rouges

Piana
At the entrance to the village on the right, coming from Porto, this grand old mansion was built in 1912. The rooms are a little dated but make up for it on the charm front, the food is good and the setting magnificent. Don't miss drinks on the terrace at sun down
Open April to mid-November
☎ 04 95 27 81 81
www.lesrochesrouges.com

Chez Felix

Ota
Simple dormitory, double and family rooms, most with dazzling views. Authentic local set menu and panoramic terrace
Open all year. Reservations essential
☎ 04 95 26 12 92

Gîte d'Étape Le Cormoran

Girolata
Basic hostel-style accommodation and restaurant in a wonderful setting overlooking the beach
Open April to September. Reservations essential
☎ 04 95 20 15 55

Hôtel le Saint-Jean

Cargèse
Modern hotel in the centre of the village
Closed in January and February
☎ 04 95 26 46 68
www.lesaintjean.com

Hôtel Continental

Cargèse
On the road to Piana
Family-run hotel
Closed 15 December to 20 January
☎ 04 95 26 42 24

Auberge des Deux Sorru

Guagno les Bains
A surprisingly good little country hotel, located deep in the valley just outside the village
☎ 04 95 28 35 14
Email: ibagni@free.fr

Auberge U Fragnu

Murzo
Converted olive mill, now a pizzeria and restaurant of character
Closed January to mid-March and Mondays out of season
☎ 04 95 26 69 26

The Asco Valley

Haut-Asco Refuge

Basic dormitory accommodation, for which you need a sleeping bag. Cooking facilities, small shop and information on walks. No advance bookings.

Hôtel Le Chalêt

Haut-Asco
Basic rooms, some with private bathroom, as well as dormitory accommodation. Copious portions of good local food in the restaurant
Open April to mid-October
☎ 04 95 47 81 08
Email: hotel-le-chalet@wanadoo.fr

The Niolo

Auberge Casa Balduina

Between Calacuccia and Albertacce
Cosy, family-run establishment with good food and eight guest rooms
Closed November. Reservations essential
☎ 04 95 48 08 57
www.casabalduina.com

Gîte d'Étape Couvent St François

Between Calacuccia and Albertacce
Dormitory accommodation and rooms with shower and WC. Kitchen facilities but no meals.
Closed November. Reservations advisable
☎ 04 95 48 00 11

Restaurant du Lac

Calacuccia
In the hamlet of Sidossi, this rather formal-looking place does genuine Niolo food
Open May to September. Reservations advisable
☎ 04 95 48 02 73

Corte and the Restonica Valley

Important: budget rooms can be impossible to find in Corte from October to May as most are rented out to students.

Hôtel de la Paix

Av. du Général de Gaulle, Corte
Central but quiet location in a newly renovated historic building
Open all year. Choice of budget rooms with basin or rooms with shower and WC
☎ 04 95 46 06 72
Email: socoget@wanadoo.fr

Hôtel du Nord

22 Cours Paoli, Corte
Mid-range, newly renovated hotel in a central location
Open all year
☎ 04 95 46 00 68
www.hoteldunord-corte.com

Hôtel Arena and Restaurant Le Refuge

Small, family-run hotel and restaurant in lovely riverside setting 2km (1.25 miles) from Corte in the Restonica Gorge. Rustic but comfortable
Open April to mid-October
☎ 04 95 46 09 13
www.lerefuge.fr.fm

Hôtel Dominique Colonna

A characterful 3* hotel with swimming pool in the Restonica Valley 1.5km (1 mile) from Corte
Open mid-March to mid-November
☎ 04 95 45 25 65

Restaurant U Paglia Orba

Av. Xavier Luciani
Traditional Corsican fare and pizzas at reasonable prices
Closed Sundays
☎ 04 95 61 07 89

Restaurant U Museu

Rampe Ribanelle, by the citadel
Busy little restaurant with an excellent and varied menu at reasonable prices. Arrive early
Closed November to April and Sundays in low season
☎ 04 95 61 08 36

Vizzavona, Vivario and the Venacais

Hotel I Laricci

Vizzavona, by the station
Popular, swiss chalet-style family-run hotel with simple but spacious rooms and wonderful views of Monte D'Oro. Dormitory accommodation in the annex
Open May to September
☎ 04 95 47 21 12
www.ilaricci.com

Vizzavona Station

Charming little restaurant in the station, serving food on an outdoor terrace with views of Monte D'Oro

Hotel du Monte D'Oro

On the Col de Vizzavona, 3km (2 miles) from the station (pick-up service offered)
Grand old nineteenth-century mansion with plenty of character, if a little dated
Open April to mid-November. Traditional Corsican menu
☎ 04 95 47 21 06

Paesotel e Caselle

A 3* hotel in lovely rural surrounds near Venaco, in the style of a stone-built *Bergerie* complex. Swimming pool
Open April to October
☎ 04 95 47 39 00
www.e-caselle.com

Casa Mathea

Poggio-di-Venaco, in the village centre
Modern self-contained studios and flats in a converted traditional family home, rented by the day. Restaurant and pizzeria. Open all year.
☎ 04 95 47 05 27
www.auberge-casamathea-corse.com

Public Holidays & Festivals

Public Holidays

The following days are public holidays:

1 January: New Year's Day
Easter Sunday and Monday
1 May: Labour Day
8 May: Victoire 1945
40th day after Easter: Ascension Day
8th Sunday and Monday after Easter: Whit Sunday & Monday
14 July: Bastille Day
15 August: Assumption Day
(and Napoleon's birthday)
1 November: All Saints' Day
11 November: Armistice Day
25 December: Christmas Day

Festivals

Corsica is an island of festivals and fairs. As might be expected in a place of staunch culinary traditions, food and drink play an important role, with events dedicated to anything from chestnuts, honey and olive oil to pigs, wine and cheese. Saints' days are fêted locally in the towns and villages, but the outstanding events of the religious calendar are the Good Friday processions, taking place in Sartène, Bastia, Calvi, Corte, Bonifacio, Erbalunga and Cargèse. Cultural events, including music festivals, are mostly confined to the summer months, when they can take place outdoors. The websites **www.corsica-isula.com** and **www.terracorsa.info** contain comprehensive lists of the island's festivals. For exact dates and venues contact the local tourist office, *mairie* or the festival organisers.

February:

Pig Fair – *A Tumbera*, in Renno, near Vico, celebrating Corsican pork and *charcuterie* with cooking demonstrations and competitions. ☎ 04 95 26 65 35

March:

Olive Oil Fair – *Festa di l'Oliu Novu*, Sainte Lucie de Tallano, celebrates the new olive oil in mid March. ☎ 04 95 78 89 13

April:

Chestnut Fair – *A Merendella*, Piedicroce in Castagniccia. ☎ 04 95 35 81 26

Cheese & Wine Fair – *Fromage et Vin*, at Cauro. ☎ 04 95 28 40 89

May

The Sea – *Fiera di u Mare*, in Solenzara. www.fieradiumare.free.fr

Brocciu Fair – *Festa di u Brocciu*, at Piana, a festival dedicated to Corsica's famous fresh cheese. ☎ 04 95 27 82 05

Cheese Fair – *A Fiera di u Casgiu*, at Venaco, one of the island's premier cheese-producing regions. www.fromages-corse.org; email: fieradicasgiu@wanadoo.fr; ☎ 04 95 47 00 15

June

Contemporary Arts – *Île Mouvante*, Sant'Antonino, Balagne. ☎ 04 95 61 70 05

St Erasmus – *I Pescadori in Festa*, Ajaccio, the fishermen's festival on 2 June (also in Propriano)

Horse Fair – *Cavall'in Festa*, Corte, featuring horses, donkeys and mules. ☎ 04 95 29 42 31

Medieval Bonifacio – *Journées Médiévales*, at Bonifacio on Whit Sunday weekend. ☎ 04 95 73 00 15

Calvi Jazz Festival – a week of formal and impromptu music events around town. www.calvi-jazz-festival.com

Ajaccio music festival – *Festival de musique*, in early July. www.fmc-corse.org; ☎ 04 95 21 12 76

July

Wine Fair – *Fiera di u Vinu*. Corsica's main wine festival takes place on the first weekend in July at Luri, Cap Corse. ☎ 04 95 35 04 17

Guitar Festival – *Nuits de la Guitare* at Patrimonio; www.festival-guitare-patrimonio.com

Lumio Fair – *Fiera di a Petra*, Lumio features Corsican fare, music and dancing. ☎ 04 95 60 89 00

Olive Fair – *A Fiera di l'Alivu*, at Montegrosso in the Balagne. ☎ 04 95 62 81 72

Calvi on the Rocks – pop festival; www.calviontherocks.com

Singing – *Festivoce*, at Pigna in the Balagne. www.festivoce.casa-musicale.org

August

Lama Film Festival. ☎ 04 95 48 21 05

Hazelnut Fair – *Fiera di a Nuciola*, at Cervione on the East Coast, in late August. ☎ 04 95 32 84 40

Fête de Ste Marie – *Paese in luce*, Nonza on Cap Corse in the evening of 15 August, lit up by an eerie procession.

Napoleon's Birthday – festivities and parades celebrating the birth date of the emperor on 15 August.

Calenzana Music Festival – *Rencontres musicales classiques et contemporaines*, Calenzana; www.musical-calenzana.com; ☎ 04 95 62 88 58

September

A Santa Festival – *A Santa di u Niolu*, at Casamaccioli in the Niolo in early September

Corsican Honey Fair – *Mele in Festa*, Murzo, near Vico. ☎ 04 95 26 68 60

Fête de Notre Dame – in Bonifacio on 8 September

October

Bastia Music Festival – *Musicales de Bastia*; email: musicalesdebastia@wanadoo.fr; ☎ 04 95 32 32 30

☎ 04 95 27 41 76

November

Wind Festival – *Festival du Vent*, Calvi; www.festival-du-vent.com

Chestnut Fair – *La Fête du Marron*, first half of November, Evisa's authentic event dedicated to the venerable chestnut. ☎ 04 95 26 20 09

December

Chestnut Festival – *A fiera di a Castagna*, Bocognano, near Ajaccio. A 3-day celebration in early December of Corsican produce. One of the island's most important events; www.fieradiacastagna.com

Information for Travellers

Passport & Visas

As part of France, Corsica is subject to EU regulations. UK visitors must present a valid passport on entry. Visitors from most non-EU European countries, the USA, Canada Australia and New Zealand do not require a visa for a stay of up to three months. Visa enquiries should be made at the French embassy or consulate in your own country.

By law, you should carry your passport with you at all times. If you lose your passport it is helpful to have a photocopy of the vital pages available and you should store this separately from your passport.

Business Hours

Opening hours for establishments vary from place to place and from one season to another but in principle are from 8am to 6pm. Most offices, businesses, museums and shops close during the middle of the day for two hours, usually between 12pm and 2pm. During the height of the summer some stay open all day. Banks are open 8.30am–noon and 1.30–4.30pm.

Time

In France the 24-hour clock is used and the hours and minutes are separated by a lower-case 'h' so 5.30pm is 17h30. Corsica, as France, is one hour later than Greenwich Mean Time. During daylight saving time, from late March to late October, it is two hours later.

Money Matters

The euro is the currency of Corsica as it is part of France. Notes are in denominations of 5, 10, 20, 50, 100, 200 and 500 euros. Coins are in denominations of 1, 2, 5, 10, 20 and 50 cents and 1 and 2 euros. There is no limit to the amount of money you may bring into France.

Credit cards such as Visa (*Carte Bleue*) and MasterCard (*Eurocard*) are most commonly used in Corsica, while American Express and Diners Club are less widely accepted. Credit cards may offer the most convenient way of paying for goods and services but are not universally accepted. Many restaurants and some shops only accept cash. Cash and traveller's cheques can be exchanged at banks and larger hotels, but it is worth noting that the commission rates vary from place to place. By far the easiest way to get local currency is by withdrawing at a *distributeur de billets* or ATM, using a debit or credit card, for which you will need your PIN number. ATM machines are found in larger towns, but not generally in small towns or villages.

Mobile Phones

Most UK mobile phones work in Corsica but check first with your service provider. Visitors from North America should also check that their phone will work in Europe. It may be worth purchasing a SIM card on a pay-as-you-go basis for the local SFR or Orange networks, from their shops in larger towns. Remember that the signal can be patchy in mountain areas and a mobile cannot be relied upon for emergencies in remote regions. Top-up cards can be bought at tobacconists and supermarkets, as well as at the service providers' own shops.

Public Telephones

Most public phones require a *télécarte*, which can be purchased at tobacconists, post offices and supermarkets. The card can be used for domestic and international calls. If the LCD display does not give instructions in English, the following may be useful:

Introduire carte – insert card
Hors service – out of order
Décrochez SVP – please hang up
Patientez SVP – please wait

Telephoning within Corsica

To phone within the island you will need to dial the full number including the regional code (04 95).

Telephoning abroad

To phone the UK dial the country code 0044 and then the local code without the first '0' and the subscriber number. For the USA and Canada the country code is 001.

The internet & useful websites

Internet cafés are found in the main towns and some hotels offer internet access. Few establishments offer wireless internet but it is always worth asking when you make a reservation for accommodation.

General Corsica websites:

www.corsica-isula.com – The definitive Corsica website in English, with plenty of cultural, historical and practical information on just about every aspect of the island. It includes useful compilations of website addresses and links to many other sites of interest to visitors.

www.terracorsa.info – Website of the group *I Muvrini*, packed full of cultural and historical information. Well worth exploring.

www.france-for-visitors.com/corsica
www.visit-corsica.com – official site of Corsica's tourist board
www.toute-la-corse.com
www.corsica-net.com
www.u-corsu.com
www.parc-naturel-corse.com – useful website on the Parc Naturel Régional Corse

Food and Wine

www.corsicaproduits.com – Corsican foods available for order
www.corsica-terroirs.com – website only in French with details of all suppliers of local produce in different regions

Tourist Information

Regional tourist offices are located in the main towns and are open all year. Smaller towns and villages also have information offices but they may only be open in high season. Details of opening hours of tourist offices are given in the regional listings for each chapter in this book.

www.bastia-tourisme.com – Bastia and surrounds
www.balagne-corsica.com – Calvi & the Balagne
www.corte-tourisme.com – Corte
www.ajaccio-tourisme.com – Ajaccio
www.porto-tourisme.com – Porto and Ota
www.oti-sartenaisvalinco.com – Propriano and Sartène
www.destination-sudcorse.co – Porto Vecchio and Alta Rocca
www.bonifacio.fr – Bonifacio

In places where there is no tourist office, the best place to head for information and advice is the *Mairie* or local town hall offices, which are found in all communities or a local bar. Those in small villages may have limited opening hours.

Visiting Village and Country Churches

Churches are usually kept locked but a key is available should you wish to visit them. The challenge is in locating the key (*clef de l'église*), which may be at the *Mairie* (town hall offices), a local bar or restaurant, or in some cases the nearest house to the church. Don't be shy about asking as local people are usually more than willing to help.

Electricity

Electricity supply is 220V at 50Hz AC. Appliances from the UK will need a Southern Europe adaptor plug for round pin sockets, which can be purchased at UK airports on departure. Appliances from other parts of the world may also need a voltage transformer in order to work. You should buy this in your home country before departure.

Photography

Corsica's stunning coastal and mountain landscapes and pretty villages provide many subjects for photography. To get the best photos, avoid the intense light of the middle of the day, particularly in summer. You will get better results by using your camera early in the morning or late in the afternoon, when the sun is lower in the sky. If you wish to take photographs of local people, it is polite to ask permission first.

Language

Increasingly, those working in tourism in Corsica speak some English, but it is helpful to have a working knowledge of French. In the main resorts, tourist office, hotel, restaurant and bar staff will probably answer you in English, even when you try to speak French. Unless you are supremely confident, arm yourself with a French phrase book, a sense of humour and plenty of patience. From time to time you may hear the Corsican language *U Corsu* spoken. If you speak Italian, you may understand some Corsican words and phrases. However, it is not expected and often not appreciated that visitors try to speak Corsican.

What to buy

As a nation, the French are passionate about food and it is little surprise that mainland French visitors to Corsica seek out small, local producers of wine, olive oil, *charcuterie*, cheese, chestnut flour, honey and jam and go home laden with Corsican delicacies. Several of the island's regions have linked their local producers under the banner of *Strada di i Sensi*, with leaflets and maps giving details of the locations where produce can be tasted and purchased. They can also be viewed on the web site **www.corsica-terroirs.com**. In the Balagne region, the *Strada di l'artigiani* is a similar scheme, listing local artists and craftsmen.

Chestnut flour: (*farine de châtaigne*) expensive but authentically Corsican and an essential ingredient of many local desserts, you can add it to home-made bread or follow one of the traditional recipes on the packet.

Olive Oil: the island's olive oil is high quality and delicate in taste and aroma, but expensive. Production is limited and small scale. Buy direct in Ste Lucie de Tallano in the Alta Rocca and Montegrosso in the Balagne.

Canistrelli: traditional biscuits with a taste of aniseed, honey or lemon.

Pottery: vivid and interesting glazes in blue, green and earthy tones are typical of many of Corsica's ceramic artists' creations. Most pottery is functional, rather than purely decorative.

Music: recordings of traditional polyphonic music and modern adaptations are available on CD and are an evocative way of recalling the island's sounds, especially if you are lucky enough to have attended a concert.

Wooden artefacts: the hard and beautifully grained wood of the olive tree is used to make chopping boards, pepper mills, corkscrews and many other useful items, that make attractive, if pricey, island souvenirs.

Local Etiquette

In general Corsicans are polite, friendly and welcoming to English-speaking visitors. Immensely proud of their island, they appreciate hearing compliments but are less open to criticism. Unless you are unhappy with a service that has been provided, it is best to avoid complaints or negative comments about the island. Above all you should avoid asking questions, making comments or giving opinions on local politics and Corsican independence.

Safety

Corsica is a safe place to travel and visitors, including solo women, are unlikely to experience problems of personal security. Just as you would anywhere else in the world, be vigilant if you're walking around urban areas on your own late at night. Occasionally there are thefts from parked vehicles so make it a rule to keep things out of sight and not leave valuables unattended. Tourists have never been the target of violence associated with the independence movement.

Useful Signs

Baignade/plage non surveillée – no lifeguard on duty

Baignade interdite – swimming prohibited

Défense de fumer – no smoking

Route barrée – road closed

Décharge interdite – no dumping of rubbish

Stationnement interdit – no parking

Propriété privée – private property

Chien méchant – beware of the dog

Attention aux chutes de pierres – beware of falling rocks

Chemin sans issue – no exit

Sentier non balisé – path without waymarks

Sentier dangereux – dangerous path

Entrée/Sortie – Entry/Exit

Ouvert/Fermé – Open/Closed

Centre Ville – town centre

Accueil - entrance to a site of interest

Forest Fires

Forest fires, sadly some started deliberately, are an ongoing problem in Corsica in the dry, hot summers. The island's constant winds and dense ground cover of the *maquis* make coastal areas especially vulnerable but fire has also ravaged inland mountain forests, including the Bavella Massif and Restonica Valley. Outdoor fires are prohibited everywhere and cigarettes must never be thrown from a car window. In fact, make it a rule never to smoke outdoors. On days of high wind when the fire risk is greatest, forest areas may be closed to walkers, with signs erected to indicate this. Report any fires immediately to the fire brigade by dialling 18 (or 112 from a mobile phone).

Emergencies and medical help

Citizens of EU countries are entitled to free emergency medical treatment and most medical expenses, but must be in possession of the European Health Insurance Card (EHIC), which replaced the E111 form in 2004 (apply online on www.ehicard.org). Visitors from all other countries should arrange travel insurance that includes medical treatment. Note that mountain rescue and helicopter evacuation are not included under the EHIC and can be very expensive, so it is essential that walkers are covered by travel insurance that includes this.

Emergency Telephone numbers:

Fire: 18   Ambulance: 15   Police: 17   From a mobile phone dial 112

Further Reading & Maps

Fauna and Flora

La Flore Endémique de La Corse
Jacques Gamisans & Jean-François Marzocchi
Edisud, 1990
ISBN 2-85744-777-9

The Birds of Corsica: An Annotated Checklist
Jean Claude Thibault & Gilles Bonacorsi
British Ornithologists' Union, 1999
ISBN 0-90744-621-3

Balades Nature en Corse
Dakota Editions, 2000
ISBN 2-910932-70-2
(useful book of nature walks in Corsica with illustrated guide to the island's fauna and flora – in French)

History, Archaeology & Culture

Granite Island
Dorothy Carrington
Penguin Books, 1984
ISBN 0-14009-524-1

The Dream-Hunters of Corsica
Dorothy Carrington
Phoenix (Orion Books), 1996, paperback
ISBN 1-85799-424-8
Blue Guide to Corsica
Roland Gant

A & C Black, London, 1992
ISBN 0-7136-3589-4

Trekking

Trekking in Corsica
David Abram
Trailblazer Publications, 2003
ISBN 1-873756-63-1

The Parc Naturel Régional Corse produces a series of books and guides on walking routes and natural history. Most are in French but a few are published also in English. They are available locally in bookshops, at the Parc's offices or through **www.parc-naturel-corse. com**

Maps

Touring Maps

It is worth picking up a copy of the Michelin map of Corsica, *Carte Routière* number 345, which is perfect for touring. It is on sale at fuel stations and bookshops and marks distances between places, as well as routes of scenic interest.

Hiking maps

With a scale of 1:25,000, these topographical maps from the Institut Géographique National (IGN) cover the island in 19 sections, with hiking routes and mountain huts marked. The whole series is also conveniently available on CD or DVD. They are available in book shops locally, or through the website **www.ign.fr**

Corsican restaurants often also serve pizzas

Index

Index

Published in the UK by:
Landmark Publishing Ltd,
Ashbourne Hall, Cokayne Avenue, Ashbourne,
Derbyshire DE6 1EJ England
E-mail landmark@clara.net Website www.landmarkpublishing.co.uk

1st Edition

ISBN 13: 978-1-84306-163-2
ISBN 10: 1-84306-163-5

© **Cathy Harlow 2007**

Britioh Library Oataloguing in Publication Data:
A catalogue record for this book is available from the British Library

Printed by: Cromwell Press, Trowbridge
Cartography and Design: Sarah Labuhn
Edited by: Ian Howe

Picture Credits:

Front cover: Capo d'Orto, near Porto
Back Cover top: Snorkelling near Porto-Vecchio
Back Cover bottom: Piana, near Porto
Phillipe Berthelin: 98l, 114, 15br

**Paintings of birds and mouflon by Penny Bains
All other images were supplied by Cathy Harlow**

DISCLAIMER
While every care has been taken to ensure that the information in this guide
is as accurate as possible at the time of publication, the publisher and author
accept no responsibility for any loss, injury or inconvenience sustained by
anyone using this book.